Dance as
Religious
Studies

Dance as Religious Studies

Edited by Doug Adams
and Diane Apostolos-Cappadona

CROSSROAD • NEW YORK

1993

The Crossroad Publishing Company
370 Lexington Avenue, New York, N.Y. 10017

Printed in the United States of America

Library of Congress Cataloging-in-Publication Data

Dance as religious studies / edited by Doug Adams and Diane Apostolos-Cappadona.
    p.   cm.
    Includes bibliographical references (p. 211).
    ISBN 0-8245-0988-9 (pbk.)
    1. Dancing—Religious aspects.   2. Religious dance, Modern.
3. Dancing—Jews—Bibliography.   4. Dancing—Religious aspects—
Christianity—Bibliography.   I. Adams, Doug.   II. Apostolos-
Cappadona, Diane.
GV1741.D24   1990
792.8—dc20   89-28388
                                                         CIP

For
Margaret Taylor Doane
and
Thomas A. Kane
Who Lead Us in Dance

Contents

Introduction

1

Changing Biblical Imagery
and Artistic Identity
in Twentieth-Century Dance

Doug Adams and Diane Apostolos-Cappadona

By studying the patterns of biblical texts and images developed in twentieth-century dance, we glimpse changing artistic identity and theological concerns. Several essays in this volume suggest the transformations of biblical images in twentieth-century dance and the connections between such transformations and theological concerns. For example, a strong prophetic spirit is noted in the images chosen by choreographers between the 1920s and the 1970s.

Modern dance pioneers Ruth St. Denis and Ted Shawn made overt religious subject matter a focus for their dances in the early twentieth century when that period's ballet had given such themes scant attention. Shawn's ministry was already moving from the church

"Changing Biblical Imagery and Artistic Identity in Twentieth-Century Dance" was originally written by Doug Adams (Austin: The Sharing Co., 1985). It has been revised by Diane Apostolos-Cappadona. It is reprinted in this revision with permission.

to the stage by 1911 when he saw St. Denis dance in Denver. Her performance convinced him that religion, dance, and drama could be combined.[1] While she stressed sacred dances from India, albeit in a loose manner, he introduced numerous dances with Hebrew and Christian scriptural themes.[2] This emphasis was indicated even in the naming of his dance center at Lee, Massachusetts, "Jacob's Pillow."[3]

Loie Fuller's *Miriam's Dance* (1911) predates any dance of scriptural theme done by Shawn. Michel Fokine's *Josephslegende* (1914) is an early twentieth-century ballet on a scriptural theme.[4] The end of World War I evoked Ruth St. Denis's *Jephthah's Daughters* (1918) and themes of Esther in *Dancer at the Court of King Ahasuerus* (1919), disquieting choices at the end of the war to end all war. Shawn's *Miriam, Sister of Moses* (1919) heralded the victory of the Exodus, while noting that the golden calf as both symbol and fact of unfaithfulness followed such seeming triumph. Between 1919 and 1920, he began to develop his unfinished *David the King;* its theme that the righteous may come to power only to be corrupted and fall from grace was a pointed criticism of American might. In 1921, Shawn presented his reassuring *Twenty-third Psalm* which he had begun as early as 1915 and developed during the time of his complete worship service in dance at a San Francisco church in 1917.

In the early 1920s, dance featured themes from the Book of Genesis and from the Christian Scriptures. There had been a mock creation of the world by Natalia Kasatkina and Vladimir Vasiliev in 1917; whereas Loie Fuller's *The Deluge* (1921) and Darius Milhaud's *Creation du Monde* (1923)[5] used black African idioms while Jean Börlin's *Creation of the World*, with the Swedish Ballet, used more classical idioms. In both 1931 and 1935, Ninette de Valois revived the *Creation du Monde* — the latter with God in white face. Heinrich Kröller produced *Joseph* in Berlin in 1921, and Kassian Goleizovsky premiered his *Joseph* in Russia in 1925.[6]

While one may detect an internationalism in such themes, the major treatments of Salome during that same period critique the cosmopolitan disposition and prosperity. Salome was treated by Alexander Gorky (1921) and Kassian Goleizovsky (1924), and continued to be treated as a theme by Ruth St. Denis (1931), Lester Horton (1931), Ruth Sorel (1933), and Mia Slavenska (1936).[7]

In the early 1930s, other themes such as Job, The Prodigal Son, and the Wise and Foolish Virgins appear in the dance. Such themes befit a period of depression and several were based on William Blake's paintings of Job: Ted Shawn's *Job, A Masque for Dancing* (1931) (fig. 1) and Ninette de Valois's *Job* (1931) with Vaughn Williams's music. Martha

Graham's *Lamentation* (fig. 20), a more universalized statement of suffering and grief, also dates from the early 1930s. The theme of the Prodigal Son, which had been done by the Paris Opera Ballet as early as 1812, reappeared in the twentieth century with George Balanchine's *Prodigal Son* (1929) (fig. 2) for the Diaghilev Ballets Russe,[8] Kurt Jooss's *Le Fils Prodigue* (1931), and David Lichine's *Prodigal Son* (1938).[9] The treatment of the parable of Wise and Foolish Virgins moved through different idioms from the folk art/folk song basis of Jean Börlin's *Les Vierges Folles* (1920) for the Swedish Ballet to the more classical idiom of Ninette de Valois's *Wise and Foolish Virgins* (1933) for the Vic Wells Ballet to the baroque, curved line paintings basis for Frederick Ashton's *The Wise Virgins* (1940).

The dances on the theme of David triumphant over Goliath appeared in the last half of the 1930s. In 1935, there were versions by Max Terpis in Switzerland and Keith Lester in London; and in 1937, Serge Lifar's *David Triumphant* opened at the Paris Opera Ballet. The emphasis in these works as opposed to Shawn's earlier but uncompleted work stressed David's triumph over Goliath rather than the later part of David's life as king. Such works were a prelude to World War II — a mocking of Goliath's military might and preparedness which Germany increasingly exemplified while other Western European countries appeared more like the poorly equipped David.

Shawn's and Ruth St. Denis's themes naturally became those of American liturgical dance. Their dances were performed in church liturgies; their Denishawn schools trained many of the earliest American liturgical dancers; and other leading twentieth-century choreographers, including Martha Graham and Doris Humphrey, first danced with Shawn and St. Denis and later taught many who became liturgical dancers. Liturgical dancers from the 1920s, 1930s, and 1940s officially joined together in the 1950s through the Sacred Dance Guild which held its first festivals and workshops at Shawn's Jacob's Pillow. Growing dance departments in colleges and universities from the 1930s further served as a channel generating common themes, for example, Martha Graham's *El Penitente* (1940) with Merce Cunningham and Erick Hawkins, and Pauline Koner's *Voice in the Wilderness* (1948).

While the events of the 1940s disrupted many dance companies and undermined the training of many men in dance,[10] the rise of women into more responsible positions throughout society as a result of the war is reflected in the dance themes chosen. Examples from this period include Graham's *Herodiade* (1944) (fig. 18) and numerous Salomes that were stimulated in part by the perfection of Lester

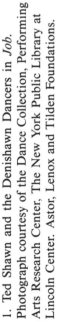

2. The Ballets Russes in George Balanchine's *The Prodigal Son*. Photograph courtesy of the Dance Collection, Performing Arts Library, The New York Public Library at Lincoln Center. Astor, Lenox and Tilden Foundations.

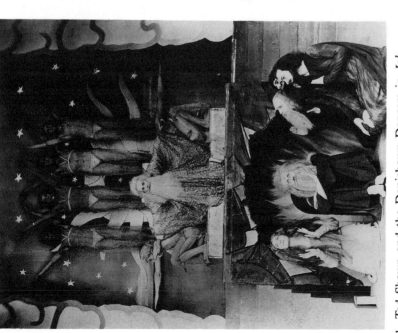

1. Ted Shawn and the Denishawn Dancers in *Job*. Photograph courtesy of the Dance Collection, Performing Arts Research Center, The New York Public Library at Lincoln Center. Astor, Lenox and Tilden Foundations.

Horton's *Face of Violence* (1950). Strong portrayals of Eve appear in José Limón's *The Exiles* (1950), Graham's *Embattled Garden* (1958) (figs. 23 and 25), and Butler's *In the Beginning* (1959). Chief among the number of dances portraying scriptural women were the stories of Judith, Deborah, Esther, and Ruth; for example, Pearl Lang's *Song of Deborah* (1959), Graham's *Judith* (1950/1962/1970) (fig. 28), and Ze'eva Cohen's *Mothers of Israel* (1975).

By the 1950s, choreographers stressed the roles of these powerful scriptural women. The emerging role of women in political and cultural life was foreshadowed in the dances of the 1950s and continued as major emphases into the early 1960s. The theme of Cain and Abel also emerged in the late 1960s. The Hebrew scriptural themes of Abraham and Isaac, Joseph's Dream, and Job, and the Christian scriptural themes of the crucifixion of Jesus and the resurrection of Lazarus were crucial themes in the 1970s. Intergenerational struggles coupled with the social and civil justice issues were seen in the dance of the late 1960s and throughout the 1970s. The choice of themes and their treatments identify the choreographers with the prophetic spirit.

Eve continued as a central figure in the dances of the 1960s and into the early 1970s even as her attention and ours became more focused on the Cain and Abel story; e.g., John Butler's *After Eden* (1966) and *According to Eve* (1972), Alvin Ailey's *According to Eve* (1973), and Paul Taylor's second section of "West of Eden" in *American Genesis* (1973). During that same period, there were numerous revivals of Prodigal Son themes; e.g., Balanchine's version and Barry Moreland's *Prodigal Son* (in ragtime). In this interpretation, the father is less open to reconciliation; the antagonism between the siblings is underscored in these works produced during the periods of upheaval in familial and international relations.

Violence and potential violence continue in the 1970s as crucifixion became a central motif from the Christian Scriptures and the sacrifice of Isaac from the Hebrew Scriptures. During this period, the crucifixion is explored through a number of the works including Graham's revival of *El Penitente* with Rudolf Nureyev; Robert Yohn's *The Man They Say* (1974) and *Cruciform* (1974); and in those dances that dealt explicitly with such diverse themes as Alvin Ailey's *Three Black Kings* (1976) and Bella Lewitzky's *Pieta*. The sacrifice of Isaac became a central focus not only in Yohn's *Abraham and Isaac* (1975), but also in the congregational dancing that became more common in the late 1960s and into the 1970s.[11]

While evil and violence were the dominant themes of the 1970s as exemplified by Graham's *Lucifer* (1975), revivals of David and

Goliath (1975) implied that America was now Goliath not David. Simultaneously there were also the themes of life spared or restored such as Abraham's near sacrifice of Isaac, Jacob's Dream in Graham's *Jacob's Dream* (1974) and *Point of Crossing* (1975), Marcus Schulkind's *Job* (1977), and Norman Walker's *Lazarus* (1973 and 1977).

Beyond its scriptural connections, producers and choreographers linked modern dance with a wider range of other art forms and artists than had been the case with classical ballets, for example, Léger's primitivist sets of 1923. To base a ballet on other art forms was not unusual in itself; but the range of the art forms did not extend beyond classical, baroque, or neoclassical. In classical ballet, the arts were rarely mutually informing. For instance, the Ballet Russe's 1914 production of *Josephslegende* with Fokine's choreography was loosely inspired by Alexandre Benois's desire to animate Paolo Veronese's *Banquets*. Commissioned to write the score, Richard Strauss had little interest in the subject; in fact, he found Joseph's piety boring. A constantly changing cast of potential dancers made it difficult for Strauss to write music for their capabilities, although he was not interested in taking such matters into account.[12] Similarly, Ballet Russe's Diaghilev asked Sergei Prokofiev to write the score for a future and undetermined ballet. The score became the basis for Balanchine's *Prodigal Son* (1929). The set designs were to be done by Georges Rouault who was only seen once by the dance company with whom he did not interact but ignored as he balanced a chair on his nose.[13]

In contrast, Goleizovsky's *Joseph the Beautiful* (1925) of the Bolshoi Ballet not only expanded the range of the arts engaged in the ballet but also coordinated the arts and artists so that they informed each other. The music was composed for the ballet by Sergei Vassilenko who knew the theme at the time of the commission. Acrobatic lifts from the circus were incorporated into the dancing. The ideas of set designer, Boris Erdman, influenced not only the sets but also the costumes (and the future of dance), for he argued that "to hide the mechanism of the body does great injustice to the dancer...ballet dancers should not be encumbered with clothes...dancers whose every muscle is employed in the dance should appear virtually naked."[14] Goleizovsky's work was an expression of its cultural era with its emphasis on the theme of freedom as personified by the Pharaoh and his court; whereas the Fokine work had little social commentary. Stalin's grip of Russian power brought an end to Goleizovsky's creativity at the Bolshoi. Nevertheless, Goleizovsky's influence in a wider collaboration of the arts and an engagement with social commentary was reflected by the generation of choreographers in Western Europe and the United States with Denishawn.

Most of the dances discussed here were prophetic in form as well as in the choice of subject matter. There are some similarities between developments in twentieth-century dance and art, such as the obscuring of the human form with fabric in Graham's *Lamentation* (fig. 3) that foretold the disappearance of the human form in abstract expressionist painting like Jackson Pollock's *Lavender Mist* (fig. 4). Overt biblical subject matter has persisted in twentieth-century dance long after it disappeared from twentieth-century art.

Canons of twentieth-century dance are essentially prophetic when they "stress realities of human life as it exists.... Such elements have been used to create dances that have been surprising and new to us; they have required us to look again more closely and have expanded our vision."[15] Many of these dances choreographically fulfill another dynamic of the prophetic:

> that which speaks the new word and calls us beyond what is. The prophetic transcends the contemporary and is allied with a yet unrealized future. Insofar as modern dance or any art simply reflects or reiterates the beliefs, tendencies, and statements of the surrounding culture, it ceases to be prophetic. The prophetic art form grows out of its time and place by calling that time and place into question and by offering a clearer and deeper vision, lest the people perish.[16]

Twentieth-century dance forms from the 1930s have influenced liturgical dance in the selection and the treatment of subjects prophetic for their periods. As other types of dance become more common in liturgy, different biblical texts will be expressed through movement. Although classical ballet explored few biblical texts, twentieth-century dance has engaged these as it has appropriated the movements of fall and gravity.[17]

Future studies may determine whether the thematic choices of choreographers correspond to choices made in similar periods by preachers and theologians as well as by novelists, playwrights, painters, poets, film makers, and composers. While the actual, and/or mutual influences upon creative artists may be difficult to trace, it is possible to discern how different art forms have an affinity for similar biblical texts or genres.

Dance as Religious Studies reveals resources for the "art of liturgical dance" in terms of both performance and scholarly interpretation.

3. Martha Graham, *Lamentation*. Photograph © Barbara Morgan.

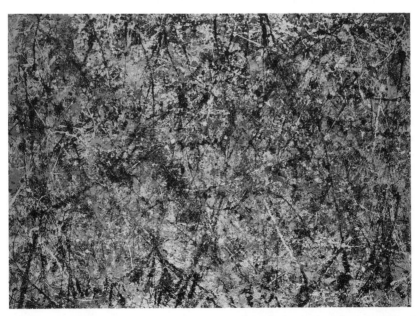

4. Jackson Pollock, *Number 1, 1950 (Lavender Mist)*, 1950. Oil, enamel, and aluminum on canvas. 87 x 118 inches. Ailsa Mellon Bruce Fund, National Gallery of Art, Washington. (1976.37.1 [2697]). © 1990 Pollock-Krasner Foundation/A.R.S., N.Y.

This collection of methodological essays has been arranged to suggest the wide spectrum and the underlying unity of these diverse and varied approaches to understanding dance as religious studies.

We begin this collection, then, with Margaret Taylor's survey of the history of liturgical dance in the Christian tradition. She presents the varied relationships between the church and the liturgical dancer starting with the scriptural tradition and extending into the nineteenth century. This chronology suggests the common patterns of mutuality and distance between the church and dance, which should be helpful to the contemporary liturgical dancer who is in search of a tradition. The remaining essays in this collection provide insights into forms of biblical dance, interpretations of the Bible in twentieth-century choreographies, and current theories and practices of liturgical dance.

Part I of *Dance as Religious Studies* concentrates on the relationship between liturgical dance and the scriptural traditions of Judaism and Christianity. Doug Adams's analysis of the scriptural precedents for communal dance in both Jewish and Christian worship assists in the retrieval of that practice for the contemporary worship service. Mayer I. Gruber's scholarly analysis of references to dance in the Hebraic tradition allows us to recognize the vital place of dance in Jewish worship and to differentiate many forms of dance and metaphorical uses of terms for dance. Hal Taussig shares insights from form criticism to help us see a wide range of liturgical dances in the Hebrew and Christian Scriptures which can provide guidance for contemporary choreographers working in worship. Employing Paul Tillich's methodology for interpreting the connections between Christian theology and the visual arts, Doug Adams and Judith Rock conclude this section with their analysis of how modern dance styles communicate prophetic biblical faith.

Part II indicates the feminist possibilities for liturgical and modern dance. The fundamental relationship between the visual arts and dance is once again emphasized as Diane Apostolos-Cappadona introduces feminist interpretation through her iconographic analysis of Miriam and Salome in Christian art and modern dance. Neil Douglas-Klotz provides us with a commentary on the work of Ruth St. Denis, a founder of modern dance tradition and a leading influence on liturgical dance. He concludes his essay with a previously unpublished exercise piece by "Miss Ruth." Martha Graham's retrieval of the female hero and its ensuing implications for both the modern and liturgical dancer are examined by Diane Apostolos-Cappadona. In concluding this section, Martha Ann Kirk applies feminist critical analysis to the treatment of scriptural women in works featuring Graham and Judith Jamison.

Part III presents a spectrum of the contemporary theory and practice of liturgical dance. Carla De Sola discusses her own development as a liturgical dancer, and offers as a model for reflection the development of her most recent choreographic work, "...And the Word Became Dance." Susan Bauer considers some of the possibilities and problems that are encountered when performing dance in liturgy and offers practical advice for the contemporary dancer and choreographer. Judith Rock illumines the role of the liturgical dancer as an artist. Valerie DeMarinis investigates the psychosocial functions of dance in liturgy.

To encourage further work, we conclude this volume with Doug Adams's bibliographic survey of sources and resources available to both liturgical dancers and students of dance as religious studies.

This current collection, *Dance as Religious Studies*, has become a reality only because of the cooperation of our colleagues. We thank them all for their support, but most especially wish to acknowledge Audrey Englert, Pacific School of Religion, for technical assistance, and Monica Moseley and Rita Waldron, Dance Collection, Performing Arts Library, New York, for their research skills. We are also pleased to acknowledge the continuing support of our work by Werner Mark Linz and Frank Oveis of the Crossroad Publishing Company.

All of us involved in the teaching of dance as religious studies have at one time or another in our lives been energized by a particular colleague, friend, or mentor. Margaret Taylor Doane and Thomas A. Kane have been both joyous companions and creative mentors in our own experience of dance as religious studies. As a token for all they have given to us, we dedicate *Dance as Religious Studies* to these two former teachers, now friends, who continue to inspire in us the wonder and delight of dance.

Notes

1. Walter Terry, *Ted Shawn: Father of American Dance* (New York: Dial Press, 1976) 42f.

2. St. Denis and Shawn disagreed as to whom credit should go for initiating any phase of their collaboration in "religion and dance," see Terry, *Ted Shawn*, 104.

3. Through the 1930s and until his death in 1972, Shawn trained numerous leading dancers and choreographers, and also gave American premieres at Jacob's Pillow to dancers and dance companies from around the world.

4. Of course, numerous ballets used scriptural themes when the Jesuits were masters of the ballet in the sixteenth, seventeenth, and eighteenth centuries: see William A. Carroll, S.J., "The Bible in Drama and Dance at the Jesuit Colleges of the Sixteenth to Eighteenth Centuries," *Papers of the International Seminar on the Bible in Dance* (Jerusalem: Israeli Center of the International Theatre Institute, 1979), the last twenty-two pages in the papers presented at the International Seminar on the Bible in Dance, Jerusalem, August 1979. See Judith Rock, *Terpsichore at Louis Le Grand: Baroque Dance on a Jesuit Stage in Paris*, Ph.D. diss., Graduate Theological Union, Berkeley, 1988.

5. The first ballet to employ Fernand Léger's primitivist sets.

6. Just before the Soviet Union banned such performances of the classical repertoire without major variation. See Gunhild Schueller, "Legend of Joseph from Fokine to Neumeier," *Papers of the International Seminar on the Bible in Dance*.

7. Richard Bizot, "Salome in Modern Dance," *Papers of the International Seminar on the Bible in Dance*.

8. This work was later revived and reworked in 1931 in Copenhagen.

9. For the context of this theme, see Selma Jeanne Cohen's "The Prodigal Son," *Papers of the International Seminar on the Bible in Dance*, and also her book, *The Modern Dance: Seven Statements of Belief* (Middletown: Wesleyan University Press, 1966). The latter compares the choreographic views of seven leading twentieth-century dance creators on how they would handle the Prodigal Son theme.

10. This no doubt contributed in part to the preponderance of themes dealing with women in the 1950s and 1960s.

11. Doug Adams, *Congregational Dancing in Christian Worship* (Austin: The Sharing Co., 1984 [1971]) 56–57.

12. Schueller, "Legend of Joseph."

13. Cohen, "The Prodigal Son."

14. Zachary L. McLove, "Russian Ballet Risen in Revolt," *New York Times Magazine* 15 November 1925, 8; and Giora Manor, "Goleizovsky's 'Joseph the Beautiful,' A Modern Ballet before Its Time," in *Papers of the International Seminar on the Bible in Dance*. For additional reading (and graphics showing something of the dances described in this article), consult Giora Manor, *The Gospel According to Dance* (New York: Dance Magazine, 1981), and Giora Manor, "The Bible as Dance," *Dance Magazine*, December 1978, 56–86.

15. Doug Adams and Judith Rock, "Biblical Criteria in Modern Dance: Modern Dance as Prophetic Form," *Focus X: Religion and Dance*, ed. Mary Jane Wolbers and Dennis J. Fallon (Reston: National Dance Association, 1981) 70.

16. Ibid., 69

17. During intermission of the Paul Taylor dance program at Zellerbach Hall on the University of California Berkeley campus, a German student in

my dance course asked, "When the two dancers fell down was it a mistake or part of the choreography?" I responded, "That is a question that modern dance has made possible; for in dance (largely ballet) before the first world war, there was no fall except by mistake." For further research on themes danced in liturgies, one may consult the *Sacred Dance Guild Newsletter* (now *Journal*) that dates back to 1958. Liturgical dancers from all over the world send in reports of their dances. To secure back issues of that journal or Sacred Dance Guild membership (which includes a subscription to that journal), write to The Sacred Dance Guild, P.O. Box 177, Peterborough, New Hampshire 03458. Many highlights from that journal are chronicled in Carlynn Reed, *And We Have Danced: A History of the Sacred Dance Guild, 1958–1978*, ed. Doug Adams (Austin: The Sharing Co., 1978). Manuscript collections such as the Margaret Taylor Collection, Graduate Theological Union Library, Berkeley, California, provide extensive details on dances done in liturgy from the 1930s to the present. Even when the use of the lectionary is becoming more widespread, changing patterns of artistic identity and theological concern may be evident in which of the Scriptures is chosen for dance.

2

A History of Symbolic Movement in Worship

Margaret Taylor

A natural expression of human beings from the earliest days through all civilizations, cultures, and religions, symbolic movement was not grafted onto Christianity in the twentieth century. The close connection between religious feeling and expressive movement has been coeval with human history.[1] As a direct outlet for religious feeling, symbolic movement was probably the first of the arts since it required no material outside of the human body. Religion was a major part of life among primitive peoples, thus religious dances were a natural way to express religious beliefs. I define *dance* as moving in rhythm with a pattern of expression.

"A History of Symbolic Movement in Worship" is excerpted and updated from Chapter 5, "The History of Symbolic Movement" of Margaret Taylor, *A Time to Dance: Symbolic Movement in Worship*, ed. Doug Adams (Austin: The Sharing Co., 1981 [1967]) 67–135, 172–75. It is included in this collection with permission.

15

Hebrew Influences

The various references to the use of dance in the Hebrew Scriptures are categorized as "spontaneous" or as "folk."[2] The qualities of Hebrew dancing are evidenced by Exodus 15:20; 1 Samuel 29:5; 2 Samuel 6:14; Psalm 149:3; Psalm 150:4; Psalm 30:11; and Ecclesiastes 3:4. The Apocryphal Book of Judith portrays the people joined together dancing (Jud. 15:12–13). Growing out of a strong Hebraic tradition, Christianity was cognizant of this natural, spontaneous, and accustomed way of human expression.

Greek Influences

In the early writings of the Christian tradition, the Greek term *chorós*, "choral dancing," was used repeatedly. Greek choral dancing had a special dignity and beauty because of its harmonious movements. The Greeks believed that dance was the art that most influenced the soul and provided the expressive way for that overflow of awareness for which there were no words. Classic Greek dramas used choral dances to emphasize a mood or to reveal a vital meaning. In the writings of the early church (which were largely in Greek), *chorós* and the plural *choroi* were used. These terms were translated as "dance," but choral movement involved folk participation in acts of worship.

The First Five Centuries

In the Aramaic that Jesus spoke and that lay beneath the Christian Scriptures, "dance" and "rejoice" were the same word. So where we read "rejoicing in the spirit," dance may be understood.[3] Jesus was not against dancing, but recognized it as a normal means of expressing joy (Luke 6:23). Similarly, in his story about the rejoicing over the return of the prodigal son, he mentioned that there was dancing (Luke 15:25).

Paul reminded the early Christians that their *bodies are temples of the Holy Spirit* and that they should glorify God in their bodies as well as in their spirits (1 Corinthians 6:19–20). That manual action was a part of prayer expression is clear in the letter to Timothy (1 Timothy 2:8). The body was respected as a channel for religious expression.

The circle dance of the disciples around Jesus was described in the apocryphal Acts of John as the "Hymn of Jesus." G. R. S. Mead suggested that this hymn was an ancient mystery ritual of early Christianity.[4] In the Acts of John, the group slowly makes a "mystic circle" and to each statement by Christ who is in the center there is the response "Amen." Although not included in canonical Christian literature, the "Hymn of Jesus" reveals that symbolic movement was employed in the second or third centuries.

The *Didache* mentions "The Cosmic Mystery of the Church,"[5] which dealt with the mystery of the creation and involved a rhythmic interpretation of the sun, moon, stars, and planets. In *Quaestiones*, we read one of the earliest references to children's choirs reflecting the fourth-century (or earlier) pattern of liturgical dance.

For third-century church leaders, the sacred *chorós* was a commendable form of expression for religious feeling. To Clement of Alexandria what was regular, rhythmical, and harmonious, was also divine. For "those who have not yet been initiated in the mysteries or have no taste for dance and song" are like that which is "dissonant, unrhythmical and material" and so "must still stand out from the divine *chorós*."[6]

Origen (c. 225) mentioned a hymn with the words "of stars dancing in heaven for the salvation of the universe."[7] To Gregory Thaumaturgus (c. 243) choral dance was a natural and spontaneous way of expressing religious joy.[8] In Alexandria, the Meletians, followers of Bishop Meletius (c. 326), danced as they sang their hymns, clapped their hands, and struck bells.

Men and women took part in circling and processional *choroi* in the fourth century. Eusebius (c. 304) stated that Philo (c. 26) in *On the Contemplative Life* described a sacred all night festival that was the same as that of the church in Eusebius's time.[9] According to Philo, this festal dance commemorated the triumphant dance of the Israelites after their miraculous passage through the Red Sea.[10]

David's dancing was the best-known justification for sacred dance (2 Samuel 6:14). Gregory of Nyssa (c. 365) felt that David's dance signified "intense joy" and that he "by the rhythmic motions of his body thus showed in public his inner state of soul."[11]

Gregory Nazianzus (c. 369) described the dance of David before the ark as "that swift course of revolution manifold ordained by God." "Dance to the honor of God" as an exercise "worthy of an emperor and of a Christian" was Gregory's advice to the Emperor Julian, who had revived "the dissolute dances of Herodias and the pagans." Gregory urged, "Rather, perform the dances of King David before the ark; dance to the honor of God. Such exercises of peace and piety are worthy of an emperor and a Christian."[12]

The "triumphant ring dance" mentioned by Gregory Nazianzus was a way to honor martyrs and to celebrate Easter.[13] This ring dance was participated in by large groups of people, so it must have been simple and for group involvement rather than observation.

Basil (c. 369), who later became the bishop of Caesarea, referred to

> those who now, together with the angels, dance the dance of the angels around God, just as in the flesh they performed a spiritual dance of life and, here on earth, a heavenly dance.[14]

At another time, Basil condemned those dances performed by women with frivolous and indecent movements. The church reacted strongly against dances performed by women, whether they were danced in the church or at the graves of martyrs.

Pantomimic dances and dramatic hymns were introduced into the liturgy and were received with enthusiasm. Arius had included a program of pantomimic dances commemorating the crucifixion in a liturgy called *Thalia*. Athanasius, his opponent, recognized the value of these additions. Beginning with the fourth century, there were more opportunities for dramatic movement in the liturgy.

There were "customary dances" that the people participated in for special services for martyrs and saints. A homily written at the close of the fourth century, on the anniversary of the martyrdom of Polyeucte, defended "our customary dances."[15]

Ambrose tried to clarify the values and dangers of the use of sacred dance.[16] Seeking a means of spiritualizing the church dance and transforming it into a symbolic dance, Ambrose wrote "The Lord bids us dance, not merely with the circling movements of the body, but with pious faith in him."[17] This was a clear statement of the need to fuse the spiritual with the physical.

Chrysostom (c. 386) noted the joy and the sense of unity expressed in sacred dance.[18] In his description of the celebration of the Whitsun festival, Chrysostom commended the Christians who "danced those spiritual dances which are...most modest."[19] "Dance to the glory of God" as David danced was Chrysostom's advice to Christians.[20] However, he cautioned against "unseemly motions" like those of pagan dances. Instead, Christians should keep their dances sacred, for God had given them feet so that they might "dance with the angels."

Augustine's warning (c. 394) to keep the sacred dances disciplined was more severe. He was against "frivolous or unseemly" dances. However, he did not object to all dancing at sacred festivals. He sensed the harmony in the dances and the need for spiritual harmony in the participants.[21]

Dancing in heaven was the occupation of the angels in the vision of Theodoret (c. 430) who wrote that he saw the martyrs in "their dance in the indestructible aeons." He urged his readers to follow their example that they might share in dance in its most spiritual form, "to dance in company with those free of all body."[22] Theodoret conceived of the sacred dance as one of the virtues in harmony with the powers above. What a change would occur when the dance came to be considered the occupation of the vices in connection with the power of evil!

During the first five centuries of the Christian era, dance was recognized by the church as a natural way of expressing *joy*, a way of *salvation*, and a way of *adoration*, as illustrated by the references to the dances of the holy ones, the martyrs, and the angels. The early Christians expressed in symbolic movement their deep joy in the coming of Christ, in the immortal life which the martyrs had earned, and in the close spiritual bond between heaven and earth. Their faith was not just an intellectual acceptance of certain beliefs but an experience of abundant life and spiritual joy. The early Christians entered into these simple dances as Christian folk, not as accomplished performers.

The Early Middle Ages (500/1100)

As the church became more authoritarian and started to regulate all forms of liturgical activity, it began to legislate against some of the dances. Although there were occasional references to councils and papal authorities that opposed religious dancing, it was difficult to know whether these disciplinary measures were indicative of the total attitude or as valid judgment against some religious dances that had degenerated. Sacred dance was a form of religious expression in which the people participated. During this period, when the general culture was not stimulating, the church preserved and fostered the religious arts. At this time, the mass developed with its definite, prescribed, and symbolic movements to the accompaniment of Gregorian chants.

It was customary to celebrate festivals and saints' days with some form of dancing. On the vigil of a saint's day, or a day of prayer, silence, and penance, dancing was not suitable to the penitential mood. The edict of the Council of Toledo (539) forbidding dancing in the churches during the vigil of saints' days was justifiable.

In the following century, the Council of Toledo suggested that Isidore, archbishop of Seville, present a ritual that would be rich in sacred choreography. This ritual became incorporated into a mass known as *Mozarabe*. Used in the seven churches of Toledo, it is still celebrated in the cathedral of Seville.

This Mozarabe with the dances of *los mozos de coro* (choristers) became known and authorized as the mass that included the dances of *los seises* according to a bull of Pope Eugenius IV in 1439. At that time, los seises danced before the ark on the altar and were "dressed as angels." Thus the dancing choristers represented the angels in heaven who had descended to the church choir in order to continue there the dance of the blessed in paradise, quite similar to the writings of Clement of Alexandria.

At the end of the seventeenth century, the archbishop of Seville forbade the performance of the los seises dance. Amazed at this ruling, the people of Seville raised the funds necessary to send los seises, whose numbers had increased from the original six to ten choristers, to Rome to perform for the pope. After the performance of their dance in full accompaniment of singing and clicking castanets, the pope said, "I see nothing in this children's dance which is offensive to God. Let them continue to dance before the high altar." Sacred dances spread throughout Europe during the eighth and ninth centuries, despite the efforts to restrain degenerate forms that were appearing. Dancing was a customary accompaniment to the processionals in which relics of saints or martyrs were carried, and it was part of the church festivals. In a liturgy of a Paris church (900), a rubric reads: "Here the canon shall dance at the first psalm." This probably involved some symbolic movements and gestures by the canon alone, or it may have pointed to a custom of the canon leading the choirboys in a circling design during the chanting of the psalms.

The Flagellants appeared in northern Italy in the eleventh century, then spread to Germany, Spain, and England. People of all classes and ages formed long processions that were headed by priests carrying crosses and banners. They walked through the streets in double file reciting prayers and drawing blood from their bodies by whipping themselves and each other with leather thongs.

Later Medieval Period (1100/1400)

The later medieval period was an age of dramatic and emotional expression. The church, which had denounced the degenerate secular, theatrical productions, decided to create its own dramatic portrayals. A definite effort to arouse public interest in the service of the church introduced more choral songs, picturesque processionals, and even ceremonial dances performed in the choir area. There were various references to hymns that mention the dance as an accepted liturgical art form. In the tenth-century hymnary of the monastery of Moissac, there is such a hymn for morning mass during the Easter festivals.[23]

The *planctus*[24] appeared as part of the mass early in the twelfth century. This is a religious play concerned with the sorrows of the three Marys. The actions to accompany the lines and musical score are specified by interlinear indications in red, or "rubrics." The actors were clergy, holy sisters, or choirboys. The play was more often chanted to music than spoken. This early form was the interrelation of gesture, music, verse, and meaning.

Mystery and miracle plays that began to take form at this time were presented in the *ballatoria* (dancing pavement), a space in the front of the church or at the west door where awnings were hung. At other times they were transported and presented on wagonstages. In France, England, and Germany, there was a thriving interest in these plays, which included, besides the dramatic action, the dancing of the follies, devils, and Salome. The follies, which represented the vices, tried to attract people in the audience; the devil, as the leading dancer, with his troupe of assisting devils, enjoyed scaring people; and the acrobatic dancing of Salome entertained them. The dancing connected with these religious dramatizations was mainly theatrical and not devotional.

Monastic orders, during the twelfth and thirteenth centuries, found the dance of religious value. For example, the Cistercian monks danced and prayed for the salvation of the universe. The Franciscans sang and danced, and called themselves the singing servants of Christ. Friar Marti of Alicante found time to write a treatise on dancing, even during the period of the Inquisition. The nuns of Villaceaux celebrated the feasts of the Holy Innocents and Mary Magdalene with appropriate dances.

Bonaventure (c. 1260) wrote that in the joys of paradise there will be endless circling in rhythmic revolutions with the heavenly spheres as the redeemed sing ceaseless songs of praise.[25] As late as the twelfth century, in the writings of the hermit Honorius, there was reference to a ritual dance similar to the one mentioned in the *Didache* as "The Cosmic Mystery of the Church."[26]

Four kinds of choral dances (*tripudia*) were mentioned by the twelfth-century rector of the University of Paris, John Beleth. The dances were customary for church festivals: the deacons' festival dance on St. Stephen's Day; the priests' festival day on St. John's Day, the choirboys' (later, the "children's") festival dance on Holy

Innocents' Day, and the subdeacons' festival dance on the Feast of the Circumcision or of the Epiphany.

Church labyrinthine dances date from the eleventh century, although there is the earlier reference in the "Naassene Hymn" of the second century. In the cathedral of Chartres (c. 1200) there was constructed in the floor a maze (or labyrinth) that was forty feet across.[27] Often people held hands as they wound around into and out of the maze.

The model for the labyrinths in Christian churches was the maze at Knossos. The Minotaur became identified with Satan and Theseus with Christ, who descended into the underworld, overcame Satan, and emerged victorious, together with those who were saved. The leader guided men and women holding each other by the hand, following the bends of the labyrinth into the center, and then out to the release of salvation.[28]

The fourteenth-century hymn writers made numerous references to ring and processional dances. In Germany, a monk composed several hymns which the choristers sang during the performance of their ring and three-step dances (*tripudia*). The term, *tripudia*, involved three steps forward and one step backward, and was used both in ring dances and in processionals.

From the fourteenth to the seventeenth century there were various dances for curing diseases; some of the participants were suffering from diseases, others were hoping to ward them off.[29] These dances were performed in honor of the Apostle John, St. Vitus, St. Anthony, or the Virgin Mary. The dancers found relief from pain in the active participation.[30]

Dance carols were a part of the medieval and renaissance periods. An Easter carol or ring dance took place in the cloisters on Easter Eve at the church in Sens and is described in a sixteenth-century manuscript. The archbishop was assisted by the clergy. They moved first round two-by-two, followed in the same manner by prominent citizens, all singing songs of the resurrection. Then the carol was performed as the dance continued from the cloister into the church, round the choir, into the nave, to the singing of the *Salvator Mundi*.

The Dance of Death (*danse macabre*) was the most widely known of all the religious dances from the twelfth to the sixteenth centuries in Italy, Spain, France, Germany, and England. It sprang from the medieval sermons on death. The preaching of the Franciscans and Dominicans emphasized the terrors of death as a means of frightening sinners into repentance. The Dance of Death started in the cemetery or churchyard with a sermon on the certainty of death. From the charnel house would come a figure, or in some cases a group of figures, in the traditional attire of Death, which was a close-fitting yellowish suit painted to resemble a skeleton. Victims were invited or coerced into accompanying Death beyond the grave. Death, although grotesque, appeared not as a destroyer but as a messenger summoning men to the world beyond.

During the period of the epidemic of the Black Plague (1347–1373), a set pattern evolved for the Dance of Death with musical accompaniment and a processional design. The whole of medieval society was represented from the pope to the common laborer, each of whom, regardless of station, was made an unwilling captive by Death. These people, arranged according to their rank, advanced in processional formation. Death indulged in grotesque and mocking dance positions.

The Dance of Death was known in fourteenth-century Spain as *La Danza General de la Muerte*. In Italy, besides the traditional dance, there was a spectacular representation of death as the all-conqueror in the *Trionfo della Morte*. In sixteenth-century Florence, there was a "Triumph of Death" procession with an oxen-drawn wagon upon which Death stood holding his scythe, surrounded by coffins. In Herder's *Kirchen Lexikon*, Baumker mentioned seven French Dances of Death, dating back to the fifteenth century, three to the sixteenth, and three to the seventeenth centuries. Five Dances of Death were known in England.

There have been numerous illustrations of the Dance of Death on the walls of cemeteries or charnel houses, in mortuary chapels, and in churches throughout Europe. One of the oldest pictures (1425) is in the *Cimetière des Innocents* near Paris. Another famous painting is *The Triumph of Death* (1450/1500) in the cemetery of Pisa. Hans Holbein made a series of drawings to illustrate the dance in 1538 (fig. 5).

In the medieval period an ecstatic dancing sect, the *Chorizantes*, sprang up in Germany with a membership in the thousands, including both sexes. They would dance through the streets, and in and out of churches until they were exhausted. They were not interested in the attention of spectators, but absorbed in their fantastic visions. Imagining that they were wading in a stream of blood, they would leap wildly in the air as if to get out of the blood. These dances first appeared during the festival of John the Baptist at Aachen in 1374, and then spread to Cologne, Metz, and other parts of Germany.

A similar display of ecstatic dancing occurred at Strasbourg in 1419. Here St. Vitus was invoked to cure a malady. Martyred under

Diocletian (c. 300), he had cured the emperor's son of demonic possession. St. Vitus became the patron saint of nervous diseases and his dance was considered to have curative value. Gradually his name became connected with the disease choreomania.

The most ancient of the Christianized pagan dances were those for St. John's Day and the "Brandons." The St. John's dance was celebrated on the eve of June 24 in Brittany, Provence, and England. In this bonfire dance the celebrants leapt over or through the fire which might have had an ancient health value as the smoke and flames destroyed vermin and miasma. The "Brandons," an ancient torch dance accompanied by chants and prayers, was performed on the first of May and at Pentecost.

Through the centuries, councils were alert to curtail excesses in sacred dancing: Auxerre (573), Toledo (589), Chalon-sur-Saone (639), Rome (826), Avignon (1209), and Paris (1212). The pagan element that was present and the undisciplined mass participation made it difficult for the consecrated and controlled religious dance to continue. Sacred dance had been overshadowed by the frenzied and grotesque Dances of Death, the wild exhausting dances of the Chorizantes, and the leaping torch dances.

The Renaissance (1400/1700)

The Renaissance is said to have begun with Dante (1265–1321) who referred to dancing as the occupation of those in paradise.[31] He described the blessed ones as dancing in such various measures that some seemed to stand still while others flew.[32] This conception of heavenly dancing, similar to Bonaventure's description,[33] became the guide for the creation of sacred dances during the Renaissance.

Elaborate dramatic presentations became popular. Allegorical masques made use of symbolic dancing to heighten the dramatic moods. In England, to celebrate the victorious return of Henry V from Agincourt (1415), maidens danced with tambourines, reminding the people of David's triumph. Another court celebration with dancing was the pageant honoring the coronation of Henry VI (1432). In this pageant there were seven maidens representing the seven celestial virtues, and another seven representing the terrestrial virtues.[34]

Corpus Christi processions were originally nothing more than ambulatory dances in which the participants, following a certain pattern, bowed in measure, swung censers in cadence, and threw flowers into the air. In Provence, King Rene sponsored an elaborate Corpus Christi masque (1463), called *Lou Gué* and also *Jeux de la Fête-Dieu*, which was presented as a series of scenes on pageant wagons. These dramatizations used no dialogue, only pantomime and dance. One scene portrayed the Jews dancing around the golden calf; another, Herod's persecution by the devils who were after his soul; at the end came Death with a scythe.

In renaissance paintings, there were glimpses of movement as the angels represented adoration. The flow of the costumes, the positions held for the moment, and the circular formations, all implied that the artists conceived of movement rather than static positions. Fra Angelico (c. 1400–1455) painted "the Dance of the Redeemed" as part of *The Last Judgment* portraying a circular dance of saints and angels entering paradise (fig. 6). Sandro Botticelli (c. 1487) portrayed angels dancing in a circle above the Nativity scene. The composer of *In Dulci Jubilo* dreamed of angels dancing as they sang, and upon waking he wrote down the melody of the carol. Donatello's *Dance of the Angels* portrays angels in symbolic movement. Renaissance artists revealed the serenity and adoration expressed in contemporary sacred dances.

Although religious dances continued to flourish during the Renaissance, certain events occurred that were to have a crippling effect upon this art. Books began to be printed after 1455, and, with the printing of tracts, pamphlets, and books, there was a growing emphasis upon the intellect. The mind would soon be considered as all-important and the body as valueless in religious growth. The Reformation, which began in 1517, tended in its extreme forms to do away with most of the visual arts, leaving only the arts of printing, preaching, and music. All dances and processions, except for funeral processions, were abolished.

Martin Luther (1525), who loved children, wrote many carols for them. In his carol, "From Heaven High," there are two little-known stanzas which support the role of song and dance.[35] Evidently Martin Luther understood the natural way that children expressed joy spontaneously with their whole beings, singing, skipping, and dancing. Luther was adamant against whatever was sham or pretense, but loved what was genuine and brought forth the total involvement of a dedicated person, whether child or adult.

In his prologue to the New Testament, William Tyndale wrote of the role of joyous song and dance. This sixteenth-century English church leader was not fearful of using the dramatic verbs "daunce" and "leepe" when he considered the joy of the good news of Christianity.

The Council of Trent (1545–1563), which represented the Roman

5. Hans Holbein, *Queen*,
from *Dance of Death*, no
date. Woodcut. Rosenwald
Collection, National Gallery of
Art, Washington.

6. Fra Angelico, *Dance in Paradise*, detail from
Last Judgment, 1425. Museo di San Marco,
Firenze. Photograph courtesy of Alinari/Art
Resource, New York.

7. *Shakers Dancing*, 19th-century American engraving. Photograph courtesy
of the Dance Collection, Performing Arts Research Center, The New York
Public Library at Lincoln Center. Astor, Lenox and Tilden Foundations.

Catholic Counter-Reformation, showed a determination to return to medieval liturgical tradition by removing literary and dramatic interpolations. The statutes of the Synod of Lyons (1566) threatened priests and other persons with excommunication if they led dances in churches or cemeteries.

The church was determined to stop religious dancing, but dancing continued in a variety of forms. St. Teresa of Avila (c. 1555) danced with holy joy. In the seventeenth century, two other noted Carmelites imitated the Spanish mystic and saint, Bienheureuse Marie de l'Incarnation and Anne de Jésus who danced before *le Saint Sacrement* at Carmel in Dijon.

The renaissance courts with their love of display often sponsored dances of a semireligious nature. The pavane, a stately dance, was performed at the death of someone in the court circle, especially a young lady. In 1507, William Dunbar described a "Dance of the Seven Deadly Sins" at the Edinburgh court on the day before "fastern's e'en" as a combination of the dance of death with a morality masque.[36]

Catherine de Medici brought to France her taste for Italian dancing and sponsored masked dances done to the accompaniment of psalms. In 1572, she produced a dance-drama called "The Defense of Paradise" that recounted the dramatic clash between the Roman Catholic King of France (Charles IX) and his brothers, who defended heaven, and the Protestant King of Navarre and his friends, who guarded hell. Navarre's knights attacked heaven. This fight, which had been planned in advance, left Charles IX victorious as his assailants were thrown back into hell which swallowed them.[37]

Such theatrical dance must have been rehearsed many times. It is, therefore, amazing to realize that men so bitterly hostile to the art of music and dance could project, even for a short time, an attitude of mutual respect and honor. It is ironic that the production of "The Defense of Paradise" was presented on 18 August 1572, just six days before the St. Bartholomew's Day massacre!

Dancing was an integral part of the first oratorio, *La Rappresentazione di Anima e di Corpo* by Emilio de' Cavalieri that was performed in the oratory of Chiesa D. Maria in Vallicella in Rome in 1600. The principal characters were Time, the World, Life, Pleasure, the Intellect, the Soul, and the Body. The original oratorio was made varied and dramatic through symbolic dances.

A traditional Easter dance, the bergerette, was performed annually in the churches of the diocese of Besançon on the afternoon of Easter Day. In a book of rites of the Church of Ste. Marie Madaleine (1582), there is a chapter for Easter Day which states that "At the end of the sermon...there are dances (*chorea*) in the cloister or in the middle of the nave of the church if it is rainy weather; they are danced to certain airs contained in the processional."[38] In spite of the synodal diocesan decrees of 1585 and 1601 that threatened severe penalties against the enthusiasts who ventured to retain the ancient custom of the labyrinthine dance, the dance continued in the churches of Besançon until 1738.

Among the numerous religious dances created for special occasions were the *ballet ambulatoire* to celebrate the canonization of Cardinal Carlo Borromeo in 1610, the dance to celebrate the canonization of Ignatius of Loyola in 1622, and the "moral ballet" composed in 1634 to commemorate the birthday of the cardinal of Savoy. The word *ballet* implied a professional dance group for theatrical performance.

A unique dance was performed by the priests at Eastertime in the cathedrals of Auxerre, Rheims, Rouen, Sens, Narbonne, and generally throughout France. The unusual feature of the dance was that it centered upon the tossing of a ball or pelota (*pilota*). When the pilota had been received from the canon or dean, the priests began to intone antiphonally the sequence appropriate to the Easter festival, "Praises to the Pascal Victim." Then, supporting the ball with his left hand, he began to dance in time with the rhythmical sounds of the chanted sequence, while the rest, holding hands, executed a choral dance round the labyrinth. Meanwhile the pilota was handed or thrown alternately by the dean to the dancers.

The passing of the ball backward and forward, in the circular dance, in which every dancer also revolved on his own axis, was thought to illustrate the apparent path or dance of the sun in the heavens throughout the year and so of its "passion." The dance at Auxerre included a variety of symbolic patterns: the resurrection of Christ-sun, the cosmic mystery of the heavenly bodies, and the labyrinthine dance.

The "Cornwall Carol" from the time of the medieval minstrels and troubadours had a peculiar mixture of religious carol and folk song. It told the story of the life of Christ in ballad form, as if related by Jesus. The ballad related such incidents as the birth in the manger, the baptism, the temptations in the desert, the betrayal by Judas, and the trial before Pilate. After the tale of the death on the cross and the descent into hell, the ballad closed with the hope that humanity "May come unto the general dance."[39] As the church gradually closed its door to religious dances, their remnants became parts of folk songs. The stanzas of the "Cornwall Carol" show an intelligent development of the life of Christ that must have had its origin within the church.

Another Christmas carol that is sung today, "Joseph Dearest, Joseph Mine," was written down in this period as *Resonnet in laudibus,* and dance was part of the carol. Another dance-carol, "Dance of the Child Jesus," was held at Roquebrussance near Brignoles. After High Mass, on the day of the patronal feast of the church, the mothers with their babies formed a group around the altar of the Christ child to sing, gesture, and dance.

There were also carols for ring dances at the time of a death. Fragments of funeral ring-dance songs or carols suggest the custom of using choral movement to express the deep joy-in-sorrow which was a Christian attitude. This expression of joy signified the release of the soul into the immortal life. Perhaps funeral services could have a more Christian character if, instead of mourning over the departed, there could be joyous acceptance of death as an onward step toward immortal life. The traditional antiphon following the "Mass for the Dead" preserved the radiant Christian faith in the spiritual immortality of the soul as it is received into the joy of paradise by a choir of angels.

Post-Renaissance Period (1700/1900)

Although sacred dance had flourished during the Renaissance in oratorio, in the interpretation of hymns and psalms in services of worship, and in theatrical allegorical ballets, in the post-renaissance period the door was firmly closed on its creative expression. Neither the Roman Catholic Church nor the Protestant Christian churches allowed sacred dances in their services. Religious dance either disappeared, survived in isolated places, changed into folk expressions, or remained submerged in the prescribed movements of the mass itself.

As the Roman Catholic Church became more centrally authoritative in Rome and published conforming edicts, there was little chance for creative and fresh exploration in the sacred dance.[40] In general, Protestant Christians felt that the portals of the spirit were to be entered with great seriousness through the mind and not through the senses. However, even in this strictness, some of the leaders were intellectually aware of the religious dances mentioned in the Hebrew Scriptures. John Cotton, a New England Puritan, wrote that "Dancing I would not simply condemn, for I see two sorts of mixt dancing in use with God's people in the Old Testament; the one religious (Exodus 15:20–21), the other civil, tending to the praise of conquerors (1 Sam.

18:6–7)."[41] In his discourse "An Arrow Against Profane and Promiscuous Dancing," Increase Mather, another Puritan, condemned only dancing that aroused the passions.

With no opportunity for creative life in conventional churches, sacred dance faded out and became unknown to church attendants. However, some sects and cults arose in this arid period, and their members experimented with symbolic movements in their rituals.

One of these new cults, "The Free and Accepted Masons," organized in 1717, grew out of a guild meeting of masons who were building English cathedrals. In this secret society (as in other later societies including the International Order of Odd Fellows and the Grange), elaborate rituals were developed in connection with initiation ceremonies and the attaining of degrees. For many members, the secret order had a stronger hold than the church, which usually asked its attendants merely to sit still and listen.

The Shakers, founded in England in 1747, were a unique group that created intricate religious dances. Their beliefs were derived from certain Huguenot groups whose ideas descended from the Albigensians of the thirteenth century, whose adherents incorporated dance as a way of adoration. This connection clarifies how Shaker dance formations came to resemble those of the early Christian church. In England, the early Shakers walked the floor while singing and swiftly passed and repassed each other "like clouds agitated by a mighty wind."

The term *Shaker* came from the rapid up-and-down movement of the hands with the action mostly in the wrists. When the participants shook their hands with the palms turned down toward the floor, the symbolic motion meant that they were shaking out "all that is carnal." When the palms were turned upward as if to receive spiritual blessing, the quick up and down, shaking movement expressed the open petition "Come, life eternal." The first ordered dance of the Shakers, the "Square Order Shuffle," was introduced by Joseph Meacham about 1785."[42] In 1820 a variation was introduced; men and women shuffled forward and backward in a series of parallel lines, weaving, in imaginative designs, a fabric of union and love (fig. 7).

Circling dances were popular at this time. Sometimes there were alternate circles of men and women, with the symbolism of Ezekiel's wheel in the middle (Ezek. 1:16). In the nineteenth century, circle dances were evident in black church worship. Whites and blacks processed together in the marching-out songs which climaxed the weeklong camp meetings that had stimulated the growth of Baptists, Methodists, and Presbyterians during the Second Great Awakening.[43]

At the close of the nineteenth century, symbolic movement was not acceptable in the established churches. However, an Anglo-Catholic, who had some influence among the leaders of the Church of England, started a growing edge of exploration in the use of interpretive movement in the liturgy. By 1884, Stewart Headlam expressed his interest in drama by directing a group of girls who participated in special services.[44] Headlam's recognition "that the poetry of dance is the expression of unseen spiritual grace" was the beginning of the revival of interest in sacred dance in the twentieth century.

Notes

1. Gerardus van der Leeuw, *Sacred and Profane Beauty. The Holy in Art* (New York: Holt, Rhinehart, and Winston, 1963).

2. For an analysis of ancient Hebrew dance, see W. O. E. Oesterley, *The Sacred Dance* (New York: Macmillan, 1923).

3. Matthew Black, *The Aramaic Approach to the Gospels and Acts* (London: Clarendon Press, 1967) 158.

4. G. R. S. Mead, *The Sacred Dance in Christendom* (London: John M. Watkins, 1926) 65.

5. *Didache* XI, 11.

6. See Clement of Alexandria, *Stromata* V, iv, 19; and idem., *Exhortation to the Heathen* xii, 199f.

7. Origin, *De Prec.* vii, 5.

8. Gregory Thaumaturgus, *Four Sermons* i; and idem., *Hom.* iv (*De Christi Bapt.*).

9. Eusebius, *DVC* xi.

10. Eusebius, *VC* II, xix.

11. Gregory of Nyssa, *Hom.* vi (*In Eccles.*) 4.

12. Gregory Nazianzus, *Oration Against Julian* 11, 171.

13. See C. H. Bromel, *Fest-Tantze der ersten Christen* (Jena, 1701).

14. Basil, *Epistle* xl.

15. B. Aubé, *Homélie inédite en append. à Polyeucte dans l'histoire* (Paris, 1882) 79.

16. See Ambrose's references to Luke 7:32 in *On Repentance* ii.6:42.

17. For his commentary on Luke 7:32, see Ambrose, *Commentary on the Gospel of St. Luke* vi. See also his commentary on Ezekiel 6:11 in *Speech* xlii.

18. Chrysostom, *Hom.* i (*In illud. vidi Dom.*) 1.

19. Chrysostom, *On the Resurrection of Lazarus* i.

20. Chrysostom, *Proaem in Pss.*

21. Augustine, *Speeches* cccxi.

22. Theodoret, *Graecarum Affectionum Curatio* xi.

23. *Analecta Hymnica* 2, 62 (Leipzig, 1890–1906).

24. *Planctus* of Cividale del Fruili. Cividale, Reale Museo Archeologico. Cividale Saec. xiv, foll. 74ff.

25. Bonaventure, *Dieta Salutis* (*Aureus Libellus*).

26. Honorius, *Gemma Animae* ("On Dancing").

27. See Mead, *The Sacred Dance in Christendom* 99n. See also T. H. Poole, "Labyrinth," in *The Catholic Encyclopedia* 4 (New York: Encyclopedia Press, 1907–22).

28. The symbolism of Christ "leading out" the people in an Easter ceremony is illustrated in the account of the processional dance in Hildesheim. See K. Bartsch, *Mittelniederdeutsche Osterlieder* (1880) 49.

29. *Analecta Hymnica* 16, 72.

30. For religious dance as healing, see E. Louis Backman, *Religious Dances in the Christian Church and in Popular Medicine* (London: Allen & Unwin, 1952).

31. Dante, *Divine Comedy: Paradise* VII.

32. Ibid., XXIV.

33. Bonaventure, "Of the Joys of Paradise," *Dieta Salutis.*

34. Lincoln Kirstein, *Dance* (New York: G. P. Putnam's Sons, 1935) 112f.

35. Roland Bainton, *The Martin Luther Christmas Book* (Philadelphia: Westminster Press, 1948) 76.

36. William Dunbar, *The Poems of William Dunbar* (Edinburgh and London: Blackwood for Scottish Text Society, 1884–5), II, 116, 119.

37. Kirstein, *Dance*, 146.

38. Rites referred to in an anonymous letter to the *Mercure de France,* September 1742. Trans. by Mead, *The Sacred Dance in Christendom*, 250.

39. See *The Oxford Book of Carols* (London: Oxford University Press, 1964) No. 71.

40. Backman, *Religious Dances in the Christian Church and in Popular Medicine*, 159f.

41. See John Cotton, *Collections by Increase Mather*, X (Boston: Massachusetts Historical Society, 1823) 183f.

42. Edward D. Andrews, "The Dance in Shaker Ritual," *Chronicles of the American Dance*, ed. Paul Magriel (New York: Henry Holt & Co., 1948) 5.

43. On the history of black dance in nineteenth-century worship, see Lynne Fauley Emery, *Black Dance in the United States from 1619 to 1970* (Palo Alto: National Press Books, 1972) esp. 119–38.

On the marching out processions of nineteenth-century camp meetings, see Charles Albert Johnson, *The Frontier Camp Meeting* (Dallas: Southern Methodist University Press, 1955) esp. 41–47, 57–61, and 122–44.

44. For his description of this sacred dance, see Stewart Headlam, *Church Reformer*, October 1884 issue.

PART I

Dance
and
Scripture

3

Communal Dance Forms and Consequences in Biblical Worship

Doug Adams

A survey of the Hebrew Scriptures suggests that group dance was normative in worship; but such dance allowed a variety of individual differences. Communal dance was not always a dance to God; but rather when included in Israelite worship, dance took a communal form. The principle word for dance in the Hebrew Scriptures is in its various forms *māḥôl, mᵉḥôlôt,* and *ḥyl* or *ḥll*. These forms denote the group dances translated by *chorós* in the Greek Septuagint and *chorea* in the Latin Vulgate. These dances are usually by a group rather than by an individual.[1]

In this group dancing, movements by the individuals could be either wild or graceful. The tendency in Judaism has been to accept a wide range of even awkward movements within the group so that all

"Communal Dance Forms and Consequences in Biblical Worship" is excerpted and updated from Doug Adams, *Congregational Dancing in Christian Worship* (Austin: The Sharing Co., 1984 [1971]). It is included in this collection with permission.

persons are included. The priestly traditions in both Judaism and Christianity have imposed standards of individual grace or group harmony into liturgical dance; and such standards eliminate some individuals. Often based on circling and leaping forms found in earlier Jewish dance, twentieth-century Israeli folk dances regularize the movements and produce more uniform results than one would find in earlier periods.

The communal nature of dance in worship has a scriptural basis, as for example in Psalm 149:3, "Let *them* praise his name with dancing." God's heavenly restoration of Zion is communal dance, "Go forth in the dances of *them* that make merry," and "Then shall the virgin rejoice in the dance, both young men and old together."[2]

Such communal dancing in worship resonates with the earliest prophetic practices, the later talmudic and midrashic vision of humanity's coming to God, and the history of Hebraic practice. In the early prophetic practice dancing is carried out in a band.[3] W. O. E. Oesterley indicated that *hebel*, "band," means rope, thus suggesting the connectedness of those dancing.[4] Throughout the Talmud and Midrash, a vision of heaven includes the communal dance.[5] Israel Abrahams asserted that throughout Jewish history, the shape of dances has been conditioned by the desire to have all caught up in the community.[6] There is debate whether the few exceptions to communal dance in the Hebrew Scriptures should be interpreted as dancing to God. Chief among these individual dances, David's dance is identified as *kirkēr*[7] and *rāqad*.[8] Later translated as *orchoumenos* in the Greek and as *saltatio* in the Latin, David's dance indicates an individual circling and jumping. Some scholarship on this dance identifies it not exclusively or primarily as a dance to God, but as a prelude to David's coronation as king and anticipated sexual union with Michal.[9]

In connecting 2 Samuel 6 with Psalm 132, J. R. Porter offered complex arguments that this event was a coronation ritual celebrated within the Jerusalem cultus.[10] His assertion that David's dance was also connected to the sexual rites with Michal that would be expected to consummate the coronation does not necessarily follow. Nevertheless, Porter noted that the elimination of much of 2 Samuel 6 in the later priestly account indicates that the priests saw at least a suggestion of sexual practice and wished to eliminate it.[11]

David's dance may be seen as appropriate to that of the prophets with whom he is seen dancing earlier.[12] Michal's anger at seeing him dance would then be understandable, for the prophets opposed the power of her father, King Saul. At the very moment when David should be coming to her to continue the line of Saul, David does a dance showing his loyalty to the prophetic tradition.

The other instances of the use of *rāqad* refer to a dance by satyrs, and by individuals.[13] In the books of Job and Ecclesiastes, these individual dances certainly were not in the mainstream of Israelite thought and practice. A rather narrow individual orientation of these books is what Israelite dance overcomes.[14]

The Christian church built upon the deepest understanding of the Jewish tradition of worship by supporting choral dancing, while suppressing individual dancing. The choral dance accompanies the return of the prodigal son to his father.[15] This return of son to father may be seen as paradigmatic for Christian worship. Thus, the inclusion of choral dancing in this passage supports my thesis of the integral role of congregational dance in worship.

The two Christian scriptural references to individual dancing, *orchoumenos*, depict decidedly nonworshipful scenes. First is the dance of Salome before Herod.[16] The second instance requires careful attention as the passage has often been misread as Jesus' call for individual dance.[17] In Luke 7:31–34 (with a comparative Matthew 11:16–19), the passage reads:

And the Lord said, Whereunto then shall I liken the men of this generation? and to what are they like? They are like unto children sitting in the marketplace, and calling one to another and saying, We have piped unto you, and ye have not danced; we have mourned to you, and ye have not wept. For John the Baptist came neither eating bread nor drinking wine; and ye say, He hath a devil. The Son of Man is come eating and drinking; and ye say, Behold a gluttonous man, and a winebibber, a friend of publicans and sinners![18]

Christ is not calling for the people to dance individual dances. Rather, "this generation" acted like the children in the marketplace expecting such a performance. This passage focuses on the false expectations and the resulting errors in judging others. From the concluding verses it is obvious that as John the Baptist does not fulfill the dancing expectation, Jesus does not fulfill the weeping one.

In Eastern Orthodoxy, the distinction between the group dance, *chorós*, and the individual dance, *orchoumenos*, with support of the former and suppression of the latter, is continued. Gregory of Nazianzus (329–388), "The Theologian" of the Eastern Orthodox Church and Bishop of Constantinople, advised the people that doing triumphant ring dances was the proper way to celebrate Easter.[19]

However, he cautioned the emperor against individual dance of the kind performed by the daughter of Herod.[20]

Basil the Great (c. 329–379), Bishop of Caesarea, urged his people to perform the ring dance.[21] He proceeded to attack individual dance performed by women as it distracted the attention of the men who sat and watched in church.[22] John Chrysostom (345–407), Bishop of Constantinople, blessed the performance of the ring dances while he censored those who through excess engaged in the individual dance.[23] One is given feet for comely ring dances,[24] while one should refrain from the unbridled dance[25] or the camel sort of dance.[26]

In Roman Catholicism, where invading hoards of pagans threatened to overwhelm the church, all forms of lay participation were restricted including dance. Even in the West, the chorea continued to command respect, albeit in a highly metaphoric form. While Ambrose (339–397), bishop of Milan, had praised bodily dance,[27] his student Augustine (354–430), writing in a more chaotic period, encouraged the people and the church to understand the dance of Psalms 149:3 and 150:4 in an exclusively metaphoric way.[28] "Dance" was a metaphor for harmonious community.

The Hebrew language, of which Augustine was ignorant, suggests that actual dance may lead to a sense of community. The Hebrews recognized the need for the people to dance literally with all their might to achieve this end. The Roman Catholic hierarchy came to recognize the power of the communal dance. The Roman Catholic objection to popular participation in dance reveals a political dimension of dancing. The superior position which Roman Catholic clergy developed over the laity required that dancing together be suppressed as too equalizing and revolutionary. Early in the twentieth century, there was approval only of dancing that will not "get out of hand."[29] The Roman Catholic hierarchy officially sanctioned an aesthetic use and understanding of dance in connection with the mass.[30] Official publications noted that individual Roman Catholics described the mass as a dance in slow motion.[31] Official Roman Catholic objection to women leading worship has complicated use of dance which is often led by women.

In considering communal dancing in worship, it is important to avoid development of an irreconcilable stress between responding to God and living in community. Worship does attempt to create a tension between the present conditions of community and the gifts and demands of God so as to stimulate our actions. Nevertheless, worship must be corporate so that the resolution of this tension is sought in corporate action and improvement rather than through individual withdrawal. For instance, many of the practices of religion, particularly the mental ways of meditation, may lead a person to look upon other persons, community, and one's own body as negatives, because such mental meditation fosters a stillness that is disturbed by activities necessitated by material life and life with others.

Without dance and other corporate expressions in worship, one could see the relationship with God as opposed to the demands of the community, and therefore withdraw from the community. In contrast to meditation and prayer, dance includes body movement which activity in life does not disturb but continues. Thus one is led to see the secular in the sacred, all caught up together. These dynamics are clarified by Gerardus van der Leeuw's suggestion that the separation that leads one to distinguish sacred from profane arises only as the dance diminishes. The reemergence of the dance, he continued, is likely to sweep away separations that the critically minded person created by sitting and not dancing.[32] Communal dance is preferable to individual dance so that one comes to look upon the constraints of living in community as a part of the response to God: a condition one should accept and not an evil one should try to escape.

Some church authorities tried to minimize the revolutionary effect of dance by restricting people to dancing with their social equals. In Paris, choir boys danced on Innocents' Day, the subdeacons on Epiphany, the deacons on St. Stephen's Day, and the priests on St. John's Day.[33] Such restrictions were difficult to enforce as dancing was often infectious. Harvey Cox analyzed the revolutionary effect of dancing and the Festival of Fools in guiding people to see all social structures as less than absolute. Even the Bible was mocked in this general effort to let God be God.[34]

The Roman Catholic Church's effort to prohibit corporate dancing from the church and graveyards and to prohibit Christians from dancing with others even outside the church extends from the times of ecclesiastical crises of Augustine into the eighteenth century.[35] My concern is to see how the dynamics of corporate dance are revealed by such prohibitions that were designed to keep Christians of differing social class from intimate contact with each other and from intimate contact with those outside the Christian community.

Dancing in the Judeo-Christian tradition has been associated with the experiences that life is not determined by the past or old self. Bondage to the past may be shaken off by dancing to free attention to feel new intentions. In the Hebrew Scriptures and subsequent Jewish traditions, dance celebrates and effects the end of slavery to the past and the beginning of new freedom to act in the world and create new community. This dynamic is present in the biblical account of the first dance at the Exodus, the Jewish commentaries on that account, and the Hasidic explanation for the Jews learning to dance.

At the Exodus, Miriam led the women in dance to celebrate the overthrow of the Egyptians and the end of the Israelite slavery.[36] In a passage of this dancing and singing in the late Beshallach Midrash, dance is linked to a forgetting of and freeing from the troubling past.[37] Of course, this does not prove that the early Israelites had such a sophisticated understanding of the effects of dance. Nevertheless, the dance from Exodus is an appropriate watershed between slavery and freedom, the past and the future.

The founder of Hasidim, Israel Baal Shem Tov (c. 1700–1760), understood the dynamic of dance in telling a story. So he learned to dance and set off the great religious revival in eastern European Judaism in the eighteenth century. He danced to aid a jailed Jew gain his freedom. Once again there is the association of dancing with the freedom to act.[38]

The prophets (*nabi*) used dance to effect the loss of preoccupation with self and with past concerns. This dynamic is revealed most clearly in Saul's contacts with the prophetic bands. In Saul's last contact with the prophets, the loss of self-consciousness in dancing is obvious in the uninhibited nakedness of Saul and the others.[39] The loss of preoccupation with the past concerns is obvious in the actions of Saul's messengers and finally Saul himself who came to the prophets with the purpose of taking David but became caught up in the spirit of prophesying (dancing) and forgot their former concern.

Christian literature testifies to a similar use of dance to effect people's freedom to act in the world. Early Christian writings and later hymnody evidence the use of dance to shake off bondage to the devil and disease. Later literature influenced by Christian ideas developed the picture of the devil and those in bondage to the devil as unmoving.

Gregory of Nazianzus, the bishop of Constantinople, stated: "May we flee from all the chains of the devil" in performing "triumphant ring dances."[40] In another address, Gregory urged the people to attend ceremonies using dances at the graves of martyrs "for the manifest casting out of devils, the prevention of sickness and the knowledge of things to come."[41] A church hymn sung and danced on Easter in the twelfth century echoed this same dynamic.[42] Another medieval hymn sings of dancing and "trampling vices under foot."[43] Although only fragments, these records reveal the common use of the dance within the early church to shake off the devil, disease, and all else that enslaves people and holds them down.

The Therapeutae (a Jewish sect that may have converted to early Christianity), did a dance in imitation of Miriam's which may have had the effect of curing disease.[44] Whether or not this group was ever Christian, their practice was common among Christians as the church historian Eusebius (260–340), bishop of Caesarea, testified in calling the Therapeutae practice Christian and a practice that is "still our custom to the present day to perform."[45]

There has been a long association between dance and healing in Christianity. Often great leaders of dance in the church were noted for their healing. Gregory the Wonder Worker (213–270), bishop of Pontus, who devised special dances on festivals for martyrs, is one example.[46] In fact, the use of dance in the treatment of disease has once again become a focus of interest in our own day.[47]

Classic Western literature influenced by Christian ideas came to associate physical illness with nonmovement and to see the devil and those in demonic bondage as nonmoving and antagonistic to dance. In the first volume of his *Divine Comedy*, Dante depicted the devil as one encased in a cake of ice, unable to move except as the devil "stood forth at mid-breast from the ice."[48] In Dante's vision, the closer one comes to God the more active one becomes — the angels dance around the Lord.

In accordance with Dante's scheme, William Shakespeare's characters expose themselves by their attitudes toward dance and music. For instance, Capulet says to his cousin what is painfully obvious in their attitude toward love and others: "You and I are past our dancing days."[49] Shylock's reaction to dancing is what one would expect from such a villain. After bidding Jessica to "lock up my doors," he decries the Christian practice of musical and dancing revelry, and cautions his daughter, "Let not the sound of shallow foppery enter my sober house."[50] Unfortunately, too many people, even into our own day, are like Shylock in their attitudes toward dance in worship and would cut the heart out of life.[51]

Nevertheless, Jesus appears to be in line with the traditional Hebraic understanding of dance when he says, "Leap for joy."[52] The Christian church continued to use dance to create greater joy in worship.[53] To enjoy the songs and music in church, one danced.

There is a strong and positive correlation between the use of dance in worship and a people's consciousness of their ability to change and affect their condition in spite of apparent setbacks. The most common dance step used in the early Christian processions was the *tripudium*, a Latin term meaning three steps. This movement pattern was interpreted as jubilation paralleling the linguistic development of the Aramaic evolution of "dance" into "joy."[54] In this dance step, one takes three steps forward and one step back. Setbacks were thus interpreted within the context of continued forward movement.[55] This movement symbolized the progress in health and welfare not only of the individual but also of the church and the entire community. One did not move in single file but rather marched in rows with arms linked to those on either side. In our own day, the Christian social movements such as the marches for civil rights and for peace are persistent signs of a people's faith and hope that they can change the conditions of the world even in face of setbacks and overwhelming odds.

A people's belief that they can shape the material world into a better placed is premised upon their belief that the material world is not inherently evil but rather is potentially good as God's creation. The Jewish and Christian practice has been based on a worldview that the material world is good and within a people's possibility and responsibility to uplift.

It is revealing that many of those who have difficulty accepting dance in Christian worship also have difficulty with communion and the other sacraments in worship. Dancing and the sacraments lead to the same realization: concern for the material world and for its increased intention toward higher forms of activity, complexity, and community. It is crucial for the continued growth of civilization that Western people (who are now tempted to resolve their tensions by escape from the world through the use of drugs), take the incarnation as their model and become recommited to the material dimension of the world.

One path for this recommitment is dance which brings movement and direction to the body, and so transforms it. Dance is not separate from the body but is more than just body not materially but intentionally. Thus, dance is to the body as spirit is to the body — one and inseparable but more. As we come to understand Christ's action of incarnation and communion as a force toward growth of activity, complexity, and community, we come to recognize not only a dimension of the Word but also the implications for direction of our words and movements for worship.

One effect of sacraments and dance in worship services is to remind us of the bodily base of all life. The dancing and the eating in worship make us aware of our material nature and hence our solidarity with and commitment to the world. By recognizing our dependence upon matter, common matter including people, we realize our solidarity with its fate and our commitment to its preservation. By recognizing our own dependence, we see the similar dependence of others and our common cause with them. The Word, then, becomes a unifying agent; and the role of words has the same quasisexual purpose. One criterion for preaching, dancing, and other worship activities is whether they have the effect of leading to awareness of the greater community and commitment to the growth of the world.

Dancing has been used in Christian worship to reveal God and those close to God as actively moving in and beyond the community to help people identify themselves with this dynamic God through their own movements. This identification through the body was used to increase Christian intentions and to transform them into actions. The process is still available to us today in Christian worship.

Notes

1. Julian Morgenstern, "The Etymological History of the Three Hebrew Synonyms for 'To Dance,'" *American Oriental Society Journal* 36 (1916) 321–32.

2. Jeremiah 31:4 and 13.

3. 1 Samuel 10:5.

4. W. O. E. Oesterley, *The Sacred Dance* (New York: Cambridge University Press, 1923) 108.

5. H. Freedman and Maurice Simon, eds., *The Midrash* (London: Soncino Press, 1939), vol. 4, trans. J. Israelstan, "Shemini" (Leviticus) XI.9, p. 151. This same story is repeated in the *Midrash*, vol. 9, trans. Maurice Simon, "Song of Songs," VII.1:2, p. 277.

Similar stories are associated with R. Jose bar Hanina of the second generation of Amoraim (257–300), *The Midrash on Psalms*, trans. William G. Braude (New Haven: Yale University Press, 1959) 9, 463; and R. Eleazar ben Pedath of the third generation Amoraim (300–330), I. Epstein, ed., *The Talmud*, trans. J. Rabbinowitz (London: Soncino Press, 1938), "Ta'anith" 31 a, Mo'ed VII, 164–65.

Other rabbis conveying this vision are R. Ulla bar Ishmael of beri (Bira'ach) of the second generation of Amoraim, and R. Helbo and R. Berekiah of the fourth generation of Amoraim. For background and dating of these rabbis and their work, see Hermann L. Strack, *Introduction to the Talmud and Midrash* (Philadelphia: Jewish Publication Society of America, 1931), supplemented by material from "Excursus III," by H. Loewe in his *Rabbinic Anthology* (New York: Meridian Books, 1938).

6. Israel Abrahams, *Jewish Life in the Middle Ages* (New York: Macmillan Company, 1896) 380.

7. 2 Samuel 6:14, 16.

8. 1 Chronicles 15:29.

9. J. R. Porter, "An Interpretation of 2 Samuel VI and Psalm CXXXII," *The Journal of Theological Studies* 5 (1954) 161–73.

10. For additional information on this cultus, see Aubrey Johnson, "The Role of the King in the Jerusalem Cultus," *The Labyrinth*, ed. Samuel Henry Hooke (New York: Macmillan Company, 1935) 73–111.

11. For the priestly account, see 1 Chronicles 15:29. R. Abba b. Kahana (c. 275) identified David's dance with a very sexual kind and sides with Michal in criticizing David for dancing in such a way; see "Bemidbar" IV.20 (Numbers) in *The Midrash*, vol. 5, trans. J. Slotki, 135. Other rabbis continued in the reaction of the writers of 1 Chronicles in reducing the dance to "he turned the front of his foot" and explain David's nakedness by "he stood on tiptoe, revealing his naked toes." See "Bemidbar," p. 133.

12. Saul's men and finally Saul himself are powerless in the face of such dance: 1 Samuel 19:19–24.

13. Isaiah 13:21; Job 21:11; and Ecclesiastes 3:4.

14. The sense of community, in its historical dimensions, would eliminate the sense of futility portrayed in Ecclesiastes and the sense of injustice portrayed in Job. The complaints in these two books result from reflecting on the fate of the individual and not the community.

15. Luke 15:25.

16. Matthew 14:6 and Mark 6:22.

17. For example, St. Ambrose of Milan misreads this passage in this exact manner; see "On Repentance," *Patrologiae Cursus Completus*, Series Latina, ed. Jacques Paul Migne, vol. 16, col. 1180. Eng. trans. in E. Louis Backman, *Religious Dances in the Christian Church and Popular Medicine* (London: Allen and Unwin, 1952) 26.

18. Luke 7:31–34.

19. Chr. Bromel, *Fest-Tantze der ersten Christen* (Jena, 1703). English trans. in Backman, *Religious Dances in the Christian Church and Popular Medicine*, 31.

20. Gregory Nazianzus, "Against Julianus II," *Patrologiae Cursus Completus*, Series Graeca, ed. Jacques Paul Migne, vol. 35, col. 710. Eng. trans. in Backman, *Religious Dances in the Christian Church*, 31.

Gregory advised that if the emperor must do individual dances, at least let him do individual ones in the spirit of David, whom Gregory considered to have approached God.

21. Basil, "Epistle ad. I, 2" in Migne, Series Graeca, vol. 32, col. 226. Eng. trans. in Backman, *Religious Dances in the Christian Church*, 25.

22. Basil, "Sermon on Drunkenness," Num. I, Migne, Series Graeca, vol. 31, col. 446, 459. Eng. trans. in Backman, *Religious Dances in the Christian Church*, 25. Even worse, such women join with others and desecrate even the group dance.

23. John Chrysostom, "On the Resurrection of Lazarus," I, Migne, Series Graeca, vol. 48, col. 963. Eng. trans. in Backman, *Religious Dances in the Christian Church*, 33.

24. John Chrysostom, "hom. ad Agricolas," in Bromel, *Fest-Tantze.* Eng. trans. in Backman, *Religious Dances in the Christian Church,* 32.

25. John Chrysostom, "Sermon on Marriage," Migne, Series Graeca, vol. 48, col. 963. Eng. trans. in Backman, *Religious Dances in the Christian Church,* 32.

26. John Chrysostom, "Commentary on the Gospel of St. Matthew," 48, Migne, Series Graeca, vol. 58, col. 492. Eng. trans. in Backman, *Religious Dances in the Christian Church,* 32.

27. Ambrose, "Commentary on Psalm 118," Migne, Series Latina, vol. 15, col. 1290. Eng. trans. in Backman, *Religious Dances in the Christian Church,* 30.

28. Augustine, "Exposition of Psalms," *The Nicene and Post-Nicene Fathers,* ed. Philip Schaff, first series, vol. 8 (Grand Rapids: Eerdmans, 1956 [1888]) 678.

29. "Dancing" in *The Catholic Encyclopedia* (New York: Robert Appleton Company, 1908) 4:618–19.

30. For example, "A Bull of Pope Eugene IV of 1439 authorizes the dances of 'los seises' ": Backman, *Religious Dances in the Christian Church,* 78.

31. D. Attwater, ed., *A Catholic Dictionary* (New York: Macmillan Company, 1962). Earlier in this century this description of the mass as a dance was given by Monsignor Robert Hugh Benson, *Papers of a Pariah* (London: Longmans, Green, and Company, 1909). Jacques Maritain has similarly described the mass in *Art and Scholasticism,* trans. J. F. Scanlow (New York: Scribner, 1930) 56. Ronald Knox elaborated this description in *The Mass in Slow Motion* (New York: Sheed and Ward, 1948).

32. Gerardus van der Leeuw, *Sacred and Profane Beauty: The Holy in Art* (New York: Holt, Rinehart, and Winston, 1963) passim.

33. Backman, *Religious Dances in the Christian Church,* 51.

34. Harvey Cox, *The Feast of Fools* (Cambridge: Harvard University Press, 1969) passim.

35. This history has been well recounted elsewhere, see for example, Backman, *Religious Dances in the Christian Church,* 154–61.

36. Exodus 15:20.

37. "Beshallach" (Exodus), XXIII.11, *The Midrash,* 290.

38. Louis I. Newman, *The Hasidic Anthology* (New York: Block Publishing Company, 1934) 66. This dynamic is further emphasized in the American experience by the fact that dance in black worship was prohibited by white legislatures, because such dancing resulted in blacks feeling too strong a sense of freedom. See Lynne Fauley Emery, "Sacred Dance," *Black Dance in the United States from 1619 to 1970* (Palo Alto: National Press Books, 1972) 119–38.

39. 1 Samuel 19:18–24.

40. Gregory of Nazianzus, "Speech II to Gregory of Nyssa," Migne, Series Graeca, vol. 35, col. 838. Eng. trans. in Backman, *Religious Dances in the Christian Church,* 31.

41. Gregory of Nazianzus, "Speech 24," Migne, Series Graeca, vol. 35, col. 1191. Eng. trans. in Backman, *Religious Dances in the Christian Church*, 42.
42. See *Analecta Hymna* 21, 37. Eng. trans. in Backman, *Religious Dances in the Christian Church*, 46.
43. See *Analecta Hymna* 1, 137. Eng. trans. in Backman, *Religious Dances in the Christian Church*, 45.
44. F. H. Colson, trans., "The Contemplative Life," *Philo* (Cambridge: Harvard University Press, 1954), 9:104–69; see esp. 165–67.
    See also Philo, *About the Contemplative Life*, ed. Fred C. Conybeare (Oxford: Clarendon Press, 1895). This latter volume sets forth the Greek, Latin, and Armenian texts of Philo's work, and the Greek and Latin versions of Eusebius' commentary and gives a conclusive defense of the commentary by Philo. Of course, the Therapeutae and their dancing rituals were dedicated to worship; but that these rituals and the very name of the group itself were connected with curing bodies as well as souls from disease, is suggested by Philo himself, see Colson, *Philo*.
45. Eusebius, *Historica Ecclesiastica* ii, 17. J. G. Davies doubts that Eusebius meant to include dance by his reference to practice: *Liturgical Dance: An Historical, Theological, and Practical Handbook* (London: SCM Press, 1984), 42–43.
46. Backman, *Religious Dances in the Christian Church*, 22. The full title of Backman's book and much of its evidence points to this same connection: *Religious Dances in the Christian Church and Popular Medicine*.
47. The literature is too vast to be recounted here. See K. Mason, ed., *Dance Therapy: Focus on Dance VII* (Reston: American Association for Health, Physical Education, Recreation, and Dance, 1980). An early graphic exposition of the use of dance "for unlocking the personalities and capabilities of retarded children" is found in Norman Canner's, *And a Time to Dance* (Boston: Beacon Press, 1968). Norman Canner, a dancer, worked with the Massachusetts Department of Mental Health.
48. Dante, *The Divine Comedy of Dante Alighieri: Inferno*, trans. John Sinclair, Canto 34 (New York: Oxford University Press, 1961) 421.
49. William Shakespeare, "Romeo and Juliet," act 1, scene 5, line 32 from *Shakespeare, Major Plays*, ed. G. G. Harrison (New York: Harcourt Brace Company, 1948), 240.
50. William Shakespeare, "The Merchant of Venice," act 2, scene 5, lines 29–36 from ibid., 313.
51. Further literary insights into the correlation of dancing with character development were collected by Gerardus van Leeuw, *Sacred and Profane Beauty*, passim.
52. Luke 6:23.
53. "Questions and Responses to the Orthodox," as quoted in Margaret Taylor, *A Time to Dance: The History of Symbolic Movement*, ed. Doug Adams (Austin: The Sharing Co., 1981 [1967]) 72–73. Although credited to Justin Martyr, this work may in fact be that of a later writer such as Diodorus,

bishop of Tarsus (c. 391) and teacher of John Chrysostom and so witness to dance in the fourth century rather than the second century.

54. In the late middle ages, the tripudium's literal meaning and practice as dance was suppressed in the general ban on dance, and tripudium came to mean simply jubilation. In a few places where dance processions survived in Christian worship into this century such at Echternach in Luxembourg, the tripudium remained the style of procession. For photographs of such processions, see Backman, *Religious Dances in the Christian Church*, 123–24.

55. Backman, *Religious Dances in the Christian Church*, passim.

4

Ten Dance-Derived Expressions in the Hebrew Bible

Mayer I. Gruber

Referring to D. Lapson's article "Dance" in the *Encyclopedia Judaica*,[1] F. Berk and D. Rosenblatt in their article "Dance" in the influential *The Second Jewish Catalogue* have written: "According to the *Encyclopedia Judaica*, the high level of interest and development in choreography can be noted by the fact that the Bible has eleven verb forms to describe dancing."[2] The eleven verbs are *ḥāgag, sābab, rāqad, qippēṣ, dillēg, kirkēr, pizzēz, pissēaḥ, ṣālaʿ, siḥēq*, and the root of the noun *māḥôl*, either *ḥyl* or *ḥll*. This list of eleven Hebrew verbs goes back to the pioneering and still basic *The Sacred Dance* by W. O. E. Oesterley.[3] In fact, two of the verbs in this list — *ṣālaʿ* 'limp' and *qippēṣ* 'jump' — are unattested in the Hebrew Bible as verbs meaning 'dance.'

"Ten Dance-Derived Expressions in the Hebrew Bible" was originally presented to the International Conference on the Bible in Dance in Jerusalem, 1979. It was originally published in *Israel Dance* (1980) 15–21, was expanded for publication in *Biblia* 62/3 (1981) 328–46, and is included in this collection with the permission of Editrice Pontifico Istituto Biblico, Piazza della Pilotta, 35-I-00187 Roma.

In her classic "Symbolic Gestures in Akkadian Contracts from Alalakh and Ugarit" A. Draffkorn Kilmer notes that it would be of general interest to trace "figures of speech... from the symbolic act in an original context to the symbolic figure of speech, attempting to establish whether the act was performed or not in the latter situation."[4] In my own comprehensive study of references to postures, gestures, and facial expressions attested in Akkadian, Ugaritic, biblical Hebrew, and biblical Aramaic, I demonstrated that criteria could indeed be established for determining when these verbs or expressions were employed in their literal meanings and when they were employed idiomatically to denote attitudes or emotions such as praise, entreaty, anger, grief, happiness, etc.[5] I showed that the most important criterion for determining when a particular verb or expression is employed literally to refer to a body movement is its being juxtaposed with other expressions denoting physical acts while the most important criterion for determining when a particular expression is employed symbolically is its being juxtaposed with other abstract expressions.

Previous studies of the verbs meaning "to dance" in biblical Hebrew relied almost exclusively upon etymology for the determination of meaning. In the present article I present the findings of my reinvestigation of the nuances of ten verbs based upon (1) the criteria explained in the previous paragraph; (2) the determination of semantic equivalents in biblical Hebrew and cognate languages; (3) traditions preserved in talmudic literature; and (4) comparisons with terminology employed in other cultures whose dance has been systematically investigated. The ten verbs to be considered are *ḥāgag, sābab, rāqad, qippēṣ, dillēg, kirkēr, pizzēz, pissēaḥ, ḥyl/ḥll,* and *śiḥēq.*

ḥāgag — 'dance in a circle'

In thirteen of its sixteen occurrences the Hebrew verb *ḥāgag* means simply 'celebrate (a prescribed festival).' In Psalm 107:27 *ḥāgag* is juxtaposed with the verb *nāʿ* 'move around,' and both verbs are said to describe the behavior of a drunk. Based on the assumed etymological relationship between the verb used in Psalm 107:27 and the verb *ḥāg* 'draw a circle' attested in Job 26:10, it has been assumed that Psalm 107:27a means "They shall move about going in circles like a drunk."[6] Hence it has seemed plausible to suggest that in 1 Samuel 30:16 and Psalm 42:5 — the only other instances where *ḥāgag* does not mean 'celebrate (a prescribed festival)' — it may mean 'dance in a circle.'[7] If so, 1 Samuel 30:16, where the verb is juxtaposed with the verbs *'ākal* 'eat,' *šātāh* 'drink,' and *nāṭaš* 'scatter,' should be rendered as follows: "So he (the Egyptian boy) led him (King David) down, and there they (Ziklag's band) were scattered all over the ground eating and drinking and dancing in a circle commemoration of the vast spoil they had taken from Philistia and Judah."

In Psalm 42:5 the words *beqôl-rinnāh wetôdāh hāmôn hōgēg* may be rendered "The multitude dances in a circle to the tune of a song of thanksgiving." It cannot be demonstrated, however, that in either 1 Samuel 30:16 or Psalm 42:5 the verb *hāgag* does not mean simply 'celebrate' as it does everywhere except in Psalm 107:27, where the context calls for a verb of motion. Nevertheless, the most plausible explanation as to how a single verb can mean 'move in circles (like a drunk)' and 'celebrate (a prescribed festival)' is that the verb *hāgag* — whose basic meaning is 'move about in a circle' — was used to refer to dancing in a circle in celebration of victory as perhaps in 1 Samuel 30:1 and to dancing in a circle in praise of God as perhaps in Psalm 42:5. The semantic development of *hāgag* 'move about in a circle' > *hāgag* 'dance in a circle to celebrate' > *hāgag* 'celebrate' thus corresponds to the semantic development *bākāh* 'weep' > *bākāh* 'weep (in mourning)' > *bākāh* 'mourn'[8] and to the semantic development *hištaḥᵃwāh* 'bend over' > *hištaḥᵃwāh* 'bend over (in worship)' > *hištaḥᵃwāh* 'worship'.[9] This does not mean that by designating a festival as *hag* the Bible means to inform us that a sacred (or nonsacred) dance was a feature of that festival although it may have been.[10]

There does seem to be one clear reference to the circle dance or processional dance about the altar that employs the noun *hag* in the sense "procession." This is Psalm 118:27, where we read, "Make a procession with branches up to the horns of the altar."[11] This interpretation of the verse, which seems to refer to the procession with *lulab* and *ethrog* on the festival of Sukkoth, is supported by reference to the Akkadian cognate of Hebrew *'isrû*, which is usually rendered 'bind.' In light of the Akkadian cognate *esēru*, which may mean 'enclose, surround,'[12] it would appear that Hebrew *'isrû hag* should mean 'make a procession, form a circle.'

sābab — 'encircle, turn about'

Especially worthy of note are the four attestations of *sābab* 'encircle, turn about' in Jeremiah 31:22; Psalm 114:3, 5; and Ecclesiastes (Qoh) 12:5 precisely because these references to dancing are generally ignored both in the previous discussions of dance in the Bible and in Bible commentaries and translations.

The most obvious instance of *sābab* 'encircle' that refers to a dance is Psalm 26:6 where the psalmist says, "I shall wash my palms with innocence so that I may walk in the procession around Your altar, O LORD." Here *sābab* refers to the same rite of worship as is described in 1 Samuel 30:16 by the verb *hāgag*.[13] That Joshua 6 (where the verb *sābab* is found six times) describes a ceremonial processional dance around the walls of Jericho is well known, and it has frequently been discussed.[14] While the aim of the circumambulation in Psalm 26:6 is worship,[15] the purpose of the circumambulations prescribed and carried out in Joshua 6 is symbolically to lay claim to the territory of Jericho.[16] Perhaps the psalmist's metaphoric description of the conspiracy of his enemies in Psalm 118:11a, *sabbûnî gam-s^ebābûnî*, "They encircled me; indeed, they encircled me," is an extension of the circumambulation as a symbolic act designed to conquer or overpower an enemy. That the same verb of motion or idiom may describe several different bodily motions or similar bodily motions with different meanings determined by context is discussed at length in my *Aspects of Nonverbal Communication in the Ancient Near East*.[17]

In Psalm 114:3–4 are additional uses of *sābab* referring to a dance performed as an act of divine worship. Here we are told that in response to the deliverance of Israel from Egypt, "The sea saw and fled, the Jordan turned around, the mountains danced like rams, the hills like young sheep." These verses combine three images. These are (1) the primordial battle between the LORD and the rebellious Sea/River;[18] (2) the splitting of the Reed Sea (Exod. 14:21 etc.) and of the Jordan River (Josh. 3:13–17) to enable the Israelites to pass over on dry land; and (3) dancing as a form of praise and worship of the LORD. Just as the personified mountains[19] are said to have danced the *riqqûd* 'skipping dance,'[20] so are Sea and Jordan said to have danced the circle dance. Similarly in Psalm 114:7 *'āreṣ* 'the land' (of Israel?) is commanded: *hûlî* "dance the *māhôl*"[21] in praise of God.

In Jeremiah 31:22 *sābab* refers neither to an act of worship nor to laying claim to territory, but to the universal phenomenon of circumambulation of the bridegroom, bride, or bridal couple.[22] According to folklorists the origin of this practice is "to obstruct the entry of demons and noxious influences" that might seek to harm the bridegroom and/or bride.[23] Bible scholars have long been puzzled as to why Jeremiah called the practice of woman circumambulating man an innovation when he says in Jeremiah 31:22b, "Indeed, the LORD creates an innovation in the land: a woman will circumambulate a man."[24] To those who had become so completely used to disaster that they said of Judah and Jerusalem, "It has been destroyed...no one lives here" (Jer. 33:10), it was indeed an innovation that weddings should again be celebrated there.[25] Using *pars pro toto* the prophet describes a wedding as "a woman will circumambulate a man."

Seeing that *sābab* 'encircle, turn about' can and does refer to the circle dance or processional dance elsewhere called *ḥag*, we may be able to appreciate the Bible's single reference to dancing as a rite of mourning. In *The Sacred Dance* Oesterley writes, "There is no instance to be found in the Old Testament of dancing being performed as a mourning or burial rite; that must be acknowledged; yet in spite of this there are strong reasons for believing that the custom did exist among the Israelites."[26] He goes on to say, "The strongest reason for believing that this custom was in vogue among the ancient Israelites is that it exists at the present day."[27] He refers specifically to the seven circumambulations of the bier that are still part of the prescribed rites of burial according to the custom of the Sephardim.[28] Perhaps the Mishnaic and Modern Hebrew term for a funeral *lᵉwāyāh* derives from the common Semitic root *l-w-y* and refers to the circumambulation of the bier.[29]

We have seen that biblical Hebrew refers to circumambulation by means of the verb *ḥāgag*, the noun *ḥag*, or the verb *sābab*.[30] Hence it is probable that *sābab*, 'participate in a circle dance or procession,' refers to the circumambulation of the bier in Ecclesiastes (Qoh) 12:5 where we read, *kî-hōlēk hā'ādām 'el-bêt 'ôlāmô wᵉsābᵉbû baššûq hassôpᵉdîm*, "When a person goes to his eternal home,[31] the mourners[32] in the street participate in the circumambulations." It is indeed remarkable that this reference to circumambulation has not been recognized in any of the major translations of the Hebrew Bible into English nor in the major critical commentaries on Ecclesiastes.[33]

rāqad — 'skip'

Curt Sachs in his monumental *World History of the Dance*[34] points out:

> *Skip dances* as movements in which either foot is used ought to be distinguished from the jump dances; in the real jump dance the dancer leaves the ground with both feet at the same time. It seems to me that only the Hebrew language discriminates carefully between the two terms.

Sachs's distinctions between *riqqûd* 'the skip dance' and *qippûṣ* 'the jump dance' derives from the assertion of Rabbi Jeremiah in the name of Rabbi Ze'ira in the name of Rab Huna (d. 296 C.E.) in the Jerusalem Talmud, Beza 5:1: "in *qippûṣ* one removes his two feet from the ground simultaneously, but in *riqqûd* one removes one foot from the ground while placing the other foot upon the ground." Sachs concludes that King David's dance before the Ark described in 1 Chronicles 15:29 was a skip dance.[35]

Sachs's conclusion seems to be corroborated by the Bible's characterization of *riqqûd* as the activity of rams (Ps. 114:4–6), calves (Ps. 29:6), and he-goats (Isa. 13:21). The similes 'dance like a calf' in Psalm 29:6, 'dance like rams' and 'dance like young sheep' in Psalm 114:4–6, suggest that in ancient Israel *riqqûd* was regarded as an imitation of the skipping or romping of large and small cattle.[36] Like Hebrew *rāqad*, Akkadian *dakāku* is employed both to refer to the romping of animals including calves, sheep, donkeys, and foxes, and to refer to the dancing of young girls. Moreover, like *rāqad* in Joel 2:5 and Nehemiah 3:2, Akkadian *dakāku* may refer to military troops' gathering together like a flock of sheep.[37]

Because the dance is frequently a feature of mourning rites, it should not be surprising that in Syriac the root *r-q-d* came to have the two meanings 'dance' and 'mourn.'[38] In the Hebrew Bible, however, *riqqûd* was understood to be a dance of joy and, perhaps like *māḥôl* in Lamentations 5:15 and in Psalm 30:12 to be a dance-derived expression for 'joy.'[39] Hence, Ecclesiastes (Qoh) 3:4 informs us "There is an appointed time to cry, and an appointed time to laugh, an appointed time to beat the breast,[40] and an appointed time to dance."[41] In Job 21:11–12 Job, describing the happiness and prosperity of the wicked, seems to characterize the *riqqûd* both as a dance imitative of the behavior of sheep and goats and as an expression of joy. There we read, "They produce their little ones like a flock, and their children continually dance. They play the tambourine and the lyre, and they rejoice at the sound of the flute."

qippûṣ and *dillûg* — 'jump'

As the above-cited passage from the Jerusalem Talmud indicates, both *riqqûd* and *qippûṣ* were attested as terms designating specific and distinct dance forms during the Amoraic period. The Jerusalem Talmud passage is useful for the light it sheds on the Hebrew Scriptures, although the single biblical attestation of *qippēṣ* in the sense of 'jump' is not in a dance context. This single attestation is Canticles 2:8, where the woman in love says of the man she loves, "Hark, my beloved! There he comes, leaping over mountains, jumping over hills." The fact that in the talmudic period *qippûṣ* designated the jumping dance and the fact that the two verbs *dilleg* and *qippēṣ* were employed as synonyms in Canticles 2:8 help us fully appreciate the single, clear reference in the Hebrew Bible to the jumping dance, Isaiah 35:6. The prophet who is generally said to have been the Second Isaiah[42] tells us that when Israel will have been vindicated by God, "Then the lame will dance like a hart, and the tongue of the dumb shall sing a joyous song." Here the parallelism 'dance like a hart'/'sing a joyous song' reflects the universal association of song and dance.

kirkēr — 'whirl, pirouette'

The verb *kirkēr* 'whirl' is twice attested in the account of King David's dancing in the procession that brought the Ark to Jerusalem (2 Samuel 6:14, 16). The interpretation of *kirkûr* as a whirling dance is based primarily on the view that *kirkēr* is an intensive (*pilpēl*) of the verb *kārar* 'rotate.'[43] Moreover, J. Morgenstern suggested that *kārar* is a secondary formation from *kwr* 'be round,' from which we get the noun *kikkar*[44] (= Akkadian *kakkaru*) 'a round loaf of bread, a round weight, a round district.'[45] Thus E. G. Hirsch in his article "Dancing — Biblical Data" suggested that *kirkēr* is "most likely the turning round and round upon the heels on one spot, as practiced by the dervishes."[46] Equally plausible from an etymological point of view and preferred by reason of its antiquity is the suggestion presented anonymously in Numbers Rabbah 4:20 that *kirkēr* designates 'pirouette.'

Notwithstanding the plausible arguments to the contrary advanced by Y. Avishur,[47] the interpretation of *kirkûr* as 'dancing,' specifically 'pirouette,' is supported by numerous uses of the verb and derived nouns in Rabbinic Hebrew and Aramaic referring either to dancing or to verbal circumlocution.[48] Nevertheless, there is evidence both in rabbinic literature and in Ugaritic literature for *kirkûr* denoting a gesture of the hand rather than a movement upon the heel or toe. That *kirkûr* may indeed denote *both* dancing and a gesture or gestures of the hand or fingers is plausible in view of the following: (1) C. Sachs's delineation of sitting dances in which all significant movement takes place from the waist upward;[49] and (2) the *hasta* 'single hand gesture' and the *samyuta hasta* 'double hand gesture,' "which have now become the hallmark of Indian dance throughout the world."[50]

The first of the two biblical attestations of *kirkûr* 'whirling, pirouette' is 2 Samuel 6:14a where we read, "David was whirling with all (his) might before the LORD." The adverbial phrase "before the LORD" indicates that the dance was performed as an act of worship.[51] The second attestation for *kirkûr* is found in 2 Samuel 6:16 where we read, "When the Ark of the LORD was coming to the City of David, Michal daughter of Saul was peering through the window when she saw King David skipping and whirling, and secretly she despised him."

The substitution of the verb *šiḥēq* 'dance' for *kirkēr* in the parallel accounts in 1 Chronicles 13:8 and 15:29 seems further to support the interpretation of *kirkûr* as 'whirling, pirouette.' Nevertheless, Number Rabbah 4:20 records the following alternative interpretation: "What is *mᵉkarkēr*? [It is that] he struck his hands against each other, clapping them and saying, 'kyry rām'." Here *kyry*, a play on the word *mᵉkarkēr*, seems to be the Greek word *kyrios* 'Lord' and the Hebrew first-person singular possessive suffix, while *rām* is Hebrew for "He (my Lord) is exalted." This interpretation underscores the fact that in 2 Samuel 6:14, *kirkûr* is an act of divine worship. The suggestion that *kirkûr* may designate a gesture of the hand is supported also by the following Ugaritic text:

il kypnh	When El saw her (Asherah),
yprq lṣb wyṣḥq	he parted his jaw, and he laughed.
p'nh lhdm ytpd	He put his foot on the footstool,[52]
wykrkr uṣb'th	and he twiddled his fingers.

pizzēz — 'skip'

The verb *pizzēz* is attested with reference to a dance step only in 2 Samuel 6:16. There the verb is usually interpreted to mean 'skip' on the basis of 1 Chronicles 15:29, which seems to equate the common verb *riqqēd* 'skip' with the rare verb *pizzēz* by substituting the former for the latter. Given the two lines of evidence that *kirkēr* means 'pirouette,' the expression *mᵉpazzēz umᵉkarkēr* 'skip and whirl' must refer to the raising of one foot (Heb. *riqqûd, pizzûz*) while the other foot, the pivot, executes the pirouette (*kirkûr*).

pāsaḥ — 'limp'

It has frequently been suggested that the festival of Pesach derives its name from a limping dance performed on this festival in hoary antiquity.[53] In fact, there is no basis for this suggestion other than the presumed derivation of the noun *pēsaḥ* from the verb *pēsaḥ* 'limp.' Nevertheless, the Bible does refer at least once to *pissûaḥ* 'a limping dance.' In 1 Kings 18:26 the behavior of the priests of Baal in their contest with Elijah is described as follows:

They took the bull that he (Elijah) had given them, and they prepared it. They called upon the name of Baal from morning until noon, saying, "Baal, answer us!" There was, however, no sound, and there was no one who answered, so they performed the limping dance about the altar which he (Elijah) had made.

This limping dance referred to in this description of the priests of Baal has been compared to the manner in which devout Muslims on pilgrimage to Mecca circle the Ka'aba "with a peculiar limping walk, dragging one foot behind the other.[54]

Some scholars hold that Elijah refers to the limping dance also in 1 Kings 18:21, "It is long enough that you are limping between two opinions." A. Ehrlich takes the Hebrew word *s^eippîm* (usually rendered 'opinions') as a biform of *sippîm* 'thresholds' (of temples), and he interprets Elijah's remark as a reference to the people who have been worshipping both Baal and the LORD by means of the limping dance. He is asking these people to perform the limping dance either for the one deity or for the other, not for both.[55] Other commentators see the two references to limping in vv. 21 and 26 as coincidental, and they hold that only in v. 26 does the verb refer to a dance. They hold that this dance is peculiar to the worship of Baal and foreign to the worship of the LORD.[56] Regardless of the tenability of this contention, there is no question that the author of the narrative deliberately employed two forms of the same verb in the two verses. It is equally certain that there is no other attestation of the limping dance in the Hebrew Bible.[57]

ḥyl/ḥll — 'perform a whirling dance' etc.

The most frequently attested and therefore the most frequently discussed term for 'dance' in the Hebrew Bible is *māḥôl*. Just as the Hebrew word *mispēd* and its Akkadian cognate *sipittu*, which originally designated a *gesture* of mourning ('beating the breast'), came by synecdoche to denote simply 'mourning,' so did *maḥôl* (which originally designed a dance associated with joyous occasions), come by extension to denote 'joy.' For example, in Lamentations 5:15, the Jews who suffered defeat at the hands of Nebuchadnezzar lament, *šābat m^eśôś libbēnû / nehpak l^e'ēbel m^eḥôlēnû*, "Our happiness has ceased / our joy has been turned into mourning." Reflecting the same semantic development *māḥôl* 'dance' > *māḥôl* 'joy,' the author of Psalm 30, a psalm of thanksgiving, gives thanks to the LORD, saying, "You turned my mourning (Heb. *misp^edî*) into joy (Heb. *l^emāḥôl*) for me: You ungirded my sackcloth, and You girt me with (a garment appropriate to) happiness" (v. 12).

It should not be surprising that of all the terms for 'dance' in biblical Hebrew the one that develops the nuance 'joy' is *māḥôl*, seeing that this is the type of dance which is danced as an expression of joy upon the safe return from battle of the armies of Israel. For example, when Jephthah returns from defeating the Ammonites, "Behold, his daughter went forth to greet him with drums and with *meḥôlōt* 'dances'" (Judg. 11:34). Likewise, in response to David's victory over Goliath, "the women went forth from all the Israelite cities for song and the *meḥôlōt* 'dances' to greet King Saul with drums, with joy, and with sistrums (1 Sam. 18:6). The dancing (Heb. *hameśaḥaqôt*) women chanted, saying, "Saul slew his thousands, and David his myriads" (1 Sam. 18:6-7). The association of *meḥôlōt* with the verb *'ānāh* 'chant'[58] is clearer still in 1 Samuel 21:11b, "They chanted in the *meḥôlōt*, saying, 'Saul slew his thousands, and David his myriads," and in 1 Samuel 29:5b, "They chanted to him in the *meḥôlōt*, saying, 'Saul slew his thousands, and David his myriads.'" The association of chanting and *māḥôl* lends support to the theory developed by Jack Sasson that *māḥôl* is both etymologically related to and semantic equivalent of Akkadian *mēlultu*, which, in turn, corresponds to the Greek *hyporchēma*, a multimedia performance including instrumental music, dance, choral singing, and mime.[59]

It is the association of *māḥôl* with military victory demonstrated in Judges 11:34; 1 Samuel 18:6-7, 21:12b and 29:5, as well as Exodus 15:20 that probably accounts for the term *meḥôlat hammaḥanayim* 'dance of the two camps" in Canticles 7:1.

> Return, return Shulamite.
> Return, return that we may see you.
> "What," (she asks) "will you see in the Shulamite?"
> (They answer): "Of course, the dance of the two camps."

Just as by synecdoche *māḥôl* came to be employed to designate 'joy' in Lamentations 5 and Psalm 30 so, apparently, the same term came to designate a musical instrument in Psalm 149 and 150. In both these psalms the term *māḥôl* appears among a list of musical instruments. The interpretation of the term *māḥôl* as the name of an instrument was advocated by the medieval philologists Ibn Janah, Abraham Ibn Ezra, and David Kimhi and in modern times by N. H. Tur-Sinai.[60] J. S. Licht argues that the term *māḥôl* has two meanings. He holds that the meaning 'dance' is alone appropriate in Judges

21:23 and Canticles 7:1, while the meaning 'flute' is appropriate in Psalm 149:3 and 150:4.[61] Perhaps, however, the noun *māḥôl*, which originally meant 'dance,' came to mean 'flute' or 'drum,' because it was used to provide music or rhythm for the dancing of the dance called *māḥôl*. Support for this suggestion is provided by the Rabbinic Hebrew term *'êrûs*, lit., 'betrothal,' which designates a gong played at weddings.[62]

If, in fact, the term *māḥôl*, which may designate a multimedia event like the Greek *hyporchēma*, can also designate 'joy' or 'drum,' we should not be surprised that in Canticles 7:1 it can designate a specific dance step rather than the entire multimedia event. Apropos of Canticle 7:1 Sachs observed: "When we read these verses from the Song of Songs we are convinced that what is referred to is a facing in all four directions."[63] Indeed, the interpretation of *māḥôl* as a whirl dance in which the dancer rotates and thereby exhibits her beauty accounts for the audience's exclamation *šûbî šûbî* "Return, return!" and their saying, "And let us look at you." This interpretation of *māḥôl* is supported by the derivation of the noun from the root *ḥwl* 'whirl, writhe.' Julian Morgenstern long ago suggested that the root *ḥll*, which is the derivation preferred by contemporary scholars such as Sasson,[64] is related to *ḥwl* as *krr* is to *kwr*.[65]

The whirling dance of the nubile woman to exhibit herself to prospective marriage partners is suggested by the passage that follows in Canticles 7:2–10 in which one of these eligible men praises her beauty from bottom to top, beginning with "How beautiful are your [dancing] feet in sandals, O noble woman!" (Canticles 7:2). Moreover, *māḥôl* refers to precisely such a dance in Judges 21:21 and in Mishnah Ta'anit 4:8. Finally, the interpretation of *māḥôl* as whirling or turning round is supported by the Rabbinic Hebrew expression *mᵉḥôl hakkerem* 'circumference of the vineyard' attested and defined in Mishnah Kilayim 4:1–2[66] in the exegetical traditional for Morgenstern's clever suggestion that this term designated an open space surrounding every vineyard, which was provided for the performance of the dances alluded to in Mishnah Ta'anit 4:8.[67]

śiḥēq — 'dance, play'

Particularly interesting is the variety of nuances of the *pi'ēl* of the verb *śḥq*. In 2 Samuel 6:21 King David tells Michal that he intends to do more of that which he is described as having done in 2 Samuel 6:14. In 2 Samuel 6:21 King David says, *wᵉśiḥaqtî* "I shall dance," while in 6:14 King David is described as *mᵉkarkēr bᵉkol-'oz*, "whirling with all (his) strength." 1 Chronicles 15:29 transforms the unusual *dāwîd m^{e}pazzēz um^{e}karkēr*, "David (was) skipping and whirling" of 2 Samuel 6:16 into *dāwîd m^{e}raqqēd ûm^{e}śaḥēq*, "David (was) skipping and dancing." Moreover, 1 Chronicles 13:8a, *w^{e}dāwîd w^{e}kol-yiśrā'ēl m^{e}śaḥ^{a}qîm lipnê hā'elohîm b^{e}kol-'oz*, "David and all Israel were dancing before God with all (their) strength," seems to be another parallel to the expression found in 2 Samuel 6:14, while 2 Samuel 6:5 seems to be a corruption of the text that has been faithfully reproduced in 1 Chronicles 13:8.

In most other cases, the *pi'ēl* of the verb *śḥq* has nothing to do with dancing, but it means 'play.' Typical of this usage are Psalm 104:26b, "Leviathan whom You created to play with him," and Proverbs 8:30–31, "...playing in His presence continually, playing on His earth..." In 1 Samuel 18:17, however, we find another nuance of the verb *śḥq*. Here we find, "The *m^{e}śaḥ^{a}qôt* women chanted, 'Saul slew his thousands, David his myriads.'" The equation of *śiḥûq* and *māḥôl* should not be surprising in that, as we have seen, *māḥôl* is both semantically and etymologically the equivalent of Akkadian *mēlulu*, which may designate both 'play' and 'dance' precisely as does Hebrew *śiḥēq*. Hence it is possible also to appreciate the expression *m^{e}ḥôl m^{e}ś^{a}ḥaqîm* "dancers' dance" in Jeremiah 31:4.

Conclusion

Once we go beyond etymological speculation to the establishment of semantic equivalents between expressions in biblical Hebrew and dance terminology in the cognate languages, we can expect to be able to clarify the Hebrew terms by reference to the rich legacy of pictorial art from the surrounding cultures. This, in turn, opens up the possibility of reconstructing the ancient Hebrew dance and accomplishing for ancient Israel what M. Emmanuel did for the classical world in *The Antique Greek Dance*[68] and what I. Lexová achieved in *Ancient Egyptian Dances*.[69] This challenge I leave for a later date.

Notes

Throughout this essay I have used the Masoretic Text (Bible in Hebrew). Versification of this text in some books, especially the Psalms, Prophets and Poetical books, differs slightly from that in the Revised Standard Version and Good News versions.

1. Dvora Lapson, "Dance," *Encyclopedia Judaica* (Jerusalem: Encyclopedia Judaica 1972) 5:1262. This chapter on the ten dance-derived expressions is a revision of a paper presented at the International Seminar on the Bible in Dance held in Jerusalem, 5–9 August 1979. I am most grateful to Professor Moshe Greenberg for his having suggested to the organizers of the conference (Barry Swersky, head of the organizing committee, and Giora Manor, head of the programming committee) and to me that I investigate the subject and present the paper. I am very glad that Professor Toby Berger Holtz of Barnard College, Columbia University, was able to present the paper on my behalf. I wish to record my thanks to Professor Shalom Paul for his having urged me to prepare the paper for publication.

2. F. Berk and D. Rosenblatt, "Dance," *The Second Jewish Catalogue*, ed. Sharon Strassfield and Michael Strassfield (Philadelphia: Jewish Publication Society of America, 1976) 337.

3. W. O. E. Oesterley, *The Sacred Dance* (New York: Cambridge University Press, 1923) 44.

4. A. Draffkorn Kilmer, "Symbolic Gestures in Akkadian Contracts from Alalakh and Ugarit," *Journal of the American Oriental Society* 94 (1974) 182, n. 24.

5. Mayer I. Gruber, *Aspects of Nonverbal Communication in the Ancient Near East* (Rome: Pontifical Biblical Institute, 1980).

6. Oesterley, *The Sacred Dance*, 44.

7. See Francis Brown, S. R. Driver, and Charles A. Briggs, *A Hebrew and English Lexicon of the Old Testament* (Oxford: Clarendon Press, 1952) 290; Ludwig Koehler and Walter Baumgartner, *Hebräisches und Aramäisches Lexicon zum Alten Testament* (Leiden: E. J. Brill, 1967) 278; commentaries of David Kimhi on these two verses.

8. M. Gruber, "Akkadian *labān appi* in the Light of Art and Literature," *Journal of the Ancient Near Eastern Society of Columbia University* 7 (1975) 74, n. 8; idem., *Aspects of Nonverbal Communication in the Ancient Near East*, 402–7.

9. Gruber, *Aspects*, 94–98.

10. T. Nöldeke, review of *Skizzen und Vorarbeiten* von J. Wellhausen, *Drittes Heft: Reste arabischen Heidenthumes, Zeitschrift der Deutschen Morgenländischen Gesellschaft* 41 (1887) 719.

11. See RSV: "Bind the festal procession with branches up to the horns of the altar."

12. Note the juxtaposition of the Akkadian synonyms *nâtu, lamû,* and *esēru,* 'enclose, encircle, surround,' in *Enuma eliš* iv 110–11: *nīta lamû na-*

paršudiš lā le'ê īsiršunūtīma kakkēšun ušabbir, "Enclosed, encircled, unable to flee (were the hosts of Tiamat); he (Marduk) surrounded them, and he smashed their weapons"; note also the juxtaposition of *esēru* and *labû* (Assyrian equivalent of Babylonian *lamû*) in *ABL* 1186:10; *šu gabīšūma ina libbi āli ēsir u emūqīya labiūšu*, "As for him, I enclosed all of him within the city, and my troops surround him;" note also the semantic equivalent of *esēru* and *lamû*, 'surround, besiege (a king, city)'; for *esēru* 'surround, besiege' see *Oriental Institute Publications* 2, 33:27–29 (= 70:28–29): *šâšu kīma iṣṣur quppi qereb Ursalimma āl šarrūtišu esiršu* "As for him (Hezekiah), I (Sennacherib) surrounded him in his capital Jerusalem like a caged bird"; see also Paul Rost, *Die Keilschrifttexte Tiglat-Pilesers III* (Leipzig: E. Pfeiffer, 1893) 34:203; for *lawû* (Old Babylonian equivalent of later *lamû*) see *Archives Royales de Mari. Textes Cunéiformes*, 1 131:10: *ālam šâti alwi*, "I besieged that city;" not the cliché *almi akšud appul aqqur*, "I surrounded, I conquered, I thoroughly devastated," passim in *Oriental Institute Publications* 2.

13. Oesterley, *The Sacred Dance*, 91; see commentaries; T. H. Gaster, *Myth, Legend, and Custom in the Old Testament* (New York and Evanston: Harper and Row, 1969) 746–47. The reference to palms washed by innocence reflects the idea expressed in Isaiah 1:5 that God will not heed prayer or worship by those whose hands are defiled by guilt, an idea that derives its poignancy from the fact that ancient Israelites supplicated with palms spread apart; see Gruber, *Aspects*, 29–31; cf. Šurpu III 44: *māmit nīš qātī lā ellūti zikir ili zakāru*, "the dire consequence of invoking the name of a god while making the prayer gesture with unclean hands."

14. See commentaries. Gaster, *Myth, Legend, and Custom*, 41 points out, "The emphasis on the sacred number seven shows clearly that the Biblical writer *is modelling his account upon a ritual ceremony*." Likewise in the Sargon legend *CT* 13 42, 17 when Sargon of Akkad says [mā]ti *tiāmat lu alm[a] 3-šu* "I circumambulated the Sealand three times" the reference to the sacred number three indicates that Sargon speaks of a rite rather than of a military procedure of surrounding a city as in the stereotypic *almi akšud* discussed in n. 12 above. Contrast B. Lewis, *The Sargon Legend* (American Schools of Oriental Research Dissertation Series 4; Cambridge, Mass., 1980) 63–64; 83, nn. 168–72; for other reference to three circumambulations in Assyrian ritual see below, n. 33. For references to symbolic circumambulation in laying claim to territory using Akk. *saḫāru* 'circumambulate,' see Ch.-F. Jean, *Tell Sifr* (Paris, 1931) #71a, 1. 19; #71, 1. 18.

15. Oesterley, *The Sacred Dance*, 91; see commentaries.

16. Gaster, *Myth, Legend, and Custom*, 411.

17. Gruber, *Aspects*, 18–19; 49, n. 1; 60, n. 2; 94–98 and passim.

18. Isaiah 51:10; Psalm 66:6; 74:13; 89:10–11; 104:6–8; Job 26:12; etc.

19. Probably Mount Lebanon (Lubnan) and Mount Sirion (Hermon); see Psalm 29:6.

20. See below.

21. For identification of *māḥôl* see below.

22. See Gaster, *Myth, Legend, and Custom*, 412; idem., *The Holy and the Profane* (New York: W. Sloane Associates, 1955) 124–45; *Funk and Wagnalls Standard Dictionary of Folklore, Mythology, and Legend*, ed. Maria Leach (New York: Funk and Wagnalls Company, 1949) 1, p. 235; M. Higger, "Haqqāpôt weʿiggûlîm," *Horeb* 1 (1934) 214 (in Hebrew); idem., *Tractate Semaḥot* (New York, 1936) 76 (in Hebrew).

23. Gaster, *Myth, Legend, and Custom*, 412.

24. See commentaries; for a survey of views see S. R. Driver, *The Book of the Prophet Jeremiah* (New York: C. Scribner's Sons, 1906) 188, 366–67; W. Rudolph, *Jeremia* (HAT 12; 2d ed., Tübingen: J. C. B. Mohr, 1958) 181–82; J. P. Hyatt, "The Book of Jeremiah: Introduction and Exegesis," *IB* 5:1034. E. Nacar, "Sobre la interpretación de 'Femina circumdabit virum,'" *Estudios Bíblicos*, 1 (1942) 405–36 argues that the innovation is that in former times when the people of Israel travelled, the women walked on the inside, the men outside to protect the women; when Israel will return from the Babylonian Exile, God will create a new circumstance of such great security that the women will be able to walk on the outside without the protection of the men; I wish to thank my former student, Mr. Ariel Zamarripa-Gesundheit for translating this article from Spanish for me. A. Ehrlich, *Mikrâ ki-Pheschutô* (Berlin: H. Itzkowski, 1899–1901) 3, pp. 244–45 (in Hebrew) explains that "a woman shall circumambulate a man" means "she shall surround him with words of endearment so as to capture his heart." *The Prophets: Nevi'im*, ed. H. L. Ginsberg (Philadelphia: Jewish Publication Society, 1978) renders "For the LORD has created something new on earth: A woman courts a man," adding in a marginal note: "Meaning of Heb. uncertain."

25. While in his prophecies of rebuke Jeremiah warns in Jeremiah 7:34 "I shall cause to cease from the cities of Judah and from the streets of Jerusalem the sound of joy and the sound of happiness, the sound of bridegroom and the sound of bride, for the land will become a ruin" (similarly Jeremiah 16:9 and 25:10), in his "Scroll of Consolations" (i.e., Jeremiah 30–33; see Y. Kaufmann, *Tôlᵉdôt hā-'emûnāh hayyisrā'ēlit* [Tel Aviv and Jerusalem, 1963] 7, p. 410); in Jeremiah 33:10–11 he says "Thus says the LORD, 'There shall again be heard in this place of which you say, "It is destroyed, it is devoid of a person, and it is devoid of cattle," in the cities of Judah and in the destroyed streets of Jerusalem which are devoid of a person and devoid of an inhabitant and devoid of cattle, people saying, "Thank the LORD of Hosts, for the LORD is kind, for His loyalty is forever" and people bringing thanksgiving offerings to the Temple of the LORD when I restore the fortunes of the land as aforetime,' said the LORD."

26. P. 194; similarly A. J. Wensinck, *Some Semitic Rites of Mourning and Religion* (Amsterdam, 1917) 44.

27. Oesterley, *The Sacred Dance*, 197.

28. Rabbi Michael Azose, spiritual leader of the Portuguese Israelite Fraternity of Evanston, Illinois, informs me (oral communication, 13 June 1980) that these circumambulations are observed by the Western Sephardim (the

communities established in Western Europe and the Western hemisphere following the expulsion of the Jews from Spain and Portugal in the fifteenth century) but not by the Eastern Sephardim (descendants of the Jews of Spanish and Portuguese origin who settled in lands of the Eastern Mediterranean). For pictorial illustration of circumambulation of the coffin among the Sephardic Jews of eighteenth-century Amsterdam see "The Acafoth, or the Seven turns round the Coffin," in B. Picart, *Ceremonies of the Jews: sixteen engravings in facsimile* (New York [n.d.]).

29. See M. D. Cassuto, "Leviathan," *Encyclopedia Miqra'it* 4:486 (in Hebrew).

30. In Rabbinic and Medieval Hebrew the preferred verb is *hiqqîp*; see sources cited in Higger, "Haqqâpôt," and in idem., *Tractate Semaḥot*, 75–76; see also Harry Rabinowicz, "Hakkafot," *Encyclopedia Judaica* 7:1153–54. In biblical Hebrew *hiqqîp* 'encircle' refers to the procession around the walls of Jericho in Joshua 6:3 and 6:11. The same verb refers to the besieging of a city also in 2 Kings 6:14. Corresponding to *sābab* in Psalm 118:11 *hiqqîp* in Psalm 17:9; 22:17; 88:18 (in the latter verse the verb is employed as the parallel word to *sābab*) and Lamentations 3:5 refers metaphorically to the psalmist's enemies' conspiracy against him. Just as in Psalm 26:6 *sābab* 'walk around' refers to an act of divine worship so does *hiqqîp* in 2 Kings 11:8 and 2 Chronicles 23:7 appear to refer to a ceremony of obeisance to King Joash of Judah. In Psalm 48:13 the two verbs *sābab* and *hiqqîp* refer to circumambulation of the walls of Jerusalem as an act of adoration of the Holy City: *sobbû Ṣiyyôn wᵉhiqqîppûāh sipᵉrû migdā-Uāh* "Encircle Zion, and march around her, count her towers."

31. Heb. *hālak* 'go (to his eternal home)' should be compared to Akkadian *alāku* 'go' in the idiomatic *ana šimti alāku* 'go to fate,' i.e., 'die'; see *Assyrian Dictionary of the Oriental Institute of the University of Chicago*, A pt. 1, p. 321.

32. On *sôpᵉdîm* 'mourners' see Gruber, *Aspects*, 350.

33. H. L. Ginsberg, *Koheleth* (Tel Aviv and Jerusalem: M. Newman, 1961) 132 (in Hebrew) correctly notes that the verb refers to a funerary rite; hence he takes the verb to mean 'they surrounded (it, i.e., the bier)'; Ginsberg's realization is not followed up in *The Five Megilloth and Jonah*, ed. H. L. Ginsberg (Philadelphia: 1969), which renders *wᵉsābᵉbû hassôpᵉdîm baššûq* "With mourners all around in the street." Circumambulation is attested as a funerary rite in the Akkadian text *Kommentar zum Alten Testament* 143, 66–67, where as in Qoh 12:5 circumambulation (*labû*) is an activity of the professional mourner. The text reads as follows: *ⁱˢnarkabtu ša ana bīt akīt tallakūni tallakanni bēlša laššu ša lā bēle tasabbu' u ᵈSakkukutu ša issu āli talabbanni bakkissu šî issu āli talabbia*, "As for the chariot which goes again and again to the festival temple, its lord [Murduk] is not (in it); without its lord it totters. Now DN who goes in a circle around the city, she, his professional mourner, goes in a circle around the city." Another attestation of circumambulation as a funerary rite is in W. von Soden, "Aus einem Ersatzopferritual für den assyrischen Hof," *Zeitschrift für Assyriologie* 45 (1939)

42, ll. 4–6: *kallatu šēpē tamassi 3-šu issu* [i]*šerši tallabia šēpē tanaššiq tallaka tuššab,* "The daughter-in-law [of the king] will wash the feet [of the dead crown prince, her husband]. Three times she shall walk in a circle around the bier; she shall kiss [his] feet; she shall go; she shall sit." Similarly in ll. 20–21 (there, p. 44) of the same text we read as follows: *3-šu issu* [i]*šerši talabbi šēpē tanaššiq* [i]*šerinnu tašarrap,* "Three times she shall walk around the bier; she shall kiss the feet [of the deceased], and she shall burn cedar." As for *eršu* 'bier,' *Assyrian Dictionary of the Oriental Institute of the University of Chicago* E 315 and Wolfrom von Soden, *Akkadisches Handwörterbuch* 246 give *eršu* only the meaning 'bed' in the extended meaning 'bier' in 2 Samuel 3:31 (so Brown-Driver-Briggs 641–42) and passim in Rabbinic Hebrew; see dictionaries of Rabbinic Hebrew. Three circumambulations of the bier before interment are attested also in Greek literature, as in *Iliad* 23, where Achilles is described as having war chariots circle the body of Patroclus three times.

34. Curt Sachs, *World History of the Dance*, trans. Bessie Schönberg (New York: W. W. Norton, 1937) 30.

35. Ibid.

36. For numerous examples from all over the world of dances imitative of animals, see Sachs, *World History of Dance*, 79–85; Beryl de Zoete and Walter Spies, *Dance and Drama in Bali* (New York and London: Harper and Brothers, 1939) 25–26; and S. Marti and G. P. Kurath, *Dances of Anáhuac* (Chicago: Aldine Publishing Company, 1964) 94–102.

37. *Assyrian Dictionary of the Oriental Institute of the University of Chicago*, D 34. Akkadian *raqādu* is also used of both people and animals; see Wolfram von Soden, *Akkadisches Handwörterbuch*, 957.

38. See dictionaries.

39. Cf. Akkadian *lurqud* "Indeed I jump for joy" (?) in H. W. F. Saggs, "The Nimrud Letters 1952 — Part III," *Iraq* 18 (1956) 54, 1. 13.

40. On Hebrew *sāpad* 'beat the breast' and the cognate Akkadian *sapādu* 'beat the breast' see Gruber, *Aspects*, 436, 449–55.

41. Contrast Ginsberg, *Koheleth*, 73.

42. See commentaries.

43. Oesterley, *The Sacred Dance*, 45.

44. J. Morgenstern, "The Etymological History of the Three Hebrew Synonyms for 'to Dance,' HGG, ḤLL and KRR, and their Cultural Significance," *Journal of the American Oriental Society* 36 (1917) 321.

45. Brown, Driver, and Briggs, 503.

46. E. G. Hirsch, *The Jewish Encyclopedia* (New York 1901) 4, p. 425a.

47. Y. Avishur, "Krkr in Biblical Hebrew and in Ugaritic," *Vetus Testamentum*, 26 (1976) 257–61.

48. See dictionaries; or G. W. Alhstrom, "Krkr and tpd," *Vetus Testamentum*, 28 (1978) 100–102.

49. Curt Sachs, *World History of the Dance*, 37–41.

50. F. Bowers, *The Dance in India* (New York: Columbia University Press, 1953) 34.

51. See Gruber, *Aspects*, 112–16.

52. For the significance of the gestus see Gruber, *Aspects* 460–63, 570, 613–14. For the full text, see Cyrus Gordon, *Ugaritic Textbook* (Rome: Pontifical Biblical Institute, 1965) 51, col. 4, 11. 27–30.

53. For the literature on this subject see J. B. Segal, *The Hebrew Passover* (London Oriental Series 12; London: Oxford University Press, 1963) 95–96; P. Laaf, *Die Pascha-Feier Israels* (BBB 36; Bonn: P. Hanstein, 1970) 144.

54. J. Robinson, *The First Book of Kings* (Cambridge, England: Cambridge University Press, 1972) 209.

55. Ehrlich, *Mikrâ ki-Pheschutô (Berlin: H. Itzkowski, 1899–1901)* 2, p. 314.

56. See J. A. Montgomery, *The Book of Kings* (ICC; Edinburgh: T. and T. Clark, 1951) 301–10.

57. See Oesterley, *The Sacred Dance*, 44.

58. For *'ānāh* 'chant' see R. Gordis, *The Book of Job: Commentary. New Translation and Special Studies* (Moreshet Series 2; New York: Jewish Theological Society of America, 1978) 32.

59. J. M. Sasson, "The Worship of the Golden Calf," *Orient and Occident: Essays Presented to Cyrus H. Gordon on the Occasion of his Sixty-fifth Birthday*, ed. Harry A. Hoffner, Jr. (*Alter Orient und Altes Testament*, 22; Kevelaer & Neukirchener-Vluyn 1973) 157–59.

60. N. H. Tur-Sinai, *Hallāšôn Wᵉhassēper* 1 (Jerusalem 1954) 369 (in Hebrew); idem., *Pᵉsûtô šel Miqrā* (Jerusalem, 1962–67) 4/1, p. 257 (in Hebrew).

61. J. S. Licht, "*Māḥôl*," *Encyclopedia Miqra'it* 4, p. 789 (in Hebrew).

62. See Babylonian Talmud, Sotah 49b; Niddah 61b. Similarly it has been argued that *mrqd*, the Ugaritic cognate of Akkadian *raqādu* and of Heb. *rāqad* 'dance' appears to designate a musical instrument in *Ugaritic Textbook* 602 (= RS 24.252), ll. 3–5: *il ytb b'ttrt il tpt bhdr'y dyšr wydmr bknr wbtlb btp wbmsltm brmqdm dšn*, "The god who is enthroned in Ashtaroth, the god who exercises sovereignty at Edrei, who sings and chants to the accompaniment of lyre and flute, of timbrel and of cymbals and of castanets of ivory." Alternatively, *mrqdm* has been taken to mean 'dancers'; so Ch. Virolleaud in *Ugaritica* 5, p. 553; A. F. Rainey, "The Ugaritic Texts in *Ugaritica* 5," *Journal of the American Oriental Society* 94 (1974) 187; C. E. L'Heureux, *Rank Among the Canaanite Gods: El, Ba'al, and the Repha'im* (Harvard Semitic Monographs 21; Missoula, Mont.: Scholars Press, 1979) 179; B. Bayer, "Dance in the Bible: The Possibilities and Limitations of the Evidence," p. 6 in *Papers of the International Seminar on the Bible in Dance* (Jerusalem: The Israeli Center of the International Theatre Institute, 1979). For the arguments in favor of interpreting *mrqdm* as 'castanets' see B. Margulis, "A Ugaritic Psalm RŠ 24.252)," *Journal of Biblical Literature* 89 (1970) 294. For *dšn* 'of ivory' see M. H. Pope, "Notes on the Rephaim Texts from Ugarit" in *Essays on the Ancient Near East in Memory of Jacob Joel Finkelstein*, ed. Maria de Jong Ellis (Memoirs of the Connecticut Academy of Arts & Sciences 19; Hamden, Conn., 1977) 170; for *tlb* 'flute' (= Akkadian *šulpu*) see J. C. de Moor, "Studies in the New Alphabetic Texts from Ras Shamra I," *Ugarit-Forschungen* 1

(1969) 177; contrast M. Dahood, Review of *Ugaritica* 5, *Or* 39 (1970) 377; L'Heureux, *Rank Among the Canaanite Gods*, 174–175. For another possible reference to *mrqdm dšn* 'castanets of ivory' see 1 Aqht 189; see Margulis, "A Ugaritic Psalm," 294.

63. Sachs, *World History of the Dance*, 43.

64. Sasson, "The Worship of the Golden Calf," *Orient and Occident*, 157–59.

65. Morgenstern, "The Etymological History," 321–24.

66. Cf. Akkadian *saḫirtu* 'circumference,' a derivative of the verb *saharu* 'circumambulate'; see *Archives Royales de Mari. Textes Cunéiformes, 13 #16*, 1:7: *saḫirtam sa gisimmarim*, "the circumference of the palm tree courtyard."

67. Morgenstern, "The Etymological History," 324.

68. M. Emmanuel, *The Antique Greek Dance*, trans. Harriet Jean Beauley (New York: John Lance Co., 1916).

69. With drawings made from reproductions of ancient Egyptian originals by Milada Lexová, *Ancient Egyptian Dances*, trans. K. Haltmar (Prague, 1935).

5

Dancing the Scriptures

Hal Taussig

How can one use the Bible and biblical scholarship in the creation of dance events in the life of the church? The twentieth century has seen the development of an apologetic for dance in the church based on biblical texts and research.[1] These passages and scholarship can provide direct material for the use of dance in worship and religious education.

Dance lives at the heart of the Hebrew Scriptures; there is scarcely a chapter that does not have at least an indirect relationship to dance. In book after book of the Hebrew Scriptures, dance either has a fundamental historical relationship or a promising literary access to the text. This not-always-recognized wedding of dance and the Hebrew Scriptures provides both a better understanding of the Scriptures themselves and a wide range of interpretive possibilities for dancers. In many cases the implicit connections between dance and the Hebrew Scriptures have not even been hinted at, much less explored, for their interpretive and artistic promise.

"Dancing the Scriptures" was originally published as *New Categories for Dancing the Old Testament* (Austin: The Sharing Co., 1981) and *Dancing the New Testament* (Austin: The Sharing Co., 1977). It is included in this collection in this revised form with permission.

This overview of connections between Hebrew Scripture texts and dance indicates the rich potential for interrelationship. In identifying the many different ways that dance intersects with the scriptural texts, a period of over one thousand years of varied cultures is involved. Rather than one specific cultural setting, there are hundreds of different cultural settings that qualify and illuminate the Hebrew Scriptures. A search for dance in the Hebrew Scriptures includes everything from primitive nomadic tribes to complex philosophical societies.

So it is not a question of discovering *the* attitude toward dance in the Hebrew Scriptures. Rather, there are the different aspects of varied cultures which exhibit some dance activity. This task includes nearly every Near Eastern culture before the time of Jesus of Nazareth.

Similarly the realization of the scriptural texts represents the continual effort of the Hebrew people to combine varied cultural influences. One particular text can represent three or four different historical moments, each of which blends several different cultural influences together.[2] One extant Hebrew Scripture text mirrors as many as ten different Near Eastern cultural settings.

Dance was a central religious act in many Near Eastern cultures and an occasional religious practice in others. In general, dance was more central to the earlier societies of the patriarchs and the Exodus. In the later, more sophisticated exilic and postexilic settings of the Hebrew Scriptures, a variety of religious dance activities were evident.

Although it is often difficult to separate the religious from the secular in Near Eastern history, where such distinctions can be made, a number of "secular" dances also can be identified throughout the cultures that intersect with the Hebrew Scripture texts. It was, of course, those explicit dance passages of the Hebrew Scriptures, e.g., 2 Samuel 6 and Psalm 149, which triggered the contemporary rebirth of sacred dance in churches and synagogues.

Now what does this all mean for dance in the church? How can that be of any help in introducing and choreographing dance in the church? Basically it signifies the discovery that the Bible as it was originally composed is not and never was intended to be simply philosophical theses or theological reflections about God. It is far more a "language event," to use the words of contemporary biblical scholars. That is, the form of a biblical passage indicates that it is often more like a happening than theory, more like a worship service than philosophy, more like a dance than a dissertation.

This has specific implications for the use of dance in the church's liturgy and education. First of all, this means that the Bible, as the church has intuited throughout its history, has much more material that applies directly to the worship moments of praise, confession, song, prayer, baptism, and communion. As dancers try to portray each of these moments in movement, they can draw upon a wealth of biblical passages that were essentially created for that purpose.

Second, many of the texts which we are called to preach or teach were meant instead to be enacted or ritualized. We can no longer relegate many of these texts to the lame function of sermon texts. They can reclaim their original context of worship when they are sung, acted out, or danced. The church dancer can expect a sense of rhythm, music, movement, position, and drama from many passages of Scripture. Form criticism is suggestive of dance as a mode of scriptural proclamation and education.

Third, it can be deduced from the biblical scholarship of the past century that a number of categories of passages encourage a dance interpretation by their own form and content. I have detailed here a categorization of passages to serve as a resource bank for dancers in the church.

The main factor in using biblical passages and scholarship for dance in the church is the development of form criticism. In isolating the particular literary and historical forms of which the Bible consists, form criticism has pointed the way to an expanded view of the use of Scriptures, while recognizing that portions of Scripture were originally hymns or songs used in early Israelite worship.

Those particular passages can be understood as both theological treatises or preaching texts, and also as musical and worship-filled events. Form criticism has achieved similar results in demonstrating the existence of creeds, oracles, covenant ceremonies, baptismal rites, ritual meals, and other action-oriented modes within the Bible itself.

Dancing the Hebrew Scriptures

Songs. There are many passages of the Hebrew Scriptures that are described by the text itself as songs.[3] Most of these are songs to God, others are simply songs.[4] Several are clearly related to dance.[5] In addition to these explicitly identified songs, there are many other texts which according to form criticism are songs not identified as such except by comparison of the passage's form with known songs in and outside of the Hebrew Scriptures. The relationship between songs and dance is obvious.

By directing attention to the many songs in the Hebrew Scriptures,

I do not mean to imply that all these songs were danced, but to reveal the implicit and constant relationship between music and dance. Where there is song, there is often dance. Even today one never knows when a song will or will not be danced. The presence of songs in the Hebrew Scriptures points toward dance and opens up new possibilities of interpreting these passages through dance.

The songs of the Hebrew Scriptures are divided into various groupings by the form critics. In addition to the major explicit types, the psalms, which will be treated as a separate category, one can identify the war songs, the mourning songs, the wedding and love songs, the watchman's songs, the taunt songs, and the workers' songs. Another group of songs identified by the form critics — the prophetic songs — is included in the formal categories of taunt or mourning song.

One of the most vivid examples of war songs is the song of Deborah and Barak in Judges 5. This is one of the most ancient songs in the Bible. It exudes the enthusiasm of the victorious armies, and as such is an excellent example of war song found in the Hebrew Scriptures. Another vivid and ancient song is found in 2 Samuel 1:19–27. This song of David's lament at the death of Saul is an early example of the mourning song. An example of the way the later prophets reinterpret this kind of song is found in Jeremiah 9:17ff.

Wedding and love songs in the Hebrew Scriptures are a part of grand celebrations.[6] However, the Song of Songs represents both the rich songs of wedding and love, and a theological appropriation of these songs.

Isaiah's lament for Babylon is formally a watchman's song with a regular structure.[7] Although this song takes on a prophetic message, and therefore theological content, the form itself exhibits six verses of the watchman's song form.

The taunt songs can be used in war or in other settings, such as Numbers 21:27–30. In the text, this taunt song is a confirmation of the Israelites' claim and conquest of Moab. However, at the same time it is a fine example of an Amorite victory taunt, which the Israelites have taken over.[8]

For dancers, the discovery of hundreds of songs in the Hebrew Scriptures presents a curious tension and opens up the texts to dance interpretation. Once it is recognized that the text was meant for music, it is accessible to the modern church dancer. However, the irony of these discovered songs is that one can only now speculate as to what the actual music sounded like. Since the songs were originally in an ancient language, it would be difficult to render the historical song in a contemporary context.

The discovery that danceable songs exist in the Hebrew Scriptures does not provide the same impetus to dance as a song where the music is available. There are two options for dance interpretation of these Hebrew Scripture songs: composing new music for song texts or reading and/or reciting the song text to existing music, live or recorded, to maintain the original musical tone.[9]

In interpreting these Hebrew Scripture songs, modern dancers can attend to three elements of the songs. These are the rhythm of the text itself, the rhythm of the music being used, and the images of the text. It is obvious how dancers can use the images of the text or the rhythm of the music to evolve choreography. Several remarks are needed concerning the rhythm of the text itself. Hebrew songs are not in measured meter that typifies contemporary songs. Ancient Hebrew songs have rhythm in that they are often in paired, tripled, or quadrupled lines. That is, the rhythm comes in lines, not words or syllables. An established rhythm evolves from the relationship of paired, quadrupled, or tripled lines to each other. For choreography, this means that the dancer cannot relate the words to measured steps and expect a workable pattern. It is often better to allot different dancers to different lines.

Among the nonpsalmic songs in the Hebrew Scriptures are Exodus 15:1-8; Deuteronomy 32:1-43; Judges 5:2-31; 1 Samuel 2:1-10; 1 Samuel 18:7; 2 Samuel 1:19-27; 2 Samuel 3:33,34; 1 Kings 8:12,13; 1 Chronicles 16:8-36; 2 Chronicles 6:41,42; Nehemiah 9:5-37; Tobit 13; Judith 10:8; Judith 15:10,11; Judith 16:1-21; The Song of Songs (at least six different songs); Isaiah 5:1-7; Isaiah 26:1-6; Isaiah 42:10-17; Isaiah 44:23; Isaiah 59:1-14; Jeremiah 22:18-23; Jeremiah 22:28-30; Jeremiah 9:17-22; Joshua 10:12; Daniel 3:25-30; Daniel 3:52-90; Daniel 3:100; Jonah 2:3-9; Micah 7:18-20; Habakkuk 3; Isaiah 47; and Habakkuk 2:6-19.

Three qualifying factors relate this list of songs to form-critical studies. First, the list is not exhaustive. There are many other texts which are held to be songs by some form critics. Second, the aforementioned forty-four songs contained two or three songs that have been combined for the purpose of the storyteller. Third, some of the cited songs are only fragments. In these cases either the rest of the song text has been lost or the editor of the biblical book simply chose to include portions of a song.

Psalms. There are important contributions that form-critical studies have made to an awareness of dance in the Hebrew Scriptures.[10] There is a general recognition that dance is related to the Book of

Psalms; for example, Psalm 149 explicitly mentions dance as a part of its praise. Less well-known are the psalms that exist in the other parts of the Hebrew Scriptures. Some are not identified within the texts, but the work of form critics have identified these passages as psalms.

Modern scholarship has painted a picture of the development of the psalms themselves. It is now clear that the psalms of the Hebrew Scriptures were not composed in one particular period of Israel's history. Rather, they were written, sung, and danced to from the early premonarchy to the late wisdom period, about eight hundred years. Thus, there were many different situations in which the Israelites worshipped in psalms. Some were the means of worship in a tribal atmosphere, while the image of ecstatic dance around the fire or of entire communities moving in unpatterned ways to the psalms certainly applies here. On the other hand, there was much movement of a different kind to the psalms as they were sung in the preexilic temple. These liturgical movements were stylized and reserved for the priestly class when the Israelites returned from exile. Similarly, there were different contexts for the psalms within one period of history.

In the early monarchy, for instance, some psalms were related to the king, the prophets, and the community at prayer. It is difficult to picture any of these settings without some movement. Through this emerging picture of the psalms' development, dancers are presented with a great variety of movement expression. Such a picture makes room for improvisational, ecstatic, and participatory treatment of the psalms as well as stylized, highly choreographed, and performed treatment.

For the modern church dancer, form criticism opens up more texts of the psalms and encourages a wide range of interpretations. Like the songs, the psalms provide a musical base and a rich collection of poetic images for the choreographer and dancer.

The psalms outside of the Book of Psalms in the Hebrew Scriptures include 2 Samuel 22; 2 Samuel 23:1–7; Isaiah 12: Isaiah 26:7–19; Isaiah 33:1–6; Isaiah 38:9–20; Isaiah 59:1–14; Nahum 1:2–8; and Zephaniah 3:14–18.

Covenant Ceremonies. If there is an identifiable center to the Hebrew faith, it is the covenant or agreement that God made with the people of God. It is then not surprising to find that Hebrew Scripture texts reflect actual ceremonies celebrating an expression of the agreement between God and Israel. Again, some of these passages are identified as covenant ceremonies by the texts themselves, while others are known as such only through form-critical studies.

There is not just one kind of covenant ceremony in the Hebrew Scriptures. As the idea of the covenant evolved, so did the ceremonies. Perhaps the most characteristic covenant ceremony is Joshua 24. This type of covenant is not unique to Israel or even to agreements between God and God's people. It is a covenant form common to the Near East, the *suzeranti*, which can also be made and ceremonialized between human beings. This covenant involves a bargain of unequal partners, the superior partner recalling what has been done for the lesser partner. Vows are made, and an object is called on to witness the agreement.

Covenant ceremonies involved ceremonial gestures relatable to dance. Contemporary dance interpretation can highlight both these ceremonial gestures and the recounting of God's mighty acts as the foundation of the covenant. Often the covenant ceremony's retelling of this narrative is highly dramatic, and therefore amenable to dance.

For interpreting covenant ceremony passages through dance, however, the fundamental guiding notion should be that of covenant itself as a relational motion which assumes movement on the part of the covenant partners. Dance has a chance to probe the expressive possibilities around the picture of God's dynamic relationship with humanity. Dancers can portray both the inner emotions and relational dynamics as they relate to these and other texts.

Among the covenant ceremony texts in the Hebrew Scriptures are Genesis 9:1–17; Genesis 15:1–21; Genesis 17:1–27; Exodus 19 and 20; Exodus 24; Exodus 34:1–28; Joshua 4:1–18; Joshua 24; 2 Kings 23:1–3; and Nehemiah 9 and 10.

Passover Texts.   In his book, *Moses*, Martin Buber provided an interesting summary of passover research in which the dancing roots of this Hebrew feast are evident. Much of the passover ritual's origins are found in the nomadic tribes of the Sinai. There the ceremonial smearing of the entrance to the tents with lamb's blood appears to have been a highly dramatic and festive act. Buber also traced the origins of the word for passover, *pesach*, to a word signifying a one-legged dance done in several Near Eastern settings. All of these origins of the passover are actually prebiblical, and do not directly describe how Israel's passover was celebrated. They do, however, show that the passover, like the agricultural feasts and monarchical ceremonies, was historically tied to dance.

The act of God passing over Israel in Egypt, sparing her own sons, is a divine dance. The graphic description of God touching down on the Egyptian households, but leaping over the Israelite homes is close to a description of a dance.

So dance interpreters have their choice of portraying God's saving action or in repeating the original movement of the Israelites, and pre-Israelites, in preparing the passover. Choreography could creatively combine the two accents in one dance event. Portrayals of God dancing from house to house or liberating God's people seem to have as many choreographic possibilities as the dance around the passover table.

Passover texts include Exodus 12 and 13; Numbers 9 and 10; Numbers 28:16–25; 2 Chronicles 30; 2 Chronicles 35:1–18; Ezekiel 45:18–24; and Deuteronomy 16:1–16.

Exodus-related Texts. One of the major themes of the Hebrew Scriptures — God leading Israel from slavery through the wilderness to freedom — is first of all a movement. In the first twenty chapters of the Book of Exodus, the dramatic movement of the individuals and the whole people is striking. The text itself shows a remarkable self-consciousness of this basic motif of movement, when the celebration of the crossing of the Red Sea — the most dramatic of the Exodus events and literarily the centerpiece of the narrative — turns out to be dance.[11]

Many texts in the Hebrew Scriptures recall the Exodus. In the Psalms and Prophets, God's post-Exodus relationship to Israel is often characterized by the Exodus experience itself. In considering the Exodus, one recognizes that this theme extends beyond those narratives dealing with the Exodus proper.

So dances here can portray the movement from slavery to freedom as Exodus metaphor for many moments in life and many texts in the Hebrew Scriptures. Treatment of the core Exodus narratives relates easily to both a dance portrayal of the story and the dancing celebration of freedom as pictured in Exodus 15.

Some Exodus-related passages in the Hebrew Scriptures outside of the Psalms are Exodus 1–20; Joshua 1:1–5; Isaiah 35: Isaiah 43:16–21; Jeremiah 24:1–10; and Jeremiah 31:1–22.[12]

Passages Related to the Figure of Wisdom. Scholarship in the last century has discovered the curious Hebrew Scripture figure of Wisdom, a goddess-like figure who helps Yahweh at the creation and attempts to save Israel.[13] In the biblical literature, Wisdom is portrayed as a figure who moves around on the earth and seeks followers for God. At the same time, she is a playful figure, who was present before the creation and had a special role in the formation of the earth and its creatures. The actual movement of Wisdom, and the joyous and creative aspects of her portrait, recommend her to dance interpretation. Othmar Keel-Leu has proved that the figure of Wisdom was danced both within and before the history of Israel.[14]

There are then historical figures and theological reasons to dance the figure of Wisdom. Indeed her playful character invites new kinds of experimentation — with the texts, dance itself, and the biblical image of God. Dancing Wisdom promises not only to unfold new possibilities for dancing the Hebrew Scriptures, but also to develop new understandings of the biblical image of God.

A number of these otherwise ignored texts include Proverbs 1:2–33; Proverbs 3:13–20; Proverbs 4:2–27; Proverbs 7:4, 5; Proverbs 8:1–9:6; Jeremiah 10:12; Jeremiah 51:15; Psalm 104; Psalm 136:1–6; Baruch 3 and 4; Wisdom 1:4–6; Wisdom 6:12–27, 8:1–21, 9:1–18, and 10:1–21; Ecclesiasticus 1:1–40, 4:11–22, 6:17–37, 24:1–47, and 51:13–38; and Job 28:1–28.

Dancing the Christian Scriptures

Hymn and Hymn Fragments. A number of texts have been identified as actual hymns or parts of hymns of the early church. As musical forms, they provide the church dancer with rhythms and poetic moods which can be choreographed. Some of these hymns were recognized before the development of form criticism, and have been set to music. For example, the hymn in Luke 1 had been set to music by Bach and others in their arrangements of the *Magnificat*. Therefore, for some of these passages, there is already music available for the church dancers as they seek to express the rhythm and mood of the passage in movement.

The other passages listed here have not yet been set to music. In order for the dancer to capture the music of the passage, I have found that one can read the passage with instrumental music as proper accompaniment for the dance and appropriate interpretation of Scripture. The nature of Greek Christian hymns usually adapts itself to jazz a bit better than to many classical pieces.

The hymns and hymn fragments of the Christian Scriptures include John 1:1–18; Philippians 2:6–11; Luke 1:46–55; 2:29–32; John 6:35–40; Colossians 1:15–20; Revelation 4:8, 11; Revelation 5:9, 10, 12–14; and Revelation 15:3, 4.

Initiation Rites. A number of rites celebrating an individual's entry into the Christian community have been detected in the Christian Scriptures. There does not seem to be one standard form or event, although they relate to baptism. These passages are significant for the church dancer, since the highly graphic character of the rites themselves recalls and inspires dance positions.

The rites themselves involve movement by the congregation, the celebrants, and the initiate. Historically these rites did inspire both ecstatic movement and a choreographed pattern by the celebrant. However, the graphic nature and the movement of the early ceremonies are starting places for the contemporary church dancer. For example, the procession by the congregation to and from the place of baptism is an excellent opportunity for both a performed dance by the celebrant or initiate and a simple dance by the entire congregation.

Highlights of these ceremonies are 1 John 1 and 2; 1 John 5:1–12; 1 Peter 2:1–10; and Revelation 2 and 3.

Enthronement Ceremonies. Form critics have shown the relationship between certain Near Eastern ceremonies of acclaiming a new king and certain Christian Scripture texts. These scriptural passages call forth the actual ceremony of a king's coronation when they are read. Although such ceremonies do not take place today, the positions and graphic nature of dance can do much to give these texts the dramatic and ceremonial context they were intended to have. Twentieth-century liturgical dance does not completely resemble that ancient Near Eastern ceremony, but does reflect some of its spirit. Liturgical dance can be a creative tie between the world of the Bible and twentieth-century life — representing both the original mode and the contemporary context.

The church dancer using a text such as Matthew's account of the Transfiguration is called to relate the implicit meaning and ceremony of the enthronement rite to the story line — the moment and action of Jesus being transfigured. In the dance, all this could have contemporary rather than ancient reference points. For instance, the throne and/or mountain could be represented by an altar in a liturgical setting.

Enthronement ceremony passages in the Christian Scriptures include the parallel treatments of the baptism, transfiguration, and crucifixion of Jesus in Matthew 3:13–17; Mark 1:9–11; Luke 3:21, 22; Matthew 17:1–8; Mark 9:2–8; Luke 9:28–36; Mark 15:33–39; Matthew 27:45–54; and Luke 23:44–47.

Eucharist-related Passages. It is not just the accounts of the Last Supper that reflect use as a part of the early church celebration of Eucharist. The formula used by the accounts of the feeding of the five thousand, for instance, are almost exact copies of the ritual of the early church's communion. Many contemporary scholars see this as either a commentary on the rite itself or a part of it.

This is significant to the church dancer in two ways. First of all, the communion is the celebration of the *body* of Christ. What better moment for the movement of the body! Secondly, as a kind of improvisation on the eucharistic event, these passages encourage a secondary event around communion, in this case — dance.

Among the communion-related passages in the Christian Scriptures are: Matthew 14:13–21; Mark 6:31–44; Luke 9:10–17; Matthew 15:32–39; Mark 8:1–10; John 6:1–15; John 6:26, 27, 32–40, 44–51, 52–58; John 13:1–20; Luke 24:13–35; Luke 24:36–45; John 20:19–29; John 21:1–23; Revelation 3:14–22; and Revelation 22:14.

Psalm-related Passages. The psalms of the Hebrew Scriptures were the first place that many church dancers found their justification. Besides the explicit exhortation to dance that we find in the psalms, church dancers have been able to infer dances from the worship-setting and music. So these have become the most danced biblical passages. Church dancers have been able to use much of the liturgical music in dancing the psalms since liturgical musicians have rarely lost contact with the liturgical use of the psalms.

What the church dancer has not seen, but what has become evident in the last century to biblical scholars, is that there are passages in the Christian Scriptures that refer to and depend on a Hebrew Scripture psalm. For example, when Jesus cries out on the cross, his words are the first line of Psalm 22. Citing the first line of the psalm, and to some extent any line, was really a reference to the entire psalm. So the death of Jesus in Matthew, Mark, and Luke is meant to be considered with reference to the Twenty-second Psalm. Since the psalm has a fairly direct tie to dance, the accounts of the death of Jesus also become dance territory.

Such psalm-related danceable passages in the Christian Scriptures include Matthew 21:1–10; Matthew 22:41–45; Matthew 4:1–11; Matthew 3:13–17; Matthew 23:37–39; Matthew 27:45–55; Mark 15:33–41; Mark 11:1–11; Mark 12:35–37; Luke 13:34, 35; Luke 20:9–19; Luke 19:28–38; Acts 2:14–36; Romans 3:9–20; and Hebrews 1:1–14.

Dramatic Narrative Passages. The dramatic narrative quality of a number of stories in the Christian Scriptures is an implicit invitation to ritual enactment. Dance, of course, is the most ancient mode of ritual reenactment. These passages quite naturally lend themselves to contemporary interpretation. This style of dance does not limit itself to straightforward reenactment of the story. There are a number of possibilities for the dancer(s) improvising on the story to highlight connections of the passage to contemporary life and to accent inherent qualities of the text that a simple reading does not emphasize enough. This category is not easily limited; therefore, I suggest watching constantly for dramatic narrative passages in the Christian Scriptures.

Some of these dramatic narrative passages are John 13:1-20; Matthew 21:1-10; Matthew 8:23-27; Revelation 12 and 13; Luke 10:29-37; and Matthew 25:31-46.

Resurrection Proclamations. The scandal of the resurrection in the Christian Scriptures lies primarily in its celebration of the human body. In its contemporary setting, it was not at all unusual to talk about a god's resurrection from the dead. However the Christian Scriptures' emphasis on the fact that it is Jesus' body which is resurrected is unusual. This highlights the Christian Scriptures' belief in the importance of the human body.

Christian faith, at least for the early church, was not abstracted from the physical but incarnated into it. The resurrection was the sign of the final victory of the spirit *in* the body. Many resurrection accounts emphasize the bodiliness of Jesus — he eats and invites Thomas to touch him. Since dance is a celebration of the body, there is a natural affinity between the Christian Scripture resurrection proclamations and dance.

Some of the resurrection proclamations are 1 Corinthians 15:3-7a; Romans 1:1-7; John 21:1-23; John 20:11-18; John 20:19-28; Luke 24:13-35; Luke 24:36-43; and Matthew 28:9, 10.

These categories of text from the Hebrew and Christian Scriptures are meant to help the church dancer in two ways. First, they identify the specific wealth of scriptural resources available for liturgical dance. Second, they point out which of the passages we use in church study and liturgy have affinities to dance. Once these affinities are identified, the introduction and use of dance in celebrating, studying, and proclaiming the Scriptures can happen more easily. In this way, dance becomes less of a novelty and more a part of the fabric of the church's life.

Notes

1. See Doug Adams, *Congregational Dancing in Christian Worship* (Austin: The Sharing Co., 1971).

2. Each moment corresponding to a stage of development of the text.

3. Exodus 15:1–18.

4. Numbers 21:17, 18.

5. Exodus 15:20, 21.

6. Genesis 29 and Judges 14.

7. Isaiah 47.

8. Numbers 21 also contains an ancient workers' song in verses 17 and 18.

9. In my own personal experience both of these options have proven quite workable. Often a contemporary musician can bring the text to life in surprising ways through an original composition. Such an effort is obviously much more elaborate than simply finding a record that seems to fit the text. This second option of using already existing music can also be highly creative when combined with the medium of dance.

10. It is not my intention to present an in-depth study of the psalms' various relationships to dance. There are a series of publications on the theme of the psalms and dance. For example, see Adams, *Congregational Dancing in Christian Worship;* Constance Fisher, *Dancing the Old Testament* (Austin: The Sharing Co., 1980); and Roland de Vaux, *Ancient Israel, Its Life and Institutions*, trans. John McHugh (New York: McGraw-Hill, 1961).

In addition, many commentaries on the psalms sometimes refer to dance in the psalms and often are helpful for a dancer's understanding. What may be needed is a dancer's handbook of the psalms that could form the basis for a dancer's ongoing work with the psalms.

11. Exodus 15.

12. In listing texts in this category, I have not included any psalms, since I have referred to all the psalms in another category. However, dance interpretation of the psalms might well keep this Exodus motif in many of the psalms.

13. In *The Lady of the Dance: A Movement Approach to the Biblical Figure of Wisdom* (Austin: The Sharing Co., 1981), I have outlined the biblical portrait of Wisdom, summarized the scholarship of the last century, and discussed her relationship to contemporary dance.

14. Othmar Keel-Leu, *Die Weisheit Spielt vor Gott* (Gottingen: Vandenhoeck and Ruprecht, 1974).

6

Biblical Criteria in Dance: Modern Dance as Prophetic Form

Doug Adams and Judith Rock

Theologian Paul Tillich advanced the discussion of "Theology and the Arts" by noting that some art is religious in style even though it is not religious in subject matter. Conversely, he argued that some art is not religious in style even though it is religious in subject matter. Similarly, some sermons and writings cite biblical passages but are essentially not expressive of biblical faiths;[1] while other sermons and writings cite few if any biblical passages but express biblical faiths.[2] To date, most discussions of the Bible in dance have focused on subject matter such as The Prodigal Son or Job,[3] rather than the less obvious but profound reflection of biblical faith and values in the aesthetics of modern dance technique and choreography.

"Religion and Art" analysis in the visual arts has proceeded fur-

"Biblical Criteria in Dance: Modern Dance as Prophetic Form" was originally presented to the International Conference on the Bible in Dance, Jerusalem, 1979. It was published in *Israel Dance* (1980), 5–9, and as *Biblical Criteria in Modern Dance: Modern Dance as Prophetic Form* (Austin: The Sharing Co., 1979). It is included in this collection in an updated revision with permission.

ther than such analysis in dance and therefore aides dance criticism on the question of biblical criteria. Tillich drew our attention to how the very style of art expresses theology. Our preoccupation with iconography in visual art or with subject matter in dance tends to reduce visual art or dance to narrative or literature, while attention to style considers each art form in its own terms and allows its unique contributions to inform us. Tillich distinguished between religion in the larger sense,[4] and religion in the narrower sense.[5] The larger sense of religion is communicated in style, while the narrower sense is communicated through subject matter. Thus, he was able to distinguish four categories of relation between religion and visual art. The first is a style expressive of no ultimate concern and a content without religious subject matter, as in Jan Steen's *The Dancing Couple* (fig. 8). The second is religious in style and nonreligious in in content as in Pablo Picasso's *Guernica* (fig. 9), a painting in which "we do not cover up anything, but have to look at the human situation in its depths."[6] The third category is nonreligious in style but religious in content, as in the case of Raphael's *Alba Madonna* (fig. 10). The visual symbols in such a painting are obviously religious; but the style is so harmonious and well-rounded that it denies the content and makes the paintings "dangerously irreligious." Tillich saw paintings of this kind as dangerous because, for example, in Raphael's *Crucifixion*, the figure on the cross reveals no dimension of suffering, which may mislead the viewer to expect an easy harmony with humanity as the goal or result of Christ's presence, an expectation that will blind the viewer to Christ's presence in much of life. The fourth category has both a religious style and religious content. Tillich's prime example of this category is Mathias Grünewald's *Crucifixion* from *The Isenheim Altarpiece* (fig. 11), where the style as well as content expresses crucifixion. He was uneasy about identifying any contemporary visual art on this level.

Tillich's four categories are thought-provoking when considered in relation to modern dance. In the first category (that of a work of art whose style shows no ultimate concern and whose subject matter is not religious), we could place many student dance compositions of the Merce Cunningham genre. The second grouping characterized by religious style and nonreligious subject matter could include Kurt Jooss's *Green Table*, Paul Taylor's *Cloven Kingdom* and *Esplanade*, José Limón's *The Moor's Pavane*, and Twyla Tharp's *Sue's Leg* (fig. 12). In the third category, we could place many of the so-called "religious" dances whose content is specifically religious but which display a nonreligious style: i.e., a style which is smooth, pretty,

8. Jan Steen, *The Dancing Couple*, 1663. Oil on canvas. 40⅜ x 56⅛ inches. Widener Collection, National Gallery of Art, Washington. (1942.9.81 [677]).

9. Pablo Picasso, *Guernica*, 1937. Oil on canvas. 11½ x 5¾ feet. Prado, Madrid. Photograph courtesy of Giraudon/Art Resource, New York. The works of Pablo Picasso are © 1990 A.R.S., N.Y./SPADEM, Paris.

10. Raphael, *The Alba Madonna*, c. 1510. Oil on wood transferred to canvas, diameter 37 1/4 inches. Andrew W. Mellon Collection, National Gallery of Art, Washington, D.C. (1937.1.24 [24]).

11. Mathias Grünewald, *Crucifixion*, detail from the *Isenheim Altarpiece*, c. 1515. Musée d'Unterlinden, Colmar. Photograph by Otto Zimmerman.

and entertaining. Norbert Vesak's *Gift to be Simple*, a ballet about American Shakers, falls into this third category. In the fourth category, that of dances with both religious style and religious content, we could place Margalit Oved's *Mothers of Israel*, Helen Tamiris's *Negro Spirituals*, and Martha Graham's *Seraphic Dialogue*.

It is the second category that radically expands our understanding of the Bible in dance as we begin to explore Tillich's observation that the very style or form of a work of art may be biblical whether or not its subject matter is.[7] The influence of the biblical faiths and their values on Western culture (and therefore on art) is diffuse, but discernible in many specific instances. Any artist within a culture is affected by its values, both those consciously accepted and rejected and those not even consciously considered. Western modern dance choreographers are no exception. Any modern dance *may* reflect biblically rooted affirmations and values, whether or not its subject matter is specifically biblical, and whether or not the choreographer had a direct intention of affirming biblical values. The reason for this is that there is in modern dance technique and choreography a prophetic element which parallels that in the biblical narrative.[8]

The first obvious question raised by this thesis is an important one. Since modern dance is such a diverse phenomenon in terms of style, technique, and choreographic intention, is it even possible to speak of a basic modern dance aesthetic? Selma Jean Cohen stated,

> The modern dance is always concerned with the unacceptable symbol, the one that startles us into awareness. The pressure may be subtle or it may be obvious, but it is always there.[9]

Modern dance, then, can be see as having a prophetic attitude toward the function of art in general, and dance in particular, in the contemporary world. The basic modern dance aesthetic has a prophetic point of view.

The biblical prophet is defined by Abraham Heschel as one who "is an iconoclast, challenging the apparently holy, revered, and awesome."[10] The prophet's language, poetry, and action is charged with agitation, anguish, and a spirit of nonacceptance.[11] The prophet "is a preacher whose purpose is not self-expression or the purgation of feeling, but communication."[12]

John Martin, former dance critic of the *New York Times*, elaborated in 1933 that modern dance was not a dance for spectacular display or self-expression, but attempted to communicate personal authentic experiences connected with a basic truth about human beings and reality.[13] Modern dance began as a prophetic form in that its purpose was the communication of personal authentic experience by means of new symbols, new forms, and new ways of moving. It called into question both the dance that had gone before, and the time and place in which it found itself.

Perhaps the modern dance of the 1920s, 1930s, and 1940s shows the basically prophetic character of the form more clearly than the dance of the 1950s, 1960s, and early 1970s. For the early modern choreographers such as Martha Graham, Doris Humphrey, and Mary Wigman, emotional motivation and human communication were primary. These choreographers believed in the potential social relevance of art that was rooted in time and space. They saw the ordinary experience of authentic human beings as valid material out of which the artist may create. They were concerned with meaning in all its dimensions. Like biblical characters and stories, they saw no necessity for happy endings.[14] While the earlier choreographers saw that dance could be communicative in itself apart from narrative or representational content, they were always concerned with form as the shape of content, rather than simply as an end in itself. As Heschel reminded us, the prophet's central concern is "the plight of man.... God Himself is described as reflecting over the plight of man, rather then as contemplating eternal ideas."[15] The early modern dances of Graham, Wigman, and Humphrey did not contemplate eternal ideas but looked at persons in human situations and told the brusque, undecorated, unlovely truth as they saw it.

Those choreographers offered us dances that lift up the ambiguity, the humor, the sorrow, the absurdity, and through these realities the truth to be found in ordinary human experience. This lifting up of things as they are is part of the prophetic voice and biblical touchstone within modern dance. Confronted with such a dance the audience has the opportunity to see some part of themselves as they really are, to hear some part of the truth of what it is to be a human being.

Heschel stated that though the prophet begins with a message of woe, he ends with a message of hope.[16] As modern dance and its choreographers grew, they developed the counterpoint side of their prophetic form. The prophetic message has a tenderness at its heart, what Heschel called the pathos of God.[17] Repent *so that* the crooked may be made straight, *so that* the barren places may bear fruit, *so that* Jacob may stand, for he is very small.[18]

While in that earlier period, modern dancers shared many of these principles of belief, this is less true today. The major change since 1950 has been the lessening role of emotional motivation and communication of universal human experience. Form has taken precedence over content. The early creators found new forms in order to communicate new content. Graham found the genesis of movement in the act of breathing — the source of human life — beginning as the biblical narrative begins with the gift of breath to the human body and its consequences. Humphrey created new movement out of her discoveries about the human body in relation to the world around it, to space, to gravity.

The middle generation of modern choreographers, however, have taken modern dance in less prophetic directions. As non-Western religions and their corresponding aesthetics permeate Western culture, this shift is reflected in modern dance styles in the work of Erick Hawkins. He states that the function of the artist is not to present life as it is, but in line with traditional Oriental aesthetics: to offer ideals of enlightenment, life as it ought to be.[19] This is directly counter to the biblically prophetic understanding that renewal or enlightenment is to be found in the midst of life as it is in all its grubbiness and ambiguity. God is at least as likely to be encountered during an invasion of the Assyrian army as in meditation in the temple.

Other choreographers such as Alwin Nikolais and Merce Cunningham have turned almost exclusively to form itself as their artistic concern. This is a potentially prophetic direction, as witnessed by Tillich's second category of art with religious style but nonreligious content. However, a requirement for the prophetic (whether in biblical narrative or in modern dance) is that it calls us as well as our favorite attitudes and assumptions into question. Insofar as choreographers have simply acknowledged the inescapability of contemporary forces of abstraction, randomness, mechanization, and meaninglessness, they have ceased to be prophetic. The prophetic is that which speaks the new word and calls us beyond what is. The prophetic transcends the contemporary and is allied with a yet unrealized future. Insofar as modern dance or any art simply reflects or reiterates the beliefs, tendencies, and statements of the surrounding culture, it ceases to be prophetic. The prophetic art form grows out of its time and place by calling that time and place into question and by offering a clearer, deeper vision, lest the people perish.

In the work of the choreographers of the 1970s, such as Twyla Tharp, Paul Taylor, Meredith Monk, Philobolus, and Kei Takei, there is a return to a concern with emotional motivation and the importance of human experience, although the result looks utterly different than the pioneering works of the early modern choreographers. A new wedding of emotional motivation and abstraction of form in dances that are religious in style suggests realities and concerns below the surface of human life. In such works, modern dance seems to be reemerging as a prophetic art form in our time and place.

In retrospect, those dances which have struck us as prophetic have certain technical elements that stress the realities of human existence, including the use of percussive movement, the center body, fall and recovery, the floor, asymmetry, and humor. These elements have been used to create dances that surprise us and strike us as new, requiring us to look again more closely and to stretch our vision. Similarly, the biblically prophetic calls us to the new song, the new wine, for repeating what used to be called prophetic will no longer be prophetic. John Cage noted that the American flag is radically asymmetrical in design, but we have seen it so often that it becomes symmetrical with our expectations of it, so we do not really look at it.[20]

New prophetic dances use movement elements in unexpected newly prophetic ways as in Twyla Tharp's *Sue's Leg* (fig. 12). Although all dancers try for a flow of movement, Tharp achieves it to a unique degree in *Sue's Leg*. She uses an extraordinary flow of movement in the dancers' bodies, together with humor, to recreate the social dance and popular music world of the 1930s and 1940s. The movement never stops; it flows through individual bodies, and from body to body, without visible drops or dead spots. The dancers meet, cling together, bounce and roll off each other, giving and receiving energy from each other's flow of movement. When body contact occurs between dancers, it is not for the purpose of spectacular lifts or other technical fireworks, but to show us real bodies — excited, moving, playing, and exhausted. Her use of humor also allows the audience to perceive a sense of community — a sense that we are all in this together — among the dancers. We see potential couples eye each other, and try each other. We see them both succeed and fail at dancing together. We see them move on. Their encounters, like ours, are both serious and absurd. Like us, they keep on dancing, stepping on each other's feet, and squeezing the last drop of life out of an era and out of themselves.[21]

Sue's Leg is a prophetic dance with secular subject matter. It is prophetic in presenting human beings not only as they were but as they are. Tharp's dances have been called merely fashionable, chic, and slick by some critics. However in this particular work she has shown us something of "the plight of man," to use Heschel's words. Watching *Sue's Leg* and listening to its music, one remembers that those people moving frenetically, throwing each other into the air, clinging together in the last hours of dance marathons, were people

12. Twyla Tharp Company, *Sue's Leg*. Photograph courtesy of the Dance Collection, Performing Arts Research Center, The New York Public Library at Lincoln Center. Astor, Lenox and Tilden Foundations.

on the brink of war and in the midst of war. Their dances came out of the heart of "the plight of man." As we watch them, recreated by Tharp, we are in our time and in the midst of our own wars, reminded of our plight.

Paul Taylor, although not a new choreographer, is a master at making prophetic dances that force us to look again at ourselves and our lives. One such dance is *Cloven Kingdom*. As the piece begins, men and women in evening dress gather and dance. We see what we expect to see on such an occasion: glamor, sophistication, courtesy, flirtation. But Taylor paints his glittering urbane picture in order spasmodically to peel it away so that we see into a more subconscious, basic, humorous, and all-too-recognizable reality.

So quickly that we are not sure whether we really saw it or only imagined it, a dancer breaks the smooth sequence to make a shambling animal-like movement toward another dancer. Just as quickly the original sequence is resumed as though it had never been broken. As the piece develops, the animal-like qualities of the apparent sophisticates emerge more completely. The dominant movement themes are now based on animal movement, which contrasts pointedly with the evening dresses and tailcoats of the dancers.

Cloven Kingdom is a biblically prophetic dance, although it has no biblical characters or religious subject matter. It is biblically prophetic because of its style, fitting the second category in Tillich's religion and art analysis. Not only does its title echo the basic human predicament; human beings are formed, as the Bible puts it, from the dust of the earth and the breath of God (Gen. 2:7). To be a person is by definition to inhabit a cloven kingdom. The dance is prophetic also because it forces us to look beneath the surface of our lives and our interactions with others, and to meet and recognize our shadow selves. Taylor, urbanely and with humor, calls into question some of our favorite assumptions about ourselves: that we are basically quite nice, civilized, courteous, and sophisticated creatures. He suggests to us that the wearing of tailcoats may be more appropriate than we realize.

A prophetic modern dance (whether religious or secular in subject matter) tells us the truth, not necessarily particular truths that God exists or that love is full of pain, but some part of the truth about ourselves. A prophetic modern dance tells us something about what it means to be a human being. Any particular truth, any particular message is soon stated. The truth about ourselves can never be told fully or too often. Biblically prophetic art is made by an iconoclast — by artists who break the holy images to shock us into new awareness of the truth about ourselves. Confronted with such a work of art, we once again have ears to hear and eyes to see. Miraculously, for a moment, we do hear and we do see.

Notes

1. Such sermons uphold the status quo without justice for many individuals.

2. Such sermons call into question the status quo and seek justice for each human life.

3. See Giora Manor, "The Bible as Dance," *Dance Magazine*, December 1978, 56–86.

4. For Tillich, religion in the wider sense was "being ultimately concerned about one's own being, about one's self and one's world, about its meaning and its estrangement and its finitude." See Paul Tillich, "Existentialist Aspects of Modern Art," in *On Art and Architecture*, ed. John Dillenberger (New York: Crossroad, 1987) 92. This essay was originally published in *Christianity and the Existentialists*, ed. Carl Michalson (New York: Charles Scribner's Sons, 1956) 132.

5. For Tillich, religion in the narrower sense was "having a set of symbols,... divine beings,... ritual activities and doctrinal formulations about their relationship to us." Ibid.

6. Ibid., 96.

7. One may perceptively see that when Tillich spoke of "religious" style he had in mind that style of biblical faiths as prophetic. One may argue that some other religions are not predominantly prophetic in style but are largely priestly in style. Although Old and New Testaments have some priestly elements, they are predominantly prophetic. For distinctions between prophetic and priestly styles, see note 8.

8. The prophetic is iconoclastic toward any standing order; for the prophet sees the limits of that order and would stretch such limits to include those left out and reform those within. Joshua C. Taylor, former Director of the National Museum of American Art, saw a parallel of the prophetic in an art style he called "will to fellowship" or "communitive"; for such art makes me aware of individual persons and our relationships. Figurative or not in subject matter, the work's painterly style (e.g., van Gogh) makes me aware that a person with a body made that and makes me aware of myself as a distinct bodily individual that can relate with others but never totally become one. In contrast, Taylor styled the priestly as "will to form" and "unitive" (e.g., classical or neoclassical works of art) that make me oblivious to persons as I am drawn beyond into perfect unity. Both "priestly-unitive" and "prophetic-communitive" art styles are religious; but they correspond to different religions. "Unitive" corresponds to Eastern religions with major concern for unity with eternal ideas and absorption into immortality of

the soul where all are one; but "communitive" corresponds to Western religions with major concern for community among persons and resurrection of the body, with each individual persisting as a distinct part in the world. See Doug Adams, "Insights from Three Perspectives on the Religious and Aesthetic Imagination," *Seedbed* III.3 (1975) 1–3, or Doug Adams, "Theological Expressions Through Visual Art Forms," in *Art, Creativity, and the Sacred*, ed. Diane Apostolos-Cappadona (New York: Crossroad, 1984) 311–18.

9. Selma Jean Cohen, *The Modern Dance: Seven Statements of Belief* (Middletown: Wesleyan University Press, 1965) 14.

10. Abraham Joshua Heschel, *The Prophets* (New York: Harper and Row, 1969) 10.

11. Ibid., 6.

12. Ibid., 7.

13. Cohen, *The Modern Dance*, 4.

14. For example, Moses never made it to the Promised Land; and the elder brother in Jesus's parable did not go to the party.

15. Heschel, *The Prophets*, 5.

16. Ibid., 12.

17. Ibid., 7.

18. Dances that come immediately to mind are Humphrey's *Day on Earth*, Graham's *Appalachian Spring*, and Charles Weidman's *On My Mother's Side*.

19. Cohen, *The Modern Dance*, 44.

20. John Cage, "Jasper Johns: Stories and Ideas," reprinted in *Jasper Johns: Paintings, Drawings, and Sculpture*, 1954–1964, ed. Alan Solomon (London: Whitechapel Gallery, 1964) 27–28.

21. Some of Paul Taylor's recent choreographies qualify for Paul Tillich's fourth category with religious subject matter and religious style: e.g., "Speaking in Tongues" (1989).

PART II

Women in Dance and Scripture

7

Scriptural Women Who Danced

Diane Apostolos-Cappadona

The Hebrew and Christian Scriptures are replete with women. In fact, the Bible can be said to begin and end with the acts of women: she who brings sin into the world and she who makes it possible for sin to be forgiven. Strong women, passive women, old women, young women, married women, single women, women with children, barren women, women beyond the age of childbearing, women of physical beauty, and women of spiritual strength — such women abound in the scriptural stories of the Judeo-Christian tradition. There are Eve, Sarah, Hagar, Rebecca, Ruth, Naomi, Miriam, Bathsheba, Jezebel, Jael, Deborah, Esther, Potiphar's wife, Jephthah's daughter, the Queen of Sheba, Herodias, Salome, Elizabeth, Ann, Mary the Mother, and Mary Magdalene. Which, if any, of these scriptural women actually danced? What is the meaning of the scriptural women who danced?

Dancing is directly related to the body. The basic instrument of the dancer is her body. Therefore, the meaning of the body is fundamental to the understanding of dance, dancer, and dancing. In his study of the relationship between religion and the arts, Gerardus van der Leeuw classified dance as the first of the arts. "[T]he art of the dance is even more primitive than verbal art. Here rhythm is all powerful, it rules the whole man and compels them to follow the right path."[1]

95

Dance, thus, was established because of the fundamental human need to communicate (through bodily gestures) with other human beings and with the gods.

From the beginning of human history, dance was used as part of religious worship. However, within that earliest human culture, there was no segregation of the body from human experience and from religion. Rather, the fundamental agrarian cycle of the seasons corresponded to the cycles of human life, especially that of the female body. As van der Leeuw noted, "The erotic function of the dance bordered on its more inclusive function as the awakener of fertility."[2] Thus, dance became associated with the creation of life.

As human history progressed, moving as Mircea Eliade has indicated from a matriarchal cyclical context into a patriarchal linear one,[3] the relationship between daily human existence and religion slowly separated. As a result, the body, especially the female body, was denigrated, and dance was slowly excised from religious worship. Simultaneously, the image of woman in Western art and culture was transformed from the duality of goddess and temptress, or Aphrodite and vampire, to that of victim and seductress, or Eve and Medea. In evoking the ambivalence of fascination and terror, the presentations of the female body symbolize woman's fundamental and powerful participation in the inscrutable mystery of life.

My analysis of the scriptural women who danced is grounded in a visual examination of the depiction of the female body, the dancer's instrument, in Western Christian art. The fundamental basis for the affinities between the visual arts and dance is the human body. The relationship between the presentation of the body in painting and sculpture parallels the attitudes toward dance, especially the inclusion of dance within Christian worship. What the art historian, Emile Mâle, used to refer to as the "mutual illumination of the arts," is helpful for understanding not only the history of liturgical dance, but also the scriptural women who danced.[4] Since we have no pictorial records of liturgical dance or dancers before the late nineteenth and early twentieth centuries, we are dependent upon how artists presented the human form in Christian art. In a thorough and precise investigation of the mutual illumination of the arts, we would find that there would be a reciprocal relationship between dance, theater, and the visual arts in terms of bodily gestures, costumes, scenery, and even, themes.

In studying the visual art tradition of each of the scriptural women who danced, then, particular attention must be paid to the depiction of their bodies. As Margaret R. Miles has noted,

For women, the continuity of physical existence is secondary to the in-
terruptions of that continuity caused by different physical conditions,
which in turn carry different social identities and personal relationships.
First menstruation, first sexual intercourse, childbearing, menopause —
all these events are primarily irreversible alterations in a woman's body
and secondarily in social identity. Change, the difference from one day
to the next, the different body, perspective, and values of different times
of life, these experiences of discontinuity, of being physically, mentally,
and socially other than one was, characterize women's experience.[5]

Therefore, an understanding of the iconographic tradition and the
portrayal of the female body in Western visual art allows for an interpretation of the role of dance, and in this instance, of the meaning
of the scriptural image of women who danced.

Ironically, the Hebrew and Christian Scriptures each have one singular woman who danced. These two women, Miriam and Salome,
represent the dichotomy of what it traditionally means to be female,
that is, to be either virgin or temptress. This dialectical symbolism
of woman is exacerbated by the fact that although Miriam and Salome both danced, they danced for different reasons, one for joy and
faith in God, the other for human pleasure. Naturally, it is this latter
image, which depicts both woman and her body as evil, that comes
to predominate in the Western visual art and dance traditions.

Miriam, whose very name means "wish" and "love," represents the
positive aspect of dance in the scriptural tradition. According to Exodus 15:20, "Miriam the prophetess, the sister of Aaron, took a timbrel
in her hand; and all the women went out after her with timbrels and
with dances." Accorded the unique epithet "the prophetess," Miriam
is singled out from other women in the Hebraic tradition, for she
both dances and prophesies.

Miriam's is a dance of praise that accompanies her triumphant
hymn in Exodus 15:21, "Sing ye to the Lord, for he both triumphed
gloriously; the horse and his rider both he has thrown into the sea."
This, then, is a song of celebration accompanied by a series of joyful
and praising movements — a dance. The image of Miriam is of a
pious and faithful female figure who dutifully obeys and worships the
Lord following the custom of her people. "It was an Israelite custom
for women to welcome the men with timbrels and dancing when they
returned from the battlefield and at other celebrations."[6] She is not
described to us in physical terms, but rather in terms of her spiritual
status, she is a prophetess, and a singer and dancer of God's praises.
This is exactly how she is depicted in the visual tradition.[7]

Miriam is characteristically dressed in a long-flowing garment that covers her body, concealing her sexuality. Thus, her physicality and sexuality are denied or disguised by both her garments and her posture. As Western history unfolds, the image of Miriam dancing before the Lord may become more gender specific, but never sensual or erotic (fig. 13). Her hair is either depicted as long and flowing in the manner of the chaste virgin, or covered with a veil in the style of the pious wife or widow. She holds an instrument, a timbrel, following the scriptural passage. Her bodily gestures indicate an attempt at movement, with an upward or transcendent thrust to her gestures.

In the varied choreographic attempts to present this virtuous and appropriate Hebrew maiden celebrating the Lord's victory, modesty prevails. Even Ruth St. Denis's interpretation of Miriam emphasized her obedience, chastity, and spirituality (fig. 14). Miriam's image, therefore, does not undergo the transformation from cultural period to cultural period as evidenced by other scriptural women such as Eve, Judith, and the Magdalene.[8] Rather, Miriam's major virtues, her modesty and her spirituality, characterize and define her both visually and choreographically throughout the history of interpretations of her story. As a form of worship and celebration, then, dance has an appropriate role when presented within the rubrics delineated by Miriam.

Salome, on the other hand, represents the inappropriate dancer; she is evil and erotic. At least that is the way she is perceived by the nineteenth and twentieth-century public. Salome's history, both in art and dance, is much more colorful than that of all other scriptural women who danced. Here is the proof to the popular adage that the story of evil is always of more interest than the story of good.

In the beginning, however, Salome didn't even have a name, let alone culpability for the death of John the Baptist. In fact, neither scriptural account of the death of John identifies the young dancer as other than "the daughter of Herodias."[9] Her dance is only described as having pleased Herod and is not defined as the infamous dance of the seven veils. The young dancer asked the happy king for the head of the Baptist only at her mother's request. In fact, a mere ten lines are devoted to the story of the young woman who becomes the most frequent scriptural character in modern dance. We know nothing of her past or her future. All we know of "the damsel" is that her dancing pleased the king and she in turn wanted to please her mother.

Salome received her name and some semblance of an identity in the writings of the Jewish historian, Flavius Josephus. Although he made no mention of her dance, Josephus stated that neither the now-

13. William Jay Bolton and John Bolton, *Miriam*, detail from a 19th-century American stained glass window, St. Ann and the Holy Trinity Episcopal Church, Brooklyn. Photograph courtesy of The Metropolitan Museum of Art, New York. (L.1985.136).

14. Ruth St. Denis and Ted Shawn in *Miriam, Sister of Moses*. Photograph courtesy of the Dance Collection, Performing Arts Research Center, The New York Public Library at Lincoln Center. Astor, Lenox and Tilden Foundations.

named Salome, or her mother, Herodias, were guilty of the Baptist's death. Rather, the guilt for this action rested with Herod.

With the establishment of Christianity as a legitimate religion and as *the* religion of the Roman Empire in the fourth century, the importance of the Christian Scriptures increased as did the status of the scriptural figures such as John the Baptist. Ironically as John's stature in Christian spirituality and theology became more significant, so did that of Salome. In fact, by the medieval period the young dancer began to become both so fused and confused with her mother, that by the nineteenth century they were collapsed into one evil female creature.

A popular image in medieval and early renaissance art and theater, Salome came to personify the evils of the flesh just as John symbolized the life of the Spirit. However, these "evils of the flesh" were not overtly erotic or pornographic in their presentation. For example, some of the finest medieval depictions of Salome are found on lesser north tympanum on the facade of Rouen Cathedral. Here the acrobatic character of her dance is emphasized as an almost prepubescent Salome garbed in a long and flowing robe bends over backwards in the performance of her "dance." The young dancer balances herself on her left hand as her body arches upwards and curves forward dramatically at her knees so that her feet hover over her upraised head. Her right arm, now broken off, most probably extended outward toward the audience entering the cathedral.

Similarly, in Benozzo Gozzoli's small oil painting from the early renaissance period, *The Dance of Salome*, a young girl occupies the foreground of the composition as she balances herself carefully on her left foot (fig. 15). The fluidity of her movement is dramatized by the curves and pleats of her long and full garment. Her bent and slightly raised right leg is highlighted by the light effects within the painting. As her left hand touches her waist, thereby defining it, her right hand is open toward Herod as her bent right arm complements the movement of her right leg. Her small and high breasts are hardly discernible, as her high-necked, low-waisted, and simple garment does not reveal the physical contours of her body.

This is in contrast to the garments worn by both Herodias and the maidservant. In both of those instances, the breasts are carefully delineated by the decorative high waists of their garments. In Herodias's case, this symbol of her sexuality is exacerbated by the puffed upper sleeves of her red garment and the decorated edges of her diaphanous headpiece which extend to the midpoint between her breasts, the maidservant's green garment is highlighted by the v-shaped neckline with the insert of the white-trimmed red undergarment accentuating her bosom.

Salome is represented twice in this painting and both times she is depicted in facial profile. Her uncovered hair flows loosely down her shoulders in contrast again to both Herodias, who has her head covered in the style appropriate to married women, and the maidservant, whose hair is piled upon her head in the fashion of the courtesan. In the second presentation of Salome in the back of the composition, she kneels at her mother's knee and hands over the decapitated head of John the Baptist. Even if mother and daughter stood next to each other, the figure of Salome would be smaller than that of Herodias, signifying two important interpretative readings.

First, this physical difference between the two women suggests the youthfulness, perhaps very young age of Salome. Second, following the classical convention that the more significant figure is physically the larger, it is Herodias's role that can be seen as primary in the action of John's death. Thus, Gozzoli's interpretation argues for a continuation of the scriptural tradition that Salome is not guilty of John's death herself; it is at her mother's request that she asks for his head.

From these two typical depictions of Salome in medieval and early renaissance art, we recognize the following simple facts, that the nature of her dance was acrobatic, that her youthfulness emphasized her as yet nonexistent sexuality, and that her mother was the cause of the Baptist's death. Such depictions of Salome are significant for the history of dance as they are contemporary to the development of the medieval theater and the continuing tradition of liturgical dance then still practiced in the church.

In the high renaissance and baroque period, the image of Salome is transformed in Western art into a vehicle for depicting female beauty. She becomes slowly disassociated from the narrative of the scriptural story. Artists begin to depict her in a demure, almost innocent demeanor as the contrast of her youthful beauty jars with the lifeless grotesque decapitated head of the Baptist. In the paintings of renaissance and baroque artists such as Titian, Sebastiano del Piombo, and Guido Reni, Salome is no longer "dancing" or involved in the action of the story. This young beauty can only be identified as Salome because she holds, or there rests beside her on a platter, the decapitated head. Herodias has disappeared from the scene as has Herod. The age of the High Renaissance and the Baroque corresponds to that time of religious turmoil identified as the Reformation and the Counter-Reformation. It was during this epoch, the age of Luther,

16. Gustave Moreau, *Salome Dancing Before Herod*, 1876. Oil on canvas, 56½ x 41 1/16 inches. The Armand Hammer Collection, Los Angeles.

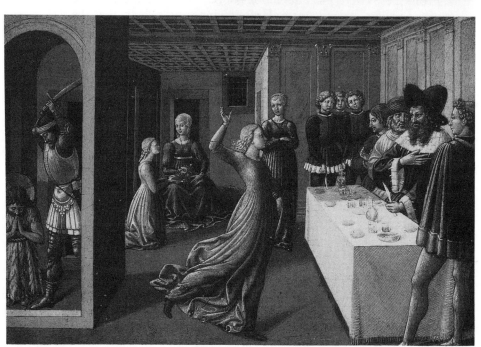

15. Benozzo Gozzoli, *The Dance of Salome*, 1461/2. Oil on wood, 9⅜ x 13½ inches. Samuel H. Kress Collection, National Gallery of Art, Washington. (1952.2.3 [1086]).

Calvin, and Zwingli, that liturgical dancing was banned from both the Roman Catholic and Reformed traditions. So it is appropriate that Salome no longer dances.

As dance becomes more and more secularized, and the ballet develops into an art form, the image of Salome wanes in religious arts. In this visual vanishing act, Salome follows all of her scriptural companions. As the art of the Baroque developed into the art of the rococo and neoclassical styles of the seventeenth and eighteenth centuries, the secularization of Christian art occurred. Religious themes in painting were replaced by genre themes, still life, portraiture, and mythological and historical themes.

However, in the nineteenth century, with the evolution of the romantic movement, there was a revival of interest in religious themes in art, literature, and music, although not always for spiritual purposes. In fact, by the end of the nineteenth century, the image of Salome erupted into one of the most popular themes of symbolist painting. With the development of the femme fatale, the classical figures of Helen of Troy, Cleopatra, and Medusa were rediscovered in conjunction with the apocryphal heroine, Judith, and the scriptural dancer, Salome.

However, this Salome was like no Salome seen before in either the visual arts or liturgical dance. She becomes *the* archetypal image of woman as the evil and destructive force whose sexuality, if not her very existence, threatened the lives of men. Salome is thus reborn and represented in the paintings of Gustave Moreau, Henri Regnault, and Henry Ossawa Tanner.

Moreau, it is probably fair to say, was obsessed with Salome. He created over one hundred images of her, all of which would influence the writers and dancers of the next twenty years. Moreau's masterpiece painting, *Salome Dancing Before Herod*, is the depiction of the erotic dancer (fig. 16). This is the first visualization of the "dance of the seven veils." The heightened tension of the moment of her dance is exacerbated by the theatrical setting of Herod's opulent palace. The aged king sits in a throne surrounded by images of the classical goddesses of fertility.

Salome, garbed in an exotic costume, has her hair piled high upon her head in the traditional manner of the courtesan. One of the infamous veils is dramatically draped over her hair and upper left arm. Her right arm is bent at the elbow and her right hand which is placed directly parallel to her facial profile holds a lotus blossom as one would normally hold a mirror. The extension of her left arm and hand forms a diagonal line that, if extended, would cut directly across

Herod's genitals. The diaphanous veiling of her strategically pleated skirt clearly reveals not only both her legs but her hips and pelvic area. Ironically, her breasts are hidden from view by the position of her right arm.

The dynamism of her bodily gestures contrasts sharply with the static forms of the seated Herod and the veiled harem girls stationed at both sides of the throne. Further, the theatrical lighting Moreau employed exacerbates the sensuality of the scene as Salome is the only figure depicted in the light; all else is seen through hazy shadows. Even the basic atmosphere of the painting reeks of an eroticism highlighted by the Oriental exoticism of the setting and costumes.

Within twenty years of Moreau's paintings, the Comedie Parisienne, Oscar Wilde, Loie Fuller, and Sergei Diaghilev created a series of independent theatrical and dance productions on the theme of Salome's dance. These new interpretations emphasized the erotic and evil dimensions of the dancer's character. A further twist to the image of Salome as the femme fatale, and by extension, of the fleshly evils of the dance, was Wilde's introduction of her obsession with the Baptist. No longer an obedient young girl who tries to please her mother, Wilde's Salome is a passionate woman tormented by her attraction for this otherwise repulsive ascetic.

The controversial opera, *Salome*, composed by Richard Strauss, was based on Wilde's play, especially the lascivious dance of the seven veils and the dramatic ending in which Salome is crushed to death by Herod's soldiers as she kisses the lips of the decapitated head of the Baptist. This is the femme fatale as the symbol of consummate evil and destruction.

Maude Allan's now classic *Dance of Salome* dates from this same period. As dramatic in her own writings as in her dance interpretation, Allan described in her autobiography "the sombre splendour of those pillared halls" where the adolescent Salome was only recently "reconciled to calling Herod Antipas . . . 'Father.'" Summoned to dance before the assembled court, Salome "weaves her most ingenious witcheries of dance."[10]

Allan choreographed her dance into two parts, "The Dance of Salome" and "The Vision of Salome." It is the division and integration of these two parts that not only mirror her artistic insight but also suggest the future treatment of heroines in the choreography of Martha Graham. For as Maude Allan's Salome finishes her dance, "she stands panting, aghast, her hands pressed to her young breasts . . . sees upon her naked flesh" the blood of the dead man.[11] In a flashback, the exhausted dancer understands the consequences of her action — the severed stern head of the man whose spiritual guidance she craved lies before her (fig. 17).

Maude Allan's Salome is not presented as the originator of her actions, nor is she responsible for them. Rather, this Salome is the victim of the fundamentally erotic power of the dance and of her mother's sinfulness. As Allan declared, "It is the atonement for her mother's awful sin!"[12]

Thus from the original scriptural passages to Maude Allan's highly interpretative choreography, we have seen Salome transformed from an anonymous damsel whose acrobatic dancing pleased a king and whose reward pleased her mother, to a victim of her own erotic desires and her mother's guilt. In this transformation, we pass into the twentieth-century's fascination with psychology, with the interior personality, impulses, motives, and resources that lie hidden within.

Martha Graham's interpretation of Salome is entitled *Herodiade*. Taking her cue from Stephen Mallarme's poem of the same title, Graham restructures the story of her dance from that of the young dancer to that of the dancer's mother who is about to set forth to an unspecified place. As Mallarme's character confesses, "I await a thing unknown."

In her most cryptic dance, Graham focuses on the psychology of waiting and preparing for "a thing unknown." The question for the audience becomes, however, not what is it that Herodias waits for, but what does she see in her mirror. The entire passage of this duet occurs within the confines of Herodias's bedroom as the queen's maidservant helps her mistress to prepare for "a thing unknown."

Recently, Graham reflected on her collaboration with Isamu Noguchi, who created the sets for over thirty of her dances, including *Herodiade* (fig. 18).

> One of the two works Isamu made for me that touched me the most deeply is the central piece for "Herodiade." I had wanted the image of a woman, waiting and wandering within the landscape of her own psyche, her own bleached bones placed before the black mirror of her fate. What Isamu brought to me was a haunting evocation. Deep within the bones was placed a small object, a bird, I sensed it was Herodiade's heart, vibrating and exposed to life. Whenever I danced "Herodiade," it was always to this animating force that moved across the stage. It was for me the core of Isamu's heart as well — that part of each artist which, as he becomes as one with the sacrificial animal, he exposes to the world.[13]

The major choreographic movement of *Herodiade* takes place before this mirror that Noguchi himself admitted was composed of the

17. Maud Allen, *Salome.* Photograph courtesy of the Dance Collection, Performing Arts Research Center, The New York Public Library at Lincoln Center. Astor, Lenox and Tilden Foundations.

18. Martha Graham, *Herodiade.* Photograph courtesy of Isamu Noguchi.

bones of the dancer's own skeleton.[14] This corresponded to the sculptural works Noguchi was then creating, single sculptures composed of bones and calligraphic forms.[15] He took the principle of his sculptural forms to the theater where they came to life by their relationship to the dancers. Thus, as she looked into this mirror of bones, Herodias (Graham) saw her own reflection, but more of a reflection than she would really like to see.[16] For in the program notes Graham herself cited Paul Valéry: "One day a woman looks into a mirror and sees her bones."

Thus this most cryptic of Graham's choreographies can be read in varied ways, including the recognition by each of the women in the audience that one day she will look into her mirror and "see her bones" as she "awaits a thing unknown." Alternatively, we see in Graham's presentation the natural extension of that late nineteenth-century reinterpretation of Salome as a femme fatale — her mother as aging femme fatale who realizes that she can no longer accomplish her aspired ends because her physicality is fading. Instead, she must send forth her youthful daughter to do the necessary deed on her behalf. Maude Allan's contention of Salome's destruction as "the atonement for her mother's awful sin" is more psychologically insightful than we might have initially thought.

Graham's *Herodiade*, however, also offers us other significant insights into the transformation of Salome and of the interpretation of scriptural women who danced. The bodily gestures Graham choreographed into this duet are concentrated on the postures of genuflection and circular rotations, liturgical prayer and the medieval labyrinth dance. These movements are paralleled in the bones of the mirror upon which Herodias's (and our) attention is fixed. In her creative genius and collaboration with Noguchi, Graham has retrieved not simply the psychological meaning of the story of Salome, and of the other scriptural women who danced, but also the fundamental relationship between religion and dance: the rhythm of movement and response of the body as symbolic of the seizing and discarding of life both sacramentally and spiritually.

Notes

1. Gerardus van der Leeuw, *Sacred and Profane Beauty: The Holy in Art* (New York: Harper and Row, 1963) 16.
2. Ibid., 21.
3. Mircea Eliade, *The Sacred and the Profane* (New York: Harper and Row, 1959 [1957]); and idem., *The Myth of the Eternal Return* (Princeton: Princeton University Press, Bollingen Series 46, 1974 [1954]).
4. For example, see Emile Mâle, *Religious Art in France from the Thirteenth to the Eighteenth Centuries* (Princeton: Princeton University Press, 1982 [1949]).
5. Margaret R. Miles, *Image as Insight: Visual Understanding in Western Christianity and Secular Culture* (Boston: Beacon Press, 1985) 25–26.
6. "Miriam" in *Encyclopedia Judaica* 12. See also Judges 11:34; 1 Samuel 18:6–7; and Psalm 68:25.
7. Curiously, the image of Miriam is a popular one with American artists in the early period of the nineteenth century. Perhaps the most famous of these images of Miriam is Washington Allston, *Miriam the Prophetess* (1821: William A. Farnsworth Library and Museum, Rockland, Maine).
8. See for further examples, Diane Apostolos-Cappadona, " 'The Lord has struck him down by the hand of a woman!' Images of Judith," in *Art as Religious Studies*, ed. Doug Adams and Diane Apostolos-Cappadona (New York: Crossroad, 1987) 81–97; and idem., "Images, Interpretations, and Traditions: A Study of the Magdalene," in *Interpreting Tradition: The Art of Theological Reflection*, ed. Jane Kopas (Chico: Scholars Press, 1984) 109–22; Jane Dillenberger, "Aspects of Eve" and "The Magdalen: Reflections on the Image of Woman as Saint and Sinner in Christian Art," in *Image and the Spirit in Sacred and Secular Art*, ed. Diane Apostolos-Cappadona (New York: Crossroad, forthcoming 1990); Margaret R. Miles, *Image as Insight*; idem., *Carnal Knowing: Female Nakedness and Religious Meaning in the Christian West* (Boston: Beacon Press, 1989); and John R. Phillips, *Eve: The History of an Idea* (New York: Harper and Row, 1984).
9. See Mark 6:22 and Matthew 14:6.
10. These quotations from Maude Allan's autobiography are as cited in *The Gospel According to Dance*, ed. Giora Manor (New York: St. Martin's Press, 1980) 60.
11. Ibid.
12. Ibid.
13. Martha Graham, "From Collaboration, a Strange Beauty Emerged," *The New York Times*, 8 January 1989, Section H:6.
14. Conversation with Isamu Noguchi, February 1987.
15. Diane Apostolos-Cappadona, "Stone as Centering: The Spiritual Sculptures of Isamu Noguchi," *Art International* 24.7/8 (1981) 79–98.
16. Interview of Isamu Noguchi by Tobi Tobias, January/February 1979, New York Performing Arts Library Oral History Program.

8

Ruth St. Denis: Sacred Dance Explorations in America

Neil Douglas-Klotz

Dance historians have long recognized the indirect influence of Ruth St. Denis (1876–1968) on the history of modern dance through her famous students Martha Graham, Doris Humphrey, Charles Weidman, and others. Yet these same historians have consistently ignored St. Denis's unpublished writings and diaries from the period after her public acclaim, essentially the last forty years of her life, claiming that she was engaged in a "deep private mysticism." It was, however, during this period that St. Denis explored unconventional and increasingly sensible approaches to sacred dance education, both solo and ensemble, liturgical and experiential.

A study of St. Denis's journey as an artist and her unpublished writings reveals contributions both to sacred dance education and choreographic technique that remain valuable today. Additionally, St. Denis's educational approaches and exercises can be integrated into a creative approach to sacred dance. These exercises include her method of sacred dance choreography and suggestions for deepening dancers' experience of the scriptural material used in liturgical dance.

The story of Ruth St. Denis's rapid rise to fame in the first decade of this century has been told with great verve by several biographers as well as in her own incomplete autobiographical account, *An Unfinished Life*.[1] From vaudeville, St. Denis found her way to a form of pageant-dance in which she embodied figures of divinity from many Eastern cultures as well as the West, including Radha, Kwan Yin, Ishtar, and Mary. The popularity of Eastern culture and the thirst for new forms of dance in the early 1900s brought Ruth St. Denis and her contemporary, Isadora Duncan, immense popular favor. Before these two, there was no modern dance in the West outside of classical ballet. Everything else was some form of vaudeville entertainment, and dancers themselves were considered little better than prostitutes.

With her partner, Ted Shawn, St. Denis founded Denishawn, one of the first schools of modern dance in America and the training ground for an explosion of twentieth-century dance innovation. When her style of dance fell out of favor due to the rise of more abstract forms,[2] St. Denis retreated to her first love, sacred dance. Even throughout the height of her popularity, St. Denis's writings lament that in order to reach large audiences her dances were performed in a theater rather than in a temple or church.

Her career was, in fact, launched by something akin to a mystical vision rather than a calculation of commercial success. St. Denis described in her autobiography the experience of seeing a poster of the Egyptian goddess Isis that caused her to change the entire direction of her career into one which would embody sacred characters and myths.

> Here was an external image which stirred into instant consciousness all that latent capacity for wonder, that still and meditative love of beauty which lay at the deepest center of my spirit.... I identified in a flash with the figure of Isis. She became the expression of all the somber mystery and beauty of Egypt, and I knew that my destiny as a dancer had sprung alive in that moment. I would become a rhythmic and impersonal instrument of spiritual revelation rather than a personal actress of comedy or tragedy. I had never before known such an inward shock of rapture.[3]

As she continued to dance and experiment into her eighties, even her critics admitted that St. Denis carried a certain presence and magnetism that overshadowed what they considered her technical deficiencies. St. Denis, however, considered her techniques to be a training in the inner landscape of the dancer's feeling, rather than physical steps. In this, she presaged other innovations in creative arts education like those of A. S. Neill, Rudolph Steiner, and Carl Orff, which deemphasized the egocentric preoccupation with product and focused on the development of the artist as the goal. While St. Denis's unpublished writings and diaries present a treasure of clear educational philosophy, the following excerpts represent some of her ideas on the potentials of sacred dance to transform education, religion, and culture.

Sacred Dance as Holistic and Creative Education

While education and psychology have recently begun to recognize the dualism inherent in educational systems that separate body, mind, emotions, and a sense of the sacred, St. Denis foresaw these problems in her work as a dance educator:

> For long have we lived constantly in two worlds, or so we supposed we did, in body and in spirit; but the new waves of release and vision that have come over the earth have shown us that in reality there are not two warring substances but only one, which is consciousness.... This being the case, our attitudes toward our bodies change, or should change. We should reverse our conceptions; we should realize in a vivid and revolutionary sense that we are not in our bodies but our bodies are in us....
>
> We are not made of one substance and our bodies of another. The whole scheme of things in reality is not two, but One. On this hangs not only the whole law and prophets of the liberating philosophy of the new age but the very starting point and method of approach of the Divine Dance.[4]

St. Denis did not separate the sacred from the scientific. She found, in the wonders of her own body, a field more worthy of study than the constant search for new technologies of comfort. In this her experiences echo those of the nineteenth-century American Transcendentalists like Walt Whitman and Henry David Thoreau, while at the same time provide a deeper understanding of Western scripture as the basis for movement.

> If we could look into an x-ray large enough to take in the entire human figure and could clearly see the transparent wonders of this organism, we would obtain a new vision of ourselves. Even by holding up our hands in the strong sunlight until the fingers are seen in a vivid glory, we can grasp a faint idea of the beauty of the body.... When we are really persuaded that the human being itself is more worthy of our intelligent thought than

any man-made object in the world, we shall unfold the infinite capacities of our inherent Sonship....

We own the most marvelous machines in the world, yet I think we value a typewriter more than our own torso. We value a radio more than our own voices, and a motor car above our legs.... We have the capacity to receive the messages of the stars and the songs of the night winds... but we are like blind people calling loudly for color to be created or deaf people saying that someone could create sound.[5]

As forms of modern dance became more popular, St. Denis decried the trend toward instant commercialization that deprived children of the joy of creative exploration and burdened them with the need to perform for the pleasure of the public. She saw this tendency to exploit art for money, rather than education and spiritual development, as one of the most harmful in Western society.

My mind was perpetually stirred to a deeper questioning of the causes of this futile and grotesque exhibition of childhood, this highest ambition of a baby of three to look like a Hollywood vamp.... We were exploiting not only immature ideas but immature children and demanding monetary results; we forced them to learn anything that could be sold and we capitalized on childish art in exactly the same way as we might capitalize on childish labor in the factory.[6]

St. Denis saw this problem as a lack of support for artists who could bring out the creativity of children. Dancers were immediately forced to affect a certain popular technique, and if not perform it, teach it in classes in order to make a living. She proposed as a solution the establishment of "community studios," which would serve not only as public-supported, noncommercial schools of the arts but as gathering places for young people.

These centers were to be scattered on the outskirts of all big cities and would take care of many more dancing teachers than were now in existence. Classes would be taught along technical, inspirational, and cultural lines. There would be noncommercial performances, where the children could dance not only for pleasure but as a sport. Then in the evening the same beautiful studios would be turned over to the adolescent boys and girls for ballroom dancing, which would be held under infinitely better conditions than the cabarets.[7]

Dance as Mystical Experience and Religious Transformer

Since she saw inner development as the key to sacred dance, Ruth St. Denis revisioned her work as an exploration into herself. In this regard, she saw her performance as being the extension of her inner spiritual attitude and reality, not something created apart from it.

> Dance is a living mantra. It is not a mere constant change of gesture and rhythm, calculated to intrigue the attention of the surface eye, but it is the very stuff and symbol of my inner creative life.[8]

In her extension of this philosophy into choreography, St. Denis did not permit herself to act out a mental composition of a sacred figure that she worshipped from afar. She felt that she actually embodied that person or sacred quality and that the training in this embodiment was the essence of her work. This led her to a unitive interpretation of the Scriptures, which found the biblical story being played out in her own flesh and blood.

> As long as we insist upon dwelling in the valley of self-condemnation and fear, looking at a far off Christ, so long shall we reap the bitter fruits of our duality.
>
> How can we achieve perfection in practice if we do not assume it first in consciousness.
>
> To manifest Him, we must first be Him!
>
> Until every least need and thrill of the full octave of human experience finds fulfillment in the Self of Christ, we shall not abandon the moral self with its world of illusions. What would we do if we were manifesting Christ?
>
> Would not the rhythm of our walk, the postures of our bodies, the gestures that we make in work and play be of a different order? And the thoughts that motivate our movements, would they not be from a higher source?[9]

In bringing dance into Christian liturgy, one of the projects of her later years, St. Denis proceeded in a gradual manner. A "rhythmic choir" could interpret hymns at the beginning or end of a service. Her real goal was the transformation of liturgy through all of the spiritual arts.

> The age of preaching is slowly passing, and the age of expression is upon us, the age of revelation by all manner of new means of beauty....
>
> I passionately want religion to have all the principalities and powers, not only the science of the intellect, the sacrifice of the heart, but I want

the Church in its highest unsectarian sense to embody Christ's gospel of Life and to have the irresistible lure of Beauty with which to heal and inspire the world.[10]

Dance as Instrument of Peacemaking

St. Denis maintained that if dance were freed from the bounds of commercialism, it would find its way back to its sacred roots, the ground beneath all arts in all cultures. The free exchange of genuine sacred dance, based on dancers' spiritual vision and experience, would change the world, she believed, and transform the insular boundaries in which we live.

> The dance of the future will no longer be concerned with meaningless dexterities of the body but will move in harmony with the compassionate and joyous rhythms of Love, and will obey in strength and balance the vital laws of Truth....
>
> As we rise higher in the understanding of ourselves, the national and racial dissonances will be forgotten in the universal rhythm of Truth and Love. We shall sense our unity with all peoples who are moving to that exalted rhythm....
>
> Toward this joyous epoch the Divine Dance will add its own deep integrative force. Not by political or material changes, but by unifying power of Harmony will the world of humanity and nature be at One.[11]

St. Denis felt that the unique capacity of people to work together selflessly, now rarely found except in war or disaster, could be released by providing a society in which people could tap their creative potential.

> I believe that instead of the tonic of war there lies in every living soul an ideal which can be as great a challenge to the ultimate reserves of his being. As we now work for war we can work instead for the building of this ideal, if once we find it. I believe that when Christ afforded us the ideal of the kingdom of heaven, He intended it to be this challenge.[12]

In her own performances, St. Denis saw her work as nothing less than dramatically changing the consciousness of her audience to appreciate a deeper level of the richness that surrounds them in nature:

> I have used my body
> As a gleaming sword
> To cut outlines of beauty
> On the mind of the world.[13]

Choreography as Meditation

In applying her philosophy to sacred dance instruction, St. Denis proceeded in a practical manner. She recognized that one must first be inspired by a sacred theme or prayer that seemed to live outside oneself, then gradually proceed to embody it.

St. Denis saw two parts of this work. In the first, a stage of prayer, the dancer "worshipped from afar" and progressed through the qualities of "supplication" (submission to an ideal), "affirmation" (the discovery of parts of that ideal in oneself), and "praise" (the less egocentric expression of joy, with neither punishment nor reward in view). The second stage would take dancers into the area of what St. Denis called "mantra" — the "less personal; response to scriptural readings." In this phase, the flexibility and training gained in the stage of prayer and submission to an ideal would enable the dancer to express from his or her whole being the essence of a scriptural passage without reliance on mental choreography.[14]

In collecting St. Denis's writing, I encountered themes for an extended sacred movement meditation in a section she called "practical application." As I applied it in my graduate classes, the meditation involves dancers choosing a sacred theme or phrase that inspires them, then lying comfortably on the floor as they go through the stages of the creative process that St. Denis outlined.

I have also found it helpful to ask dancers to focus on the pulsation of their heartbeat and blood, along with their breathing, so that the expression of the sacred theme would issue, as St. Denis proposed, from the "heart's offering upon the altar." The physical heart directly connects with that more emotional/spiritual sense of what "gets our blood moving" and causes us to pulse outward from a center of potent energy.

The process St. Denis outlined can prove useful both when dancers initially explore a theme for their personal development and when they wish to check a more finished dance for its authenticity with their own feeling. I have used variations of this meditation process with dancers in the creation of group sacred dances and circle dances, especially Dances of Universal Peace.[15] There is no doubt in my mind that St. Denis used a similar meditative process in her own work to balance the intellectual and feeling parts of her dance research.

Included here in conclusion is an edited version of St. Denis's scenario of creation, which can be modified for use as a meditation by guiding the stages in more experiential language. This is best done by the instructor engaging in the process at the same time and sensing the availability of students to take the next step. In this case, the "vision" and the "teacher" involve the sacred phrase/theme chosen and the difficult lessons that theme presents for the student personally.

Act I

1. The student enters the Classroom and is shown the Vision. She resolves to become one with the Vision.

2. She comes to the feet of the teacher and is given her first discipline.

3. She becomes discouraged and rebellious and starts to retreat.

4. She is now in a period of great bewilderment and mental suffering and only after great struggle, she brings herself to...

5. The point of surrender. Here she lays herself prone upon the floor in an abandonment of surrender. This is the heart's offering upon the Altar. The last scene of our drama of discipline is the mental receptivity of the student who now sits quietly in an attitude of expectancy and enters into the great Silence.

Act II

1. The response of the Body to the Divine Will begins with breath and the gestures growing out of this communion.

2. Rising... there are many ways of rising from the floor to standing position where the full articulation of the body is used. The simplest manner of rising will be done but as the student progresses more beautiful and controlled ways of rising will be attained.

3. Response... of the whole body to various forms of rhythmic discipline, which is symbolic of the discipline of the acolyte on all planes of her being.

4. Space... covering, taking all forms of walking, running, leaping and turning or the circumference activities.

5. Conscious control... of the entire body or perfect coordination and includes examples of complete dance phrases.

6. Spontaneity and improvisation... The instant response to thought and music, expressed in co-ordinated movement.

7. Mystical union... between the realization of Spiritual Being and sovereignty over the body.

Act III

Radiation... filled with the dynamic energy of Spirit, we ray forth our countless manifestations of Beauty. These expressions range from the solo dance to the greatest complexity to the large ensembles.

In the highest Radiation of our present manifestation, we shall utilize the full palette of colors composed of the finest contributions of the cultures of the world.[16]

Notes

1. Ruth St. Denis, *An Unfinished Life* (New York: Harper and Brothers, 1939). See also her *Lotus Light* (Boston: Houghton Mifflin, 1932), and *The Divine Dance*, ed. Neil Douglas-Klotz (San Francisco: PeaceWorks Press, 1989).

The major biographical accounts of Ruth St. Denis are Suzanne Shelton, *Divine Dancer: A Biography of Ruth St. Denis* (Garden Grove: Doubleday, 1981); Elizabeth Kendall, *Where She Danced: The Birth of American Art-Dance* (Berkeley: University of California Press, 1979); and Walter Terry, *The 'More Living Life' of Ruth St. Denis* (New York: Dodd, Mead, and Company, 1969).

2. For example, the choreography of Mary Wigman.

3. Ruth St. Denis, *An Unfinished Life* (New York: Harper & Brothers, 1939) 52.

4. St. Denis, *The Divine Dance*, 5.

5. Ibid., 35.

6. St. Denis, *Unfinished Life*, 251.

7. Ibid., 253.

8. Ruth St. Denis, Unpublished diaries, entry dated 28 June 1934, University of California at Los Angeles Collection.

9. St. Denis, *The Divine Dance*, 36.

10. Ibid., 28–29.

11. Ibid., 38.

12. St. Denis, *Unfinished Life*, 197.

13. Ruth St. Denis, *Lotus Light* (Boston: Houghton Mifflin, 1932) 5.

14. St. Denis, *Divine Dance*, 32.

15. The Dances of Universal Peace were begun by one of St. Denis's students, Samuel L. Lewis.

16. St. Denis, *Divine Dance*, 16.

9

Martha Graham and the Quest for the Feminine in Eve, Lilith, and Judith

Diane Apostolos-Cappadona

The choreography of Martha Graham has influenced the development of twentieth-century dance, including liturgical dance. One of the leading "modernist" pioneers in the world of dance, Graham's work has always been characterized by her interest in the emotive and spiritual qualities of dance. Basing her style of interpretation on the classical Greek tenet that dance was the only art form capable of expressing the inexpressible, she stripped away the unnecessary obstructions from both the stage and the dancer's body. The absolute simplicity of her search for gesture, movement, emotion, and spirituality has led to the development of her singular and influential choreography.

Graham reinterpreted classical mythological and scriptural stories from the perspective of the hero to the heroine. In that process, she helped modern dancers and modern liturgical dancers to identify with the authenticity of the spiritual quest for the feminine. In her choreographies for *Embattled Garden* (1958) and *Judith* (1955/1962/1970), Graham's dances focus on three female figures from the Judeo-Christian tradition, Eve, Lilith, and Judith. Ironically, both dances were accompanied by sets designed by Isamu Noguchi. His carefully conceived sets exemplify the height of deceptive simplicity that successfully augmented Graham's choreographic and psychological intentions.

Born at the end of the nineteenth century, Martha Graham matured as a dancer-choreographer during the artistic revolution known as "modernism." This tendency of all the arts in the 1920s and 1930s to pare away the surface decorations and disguises led to a shift toward the "essence" of things. In this, modernism became the first formal abstract movement; for *ab-stract* means to take the essence from. Influential on the development of modernism was Vassily Kandinsky's now classic manifesto of modern art, *Concerning the Spiritual in Art and Painting in Particular.* First published in English in Alfred Stieglitz's journal, *Cameraworks,* Kandinsky expanded James Abbott McNeill Whistler's earlier attempts to visualize the analogy between music and painting. Taking this relationship to its logical conclusion, Kandinsky argued that the true artist was the one who painted from his/her emotional depths outward, as one who was able to do with color what Mozart did with chords. Visual artists, among them Georgia O'Keeffe, began to paint to music, to paint what the music made them feel. With the further introduction of modern art through exhibitions at Stieglitz's gallery, "291," and the Armory Show of 1913, modernism came to signify the search for the detail, not the panorama.

A further influence on both the development of modernism and Graham was the late nineteenth and early twentieth-century fascination with Orientalism. This interest varied from complete intellectual and spiritual absorption into the philosophy of the Orient to a superficial costuming of works of art with Oriental paraphernalia. Whereas Graham's teacher and inspiration, Ruth St. Denis, not only absorbed but was absorbed by the Orient, Graham on the other hand proceeded to submerge herself (but not lose her individuality) in Orientalism. Thus, she was able to fuse her Oriental nature with her later interests in Greek mythology and Jungian psychology.

Like her contemporary, Georgia O'Keeffe, Martha Graham's work and persona became a reflection and a reflector of the modernist ethos. As O'Keeffe pared down the composition and formal elements of her paintings to just the necessary essentials, so too, Graham eliminated the unnecessary, i.e., dramatic sets, elaborate costumes, and detailed movement, from her choreography. A helpful comparison can be made between O'Keeffe's early paintings, that is, those from the 1920s and 1930s, and Graham's choreography. Each in her own way sought to express the inexpressible through the simplicity of the essential. In their initial (and contemporary) interpretations of the frontier landscape and American sources, these two female modernists sought for an integrity of form, beauty with austerity, and truth to materials.

Both O'Keeffe and Graham were enamored of the fervent simplicity of both Shaker and American Indian art and ritual. Just as O'Keeffe sought to visualize through her paintings the uncluttered view of the distant horizon, thus emphasizing the unique characteristic of America, the vastness of the landscape, Graham endeavored with the help of Isamu Noguchi to project this same sense of vast space in *Frontier*. As O'Keeffe depicted the sensuality and abstraction of human gestures through *Black Abstraction* (fig. 19), so Graham choreographed the singularity of the essence of grief-ridden gesticulation in *Lamentation* (fig. 20). For both of these women, emotion and its expression were fundamental to the human condition. Thus, what O'Keeffe presented through the painted image, Graham signified through the human body.

It is the recognition of this emotive bodiliness that distinguishes Martha Graham from other choreographers. Raised in a puritanical Presbyterian household, Graham was taught from an early age that "the body never lies." If we translate "the body" into "movement," then we recognize a classic Christian doctrine that God is pure act, that his mobility, that is, his freedom to move, characterizes him as the divine. There is in Graham's interpretation of the dance, then, both the emphasis on contraction and release that signify restriction and freedom of movement. With this foundation, then, Martha Graham becomes empowered to bring into being an intense physical expression of her private world and to make this private world not merely public but classic and universal.

Because Graham perceives the world through feminine categories and has an interest in Jungian understandings of "the Great Mother," she comes to reinterpret the classical Greek myths, biblical stories, and American legends through the eyes of the female protagonist. Thus, her story becomes their stories, her eyes their eyes, her body their bodies, her movement their movement, her choreography their voices. For Graham, the female, given her cyclical physicality and native intuition, is more attuned to nature; she is therefore the more

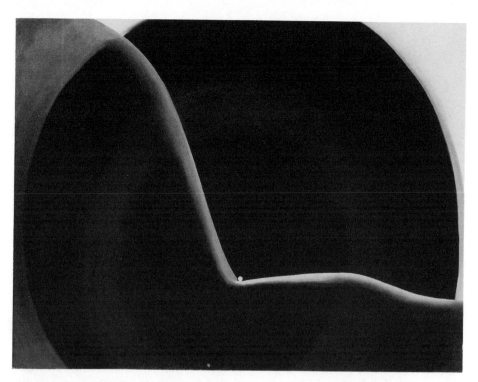

19. Georgia O'Keeffe, *Black Abstraction*, 1927. Oil on canvas, 30 x 40¼ inches. The Metropolitan Museum of Art, The Alfred Stieglitz Collection, 1949. (68.278.2).

20. Martha Graham, *Lamentation*. Photograph © Barbara Morgan.

receptive and expressive vehicle of human experience. In her *Notebooks*, Graham wrote,

> Thus the woman is the original seeress, the lady of the wisdom-bringing waters of the depths, of the murmuring springs and fountains, for the "original utterance of seerdom in the language of water." But the woman also understands the rustling of the trees & all the signs of nature, with whose life she is so closely bound up.[1]

In her bodiliness, then, the female is capable of extending the spirituality of nature and the fundamental experience of being human. The dramatization of these is necessary to evoke transformation in the spiritual consciousness of others as the past, present, and future commingle into an inescapable unity of movement and emotion. For Graham the theater is a form of ritual space, a hypothetical world in which we, the spectators, simultaneously observe and participate by proxy through the dancers.

In *Embattled Garden*, Graham retrieves our first home, the Garden of Eden, and returns us to the moment when historicity began. The basic elements of the well-known story of the temptation and fall of Adam and Eve are expanded from three (Adam, Eve, and the Serpent) to include a fourth player, Lilith. This extension of the necessary characters is a genial move on Graham's part, for it not only adds drama to the action between Adam and Eve, but also engages the audience who must come to recognize (perhaps for the first time) the dual nature, not merely the duality, of male and female. For as man can be both innocent and devious as signified by Adam and the Serpent, so woman can be both naive and seductive. The focus of *Embattled Garden* is the expression of the fundamental human emotion of love, but love comes in many different guises such as adoration, infatuation, passion, obsession, and mutuality. In her program notes for this dance, Graham writes

> Love, it has been said, does not obey the rules of love but yields to some more ancient ruder law. The Garden of Love seems always to be threatened by the Stranger's knowledge of the world outside and by the old knowledge of those like Lilith (according to legend, Adam's wife before Eve) who lived there first.

The Book of Genesis relates two accounts of the creation of the first human beings. Genesis 1:27 reads,

> So God created man in his own image, in the image of God created he him; *male and female* created he them.

Whereas Genesis 2:22 states that

> And the rib, which the LORD God had taken from man, made he *a woman*, and brought her to the man.

According to Jewish tradition, the first wife of Adam (the one whose creation is described in Genesis 1:27) has been identified as Lilith.[2] As the created equal of Adam, Lilith comes to a recognition of the world and her own validity more quickly than Eve will in the later narrative. In fact, given her own sense of individual identity, Lilith rebels against both Adam and God, and is therefore expelled from the Garden and from Adam. She becomes then like the screech owl, a demon creature who visits lonely men and pregnant women in the middle of the night. Graham noted that

> Adam, before Eve, already possessed a demon wife, Lilith, with whom he *quarreled for mastership.* But Lilith raised herself into the air thru the magic of the name of God & hid herself in the sea. Adam forced her back with the help of 3 angels. Lilith became a nightmare, a Lamia, who threatened those with child, & who kidnapped the new-born child.[3]

Both the legendary accounts and Graham's choreography suggest that the root of Lilith's disobedience is her sexuality; perhaps it can be inferred she not only initiates sexual activity with Adam, perhaps she also actually enjoyed it. As *Embattled Garden* opens, Graham places Lilith underneath the Tree of Knowledge, upon which the Serpent will slither up and down throughout the dance. In this placement and bodily position that Lilith assumes in *Embattled Garden*, Graham follows an established iconographic tradition for Adam's first wife, to languish provocatively on her side like a classical image of the goddess Venus (fig. 21).[4] Further, Graham's Lilith holds as her attribute a fan, which is

> the mythical symbol of betrayal and deceit. When held at the breast it creates the triangular design of the arms so necessary to the Goddess; when held on the head it becomes a crown; when used by Lilith reclining at the base of the tree it underscores her cool, sophisticated detachment.[5]

In its triangular form, the fan also symbolizes the female genital area which is, as a result of the Fall, hidden and forbidden.

Significantly in Graham's interpretation, it is Lilith who brings Eve to a recognition of her female sexuality and initiates her into womanhood. This relationship between Lilith and Eve does not follow the line of the scriptural or legendary accounts, but rather Graham's own understanding of the Jungian symbolism of the Great Mother in which the older woman (most regularly a hag), initiates the man into his journey toward death. In *Embattled Garden*, however, the older — read here more knowledgeable — woman introduces the younger — read here more naive — woman into the journey toward womanhood through the experience of her sexual nature (fig. 22).

This initiation is again a series of re-presentations of classic iconography, thus, emphasizing Graham's genial and subliminal manipulation of the human psyche. For as the dance begins, the Serpent slides down the Tree of Knowledge and moves toward the garden of innocence. The placement of these two areas on the left and right sides of the stage area highlight Graham's recognition of the fundamental duality (the *coincidentia oppositorum*) of human existence. Given the classical Western tradition that signifies that the left is evil and the right is good, the deployment of the Serpent and Lilith with the Tree of Knowledge at audience left and of Adam and Eve in the garden of innocence at audience right, subliminally reaffirms the audience's recognition of the characters' basic natures. As the Serpent approaches the garden, he comes close enough to kiss Eve who is quickly retrieved by Adam. In a quick encounter, the Serpent overcomes Adam who collapses into the shape of a young child. Lilith then enters the garden, first passing by Eve and then waking Adam with a kiss. In the movements that ensue, Lilith seduces Adam, and retreats with the Serpent to watch what will transpire between the now sexually initiated Adam and the sexually awakened Eve.

At this point, Graham's study of the power of visual imagery takes over as the movement of the dancers' bodies is directed by Eve's hair. In classical mythology and Christian iconography, hair has a powerful symbolic history.[6] Simply, hair signifies energy and power (consider merely the importance of hair to the biblical hero, Samson). In classical Western culture, the different stages of a woman's life were denoted by the manner in which she dressed her hair; young unmarried women wore their hair loose and flowing, chaste married women covered their hair with a veil or mantle, and courtesans piled their hair high upon their heads and adorned with jewels and flowers.

As the sexually awakened Eve (recently kissed by the Serpent) approaches Adam, her hair is loose and flowing. After she flails him with her tresses, he caresses her hair and flagellates himself with it. Then in an action that both signifies his power and control, Adam grasps Eve's hair tightly, turning her head in a circular movement, and then throws her down to the ground. Eve seeks solace in the

21. "Lilith" from the base for a statuette, carved with high relief of Eve and Serpent on either side of Tree of Life. 15th century, French miniature. Boxwood, H. 3½, L. 4 13/16, W. 3 9/16 inches. ¾ view from left. The Metropolitan Museum of Art, The Cloisters Collection, 1955. (55.116.2).

22. "Eve" from the base for a statuette, carved with high relief of Eve and Serpent on either side of Tree of Life. 15th century, French miniature. Boxwood, H. 3½, L. 4 13/16, W. 3 9/16 inches. ¾ view from right. The Metropolitan Museum of Art, The Cloisters Collection, 1955. (55.116.2).

23. Martha Graham, *Embattled Garden*. Photograph courtesy of Isamu Noguchi.

arms of the Serpent who carries her to Lilith. Under the Tree of Knowledge, then, Lilith binds Eve's hair as these three figures, Eve, Lilith, and the Serpent, are united in a movement profile (fig. 23). Thus, Eve is fully initiated into womanhood.

As part of the action that ensues, Adam and Eve perform a dance of sexual possession. Later when Eve approaches Lilith in a posture of respect, Adam retrieves and pulls her across stage by her bound hair. He then dramatically throws her into the garden, establishes his authority over the place and Eve. A quadrille follows, performed by the four characters, and ends with Lilith's seduction of Adam. After she has spent Adam's sexuality, Lilith allows Eve to retrieve him in the climactic movements of *Embattled Garden*.

Through a carefully orchestrated series of emotive bodily contractions, Eve lowers herself to the floor with her legs splayed out to either side as she accepts Adam's body on her lap, cradling and rocking him as she would a child, their posture reminiscent of the images of the Pietà (fig. 24).[7] If we remember the Jungian motif of the man's initiation toward death by the older woman, we recognize that these climactic moments mimic both the life and death cycle. Eve's bodily contractions symbolize both sexual intercourse and the birth process, while Lilith's ravishment of Adam's sexual energy signifies his journey to death. The simple fact that these two actions are activated by two different women exacerbates the classical interpretation of woman as virgin and whore; the positive and negative aspects of the *vagina dentata* are presented by Graham's masterful choreography (fig. 25).

The closing movement of *Embattled Garden* has Adam carrying Eve back to paradise as Lilith and the Serpent return to their original positions beneath the Tree of Knowledge. As the curtain closes, Adam seats himself behind Eve in the garden of their innocence and gently strokes her hair. The return to the opening motif is significant; nothing is as it seems, for although the group on the side of evil is perhaps unchanged, the group on the side of good are irrevocably transformed.

The return to this particular placement thus signifies the fundamental human hunger for the return to the garden, of the nostalgia for our lost innocence, as revealed by Adam's gesture of gently stroking Eve's hair. This gesture tells all: the loss of sexual innocence, the sexual initiation, the power of female sexuality, the domination of the female, and the journey of the male toward death, the now united fate of man and woman. Graham described Eve as "the quester" who "otherwise would not have heard the voice of the serpent." The expulsion from the Garden of Eden was, for Graham, the "1st step towards

24. Andrea del Solario, *Lamentation*, c. 1505/7. Oil on wood, 66⅜ x 59⅞ inches. Samuel H. Kress Collection, National Gallery of Art, Washington. (1961.9.40 [1402]).

25. Martha Graham, *Embattled Garden*. Photograph courtesy of Isamu Noguchi.

maturity." As all the descendants of Eve have learned, knowledge, especially knowledge of our own bodies, is a dangerous thing.

If Graham characterized Eve as "the one who questions," then Judith was "the one who participates."[8] The apocryphal story of the Jewish heroine who saved her city, has inspired writers and artists throughout the ages.[9] In the late nineteenth and early twentieth centuries with the artistic development of the femme fatale, Judith was resurrected from the annals of Western art history (fig. 26). This new Judith, however, became a visualization of castration anxiety and the destructive character of female heroism. This was the Judith who would have been most familiar to Martha Graham.

Nevertheless, Graham was able to retrieve the original apocryphal story of the beautiful and righteous widow, who by the strength of her character and her faith in God, was able to conquer God's enemy (fig. 27). Empowered as much by wisdom as feminine intuition, Judith reversed the traditional story of the damsel in distress into the damsel who resolves the distress. Graham, however, did not concentrate her presentation of Judith upon either female heroism or faith in God. Rather she delved into her own life experience, for the dancer-choreographer was sixty-one when she first choreographed *Judith* and seventy-six when she revised her presentation in 1970.

Graham's Judith is not the young pious widow of the apocryphal text. This Judith was an aged woman who would review her life as a widow and relive her mission as the heroine of her people. Graham's interpretation was premised upon the complex theme of introspection — the principle of the flashback predicated upon individual and collective memory. To augment the psychological appeal of *Judith*, Graham introduced the "flashback-within-the-flashback"; for as the aged Judith remembered the story of the young Judith, so the widow Judith remembered Judith the young bride. Once again in a Graham work would past, present, and future be commingled and indistinguishable.

In her *Notebooks*, Graham described the intention of her flashback technique without particular reference to any single work.

The drama of love is played in the mind. It is lyricism of one moment, a flash of time, that is never over, that is anonymous & universal & hence mystical. The mind appears before itself, filled with the image of woman, so resplendent in her nudity that she is all degrees of light: angelic & demonic, carnal & spiritual, unique & universal.[10]

So she transformed Judith from the Jewess to Everywoman — to

26. Gustav
Klimt, *Judith
II/Salome*, 1909.
Oil on canvas,
176 x 46 cm.
Ca'Pesaro Galleria
Internazionale
D'Arte Moderna

27. Francesco del Cairo, *Judith with the Head of Holofernes*,
c. 1630–5. Oil on canvas, 46⅞ x 37⅛ inches. State
No. 798. The John and Mable Ringling Museum of Art,
Sarasota, Florida.

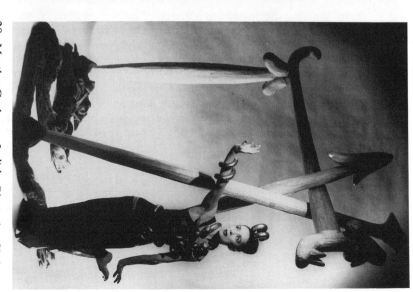

28. Martha Graham, *Judith*. Photo by Chris
Alexander. Photograph courtesy of Isamu
Noguchi.

that Everywoman within each of us who remembers at the moment of confrontation and trial that one singular moment of freedom and ecstasy. As she stands at the edge of the dreaded general Holofernes's tent, Judith intuits what Graham has always known, that "[t]he experience of love" has "finally dominated the experience of solitude."[11] So as the about-to-be heroine recalls with tenderness the feeling the virginal bride had as she entered her new husband's tent on their wedding night, the widowed and ostensibly lonely Judith anticipates for one brief moment, masked by the joy of that now departed love, her encounter with the man inside this tent. As she stands on the brink of a disastrous surrender, Judith miraculously retrieves her sense of time and place, and thus enters Holofernes's tent not to make love but, to paraphrase the Scripture, to astonish the world.

As in *Embattled Garden*, a significant element of the successful reinterpretation of a classic story into a universal experience in *Judith* was Graham's collaboration with Isamu Noguchi. Also influenced by the evolution of the modernist ethos, Noguchi's fundamental Japanese orientation was empathetic to Noh theater, where the almost bare stage is implemented with the most minimal of props that become elevated to symbolic values. Just as his set for *Embattled Garden* bisected the stage with the two spaces for the Tree of Knowledge and the Garden of Innocence, Noguchi divided *Judith* into a woman's space and a man's place. In the former, the pious widow removes her mourning garments and adorns herself with jewels and perfumes. In the latter, the necessary murder will occur. Recently, Graham herself reflected on the empowering energy of Noguchi's set for *Judith* (fig. 28).

> In "Judith," the episode to represent "her putting aside of her garments of sadness and putting on her garments of gladness" suggested to me a jewel to be worn and revealed on stage. But I was unprepared for the barbaric carved-jewel necklace and headpiece that Isamu brought to me with which to dress myself within the dance. They intensified and gave me a deeper image of myself as Judith, a feeling they possessed in some way the spirit of this Jewish heroine. The gesture of triumph I made toward the tent of Holofernes, which Isamu created as a rampant animal, came to me with an added power in the coiled bracelet he had devised for my arm.[12]

Again, following a classical tradition in the iconography of Judith, Noguchi and Graham visually empowered her right arm with the symbolism of the bracelet.[13] This is the arm with which Judith would slay Holofernes, with which a woman would strike down a man! The symbol of that action, of the inherent and necessary strength of a woman, was not the feared vagina dentata, but Judith's right arm, a sign of justice and valor highlighted by the bracelet.

In the shapes of both the jewelry Noguchi designed for Judith, and the fixtures of the woman's space and the man's place, the sculptor intertwined the basic elements of the male and female bodies. Thus, he physically stripped Judith and Holofernes down to their bones, to the universal femaleness and maleness, just as Graham would strip them down to the essential drives of their emotions. Noguchi believed that one keystone to their successful collaboration was his ability to create "objects not props." These objects, such as Judith's jewelry, became "natural extensions of Martha's body." Thus, the "fluidity of movement" within the dance was heightened not disturbed by his sets.[14] The fundamental emotive bodiliness that has been Graham's trademark was enhanced by Noguchi's art. His interest in transformations of spatial relationships was complimented by her interest in transformations of human consciousness. Their connecting link was the human body, in particular, the female body. As Graham herself indicated, her reinterpretation of these classic stories around the female figure, of the universalizing of the otherwise particular, is premised upon her conviction of the collectivity and authenticity of human experience.

> I do not want her to be remote
> I do not want her to be a goddess, but a woman[15]

The common denominator of human experience is the human body. The basic instrument of the dancer is her body. The dancer's goal is to communicate meaning and value for "Gesture is the first (language)" and "movement is the seed of gesture."[16] In her retrieval of the female protagonist, in the simplification of movement, and in the search for emotive bodiliness, Martha Graham has redefined the meaning of gesture through the spirituality of the feminine.

Notes

1. Martha Graham, *The Notebooks of Martha Graham* (New York: Harcourt, Brace, Jovanovich, 1973) 10.

2. For information on Lilith and her place in Jewish literature and spirituality, see Gershom Scholem, "Lilith," *Encyclopedia Judaica*, 11:245–49. For a helpful discussion of the iconography of Lilith in Western Christian art, see Jeffrey M. Hoffeld, "Adam's Two Wives," *The Metropolitan Museum of Art Bulletin* 26.10 (1968) 430–40. For an alternative, but not exclusive, study of Lilith's role in *Embattled Garden*, see Genevieve Oswald, "A Vision of Paradise: Myth and Symbol in the 'Embattled Garden,'" unpublished paper presented to the Jerusalem Conference on the Bible in Dance, Session II, 13 July 1979.

3. Graham, *Notebooks*, 193.

4. Although he does not say this directly, Hoffeld suggests this iconography, and classical source for this posture, in his study of Lilith. My own intuition is that Lilith does in fact through literary and visual sources become the expression of the fertility goddess in the Hebraic tradition, whereas Eve becomes the fallen woman.

5. Oswald, "A Vision of Paradise," ms. pp. 11–12.

6. For an introduction to the importance of the symbolism of hair, especially of a woman's hair, see Diane Apostolos-Cappadona, "Images, Interpretations, and Tradition: A Study of the Magdalene," in *Interpreting the Tradition*, ed. Jane Kopas (Chico: Scholars Press, 1984).

7. The movements of Adam and Eve in this highly dramatic moment can also be seen as a conflation of the classic imagery of the crucifixion, deposition, and lamentation of Jesus of Nazareth. For example,

> And for a chosen few, the climax came at one breathless moment when Adam, standing with tautly outstretched arms as though hanging on a cross, collapsed onto Eve's wide-spread knees. The vision of a Pietà was distinctly drawn, as if the Old and New Testaments suddenly coalesced into one blinding revelation that associated Adam's fall from grace with Christ's descent from the Cross, both figures being heroic embodiments of their Father's will: the first to people on earth in His name; the second, to bring His word unto the erring race of man.

Ernestine Stodelle, *Deep Song: The Dance Story of Martha Graham* (New York: Schirmer Books, 1984) 203.

8. Graham, *Notebooks*, 330.

9. For an analysis of the iconography of Judith through the history of Western Christianity, see Diane Apostolos-Cappadona, "'The Lord has struck him down by the hand of a woman!' . . . Images of Judith," in *Art as Religious Studies*, ed. Doug Adams and Diane Apostolos-Cappadona (New York: Crossroad Publishing, 1987).

10. Graham, *Notebooks*, 221.

11. Ibid., 221.

12. Martha Graham, "From Collaboration, a Strange Beauty Emerged," *The New York Times*, Arts and Leisure Section, 8 January 1989, 6.

13. See for example the images of Judith by Donatello and Artemesia Gentileschi for the visual evidence of the elaborate bracelet on her right arm.

14. Interview of Isamu Noguchi by Tobi Tobias, January/February 1979. Oral History Archives, Dance Collection, The New York Public Library.

15. Graham, *Notebooks*, 292.

16. Ibid., 325.

10

Biblical Women and Feminist Exegesis: Woman Dancing Men's Ideas or Women Dancing Women

Martha Ann Kirk

Throughout the nineteenth and early twentieth centuries, more women than men were churchgoers and professional dancers. Women churchgoers accepted the Bible as taught by male leaders, while women dancers performed the dances taught by male choreographers. Both the interpretations of the Bible, and the forms and subject matter of the dances perpetuated male dominance over females.

Feminist exegesis of the Bible explores how biblical studies can be part of the feminist movement, can provide a critique of male dominance over females. I consider which biblical women have been selected most often for contemporary professional dances, and reflect on which of these dances received more attention from audiences and critics. My study of the strength and vulnerability of dancer Judith Jamison and choreographer Martha Graham, both of whom have portrayed biblical women, is based on a feminist perspective. In the future, more in-depth studies of the forms of individual dances and their relationship to gender roles will be needed.[1]

Patriarchal culture has taught men that they are dominant, powerful, virile, and good. As men stand next to women, they begin to question these things because men find themselves attracted to women. This attraction often makes men afraid. Sometimes this fear takes the form of hatred, but more often the fear becomes anxiety. In literature and the arts, when men allow their deepest feeling to surface, they often reduce women to stereotypes that can be controlled. Most of the visual art and literature of the Western world has been created by men and for men with women frequently the objects depicted or described. Edwin Mullins writes about

> the temptresses and the whores, the witches and hags, the sanitized virgins and penitent sinners — images that are chimeras of men's buried terrors of what women might do if allowed to be themselves unchecked.[2]

The idea that beautiful women can take away men's power and are even deadly comes through in myths and stories such as those of Medusa, Artemis, Clytemnestra, the Sphinx, the Amazons, the Sirens, the Fates, and witches. Women as the creators of literature, arts, and dance, sometimes recreate the femme fatale and other patriarchal stereotypes, but they also portray multidimensional women.

Christian literature, preaching, and religious education have reduced women and their activities to a few types and then used biblical women as illustrations of these types. Women were either ideals or temptresses, virgins or whores — Mary on the pedestal or Eve the source of all evil. Women who had power were bad women: Potiphar's wife, Delilah, Bathsheba, Jezebel, Athalia, and Salome. Even the good women were tainted by using deceit or seduction — Jael, Esther, Ruth, and Judith — or they had backgrounds of promiscuity — the Samaritan woman at the well, the legendary development of Mary Magdalene. Women were victims — the daughter of Jephthah, Hagar, the concubine of the Levite of Judges 19, and Tamar — and they endured suffering because of the men they loved — Mary at the cross. Women were passive: their importance was in carrying the male seed — the wives of the patriarchs — or they needed to be helped or rescued by males — the women cured by Jesus. Women prophetesses were mentioned as striking exceptions: Miriam, Deborah, and Huldah. They are probably representative of large numbers of women whose words and activities have been suppressed by patriarchal historians.

Historical Examples

Citing some of the biblical dance works before the last hundred years
gives modern biblical dance a context. In Spain after the Moors were
expelled, there was an Annunciation *pas de deux* of Mary and the
Angel. Mary's being lifted up was explained as symbolic of women's
elevated position in society at that time. The Passion Plays and Mystery Plays that developed during the medieval era included dances
such as Salome entertaining Herod or Mary Magdalene dancing with
demons. The *Minuet of the Queen of Sheba* was in a choreographic
procession for the festival of Corpus Christi in Provenance in 1462.

From the sixteenth to the eighteenth centuries, the Jesuits who
founded schools throughout Europe and Latin America extensively
used biblical dramas with ballet to instruct and inspire their students. William A. Carroll compiled a list of Jesuit dramas in the
German-speaking provinces that dealt with women's stories. Athalia
was portrayed twelve times, Esther twenty-two, the daughter of Jephthah six, Jezebel nine, Judith thirteen, Rebecca two, and Susanna
five.[3]

Sometimes the allegory of the ballets involved a current event.
When the Swedish armies were invading the Germanic area in 1642,
the play *Judith* was performed. The evil biblical leader, Holofernes,
was associated with the Swedish military leader. Many artistic and
social factors influenced the selection of dramatic characters. However, certain ideas flowing from the stereotypes of women may also
have had an influence on the selection of these ballets: strong women
are evil (twenty-one selections of Athalia and Jezebel); women are
seductive or deceitful, but that power can be used for good (thirty-
seven selections of Esther, Judith, and Rebecca); wives faithful to
their husbands are protected by God (five selections of Susanna);
and women are sacrificial victims (six selections of the daughter of
Jephthah).

Jesuit students performed the biblical drama *Jephthah's Daughter*
in Belgium in 1613, and another group in Ingolstadt, Germany, in
1637. In the eleventh chapter of the book of Judges, Jephthah, a
proud warrior, vowed that he would slay as a sacrifice the first thing
he saw when he returned from battle if God would grant him victory.
When the man returned, his unnamed daughter came out dancing
for joy to celebrate his triumph. While Isaac the son is not actually
sacrificed by his father Abraham, the daughter is sacrificed by her
father. The version of this story done in dance at the Jesuit school
of Hildesheim in 1755 dramatically had the meeting of daughter and

father by torchlight. Then she did an allegorical dance with death personified.

The version of *Jepthitas* by Jacob Balde (1604–1668) considered the sacrificed daughter as an image of the sacrificed Christ. Balde also wove in the story of Iphigenia, the Greek girl sacrificed by her father Agamemnon, as another level of symbolism. While biblical men such as Adam, Melchizedek, Moses, and David have been frequently used as figures of Christ, very rarely have women been used as Christ figures. In the monastery of St. Catherine on Mount Sinai, while Isaac is painted on one side of the altar where the sacrifice of Christ will be commemorated in the Eucharist, on the other side is an image of the daughter of Jephthah.[4]

After the extensive use of biblical material for ballets by the Jesuits, this source of content was hardly ever used until the late nineteenth century when pioneers of modern dance turned to Scripture. The stages of modern dance have provided women an opportunity to proclaim biblical women's stories as interpreted by women before pulpits of Christian churches, to preach these stories as interpreted by women. Though Antionette Brown was ordained by the Congregational Church in 1851, and Elizabeth Cady Stanton and others developed the *Women's Bible* in 1898, women's interpretation of Scripture has had little influence in Christianity until the 1970s.[5]

The Sensation of Salome

Salome seems to be the most frequently danced female biblical character on the professional stage from 1895 when Loie Fuller danced as Salome with shimmering veils until the present day. Giora Manor has written about seven times as much in "The Scandals of Salome" as he has in "Biblical Women" where he treats eight other female characters.[6] This might reflect Manor's bias in selection of material, but it appears to represent the proportion of attention given Salome in relation to other biblical women in twentieth-century dance. Richard Bizot listed thirty-nine choreographies based on Salome between 1895 and 1977.[7]

Herod married Herodias, the wife of his brother Philip, and John the Baptist criticized this adulterous union. At a banquet, Herodias's daughter danced and Herod was so charmed by her that he offered her anything she wanted. Her mother told her to ask for the head of John the Baptist on a platter. The text does not indicate if the dancer is an innocent young child incestuously coveted by a stepfather and psychologically manipulated by an evil mother, or if Salome is mature and malicious. Scripture does not even give the dancing daughter a name and only devotes ten lines to her in telling of John the Baptist in the sixth chapter of Mark's gospel.

Medieval and Renaissance art and literature depicted Salome as young and innocent, but nineteenth-century works of art developed her as erotic and exotic (figs. 15 and 16). Likewise, the biblical victims, Bathsheba and Susanna, during the seventeenth century are transformed from those who suffer to seductresses in works of art that exploited tales of unclothed women. The poses and costumes of the dances on Salome indicate connections with the visual arts.

In 1891, Oscar Wilde wrote a play *Salome* and three years later Aubrey Beardsley illustrated it. Wilde's text was the basis of Richard Strauss's opera of 1905. Wilde developed Salome as a lascivious woman whose unrequited love for John the Baptist turned into revenge. In 1909, Gustav Klimt painted *Judith II/Salome* (fig. 26), which merges the two women into one version of the femme fatale. Diane Apostolos-Cappadona has developed how Salome and Judith who indirectly or directly decapitate males suggest "castrating females."[8]

In 1895, Loie Fuller danced Salome as an innocent young girl in a flowered costume, but audiences who had been shaped by the lurid literature and art of the woman wanted a femme fatale. Maude Allan performed her *Dance of Salome* throughout Europe in 1907, and presented over two hundred performances in London the next year (fig. 17). She wore only strings of pearls forming a bra and a loincloth, which upset the censors. Noel Pemberton Billing, a member of the British Parliament, wrote an article, "The Cult of the Clitoris," in his paper, *The Vigilante*, and called Allan a lesbian and a sadist.[9] In America, the actress Marie Cahill wrote President Theodore Roosevelt and other political leaders asking that they censor the stage and stop the "Salome craze" because it was a disgraceful, vulgar exhibition.

In 1907, the Metropolitan Opera performed *Salome* by Richard Strauss that included the nonbiblical striptease-like dance of the seven veils. Salome held and played with the decapitated head of John the Baptist. Angry supporters of the opera had *Salome* closed after the first performance. Right after that Bianca Froelich, the Metropolitan's prima ballerina, danced Salome as a solo in vaudeville at Lincoln Variety Theater. That same year Florenz Ziegfeld had a version of the dance by Mlle. Dazié in his follies. The success of this performance led Dazié to teach "Salome classes" two hours each day, training about one-hundred-fifty women each month to take this dance to vaudeville theaters throughout the country. The risque costume and gruesome head created a sensation while the dance had little artistic merit. The popularity of this came to be called "Salomania."

Gertrude Hoffman, a talented vaudeville player, was sent by Oscar Hammerstein to see Maude Allan's successful version of Salome in London and to copy it for the American stage. Hoffman did create a dance with some substance and began touring the United States in 1908, offering a little more than the eroticism and gore of the first wave of touring Salomes.

Ruth St. Denis returned from Europe in 1909 and appeared at the Hudson Theater. Reviews said, "Out-Salomeing all the Salomes, Miss St. Denis burst upon dazzled audiences."[10] Her experience doing the dance she had created on the Indian goddess Radha had given St. Denis a sense of the exotic and reinforced her power to enchant audiences. The poet philosopher, Hugo von Hofmannsthal, who had written beautiful critiques of St. Denis performances in Austria and Germany from 1906 to 1909, started writing an unfinished Salome scenario for her.

Many other dances of Salome could be cited throughout the years since Ruth St. Denis's version.[11] More of the dances have been choreographed by men than by women. Some of the women choreographers, such as Gertrude Kraus, have not focused on the nonbiblical "striptease" dance of the seven veils, but on the emotions of the characters. Salome has intrigued artists and writers. Why? The story of Salome is one that allows titilation of the male sexual appetite in lascivious dancing and reinforces the male ego, suggesting that women would kill for the men they love. The story has been interpreted as a story of Herodias who wants to be with Herod rather than her husband Philip and would have John the Baptist killed to stop his objections to the illicit union, or the story of Salome's unrequited love for John.

Other Seductive Women

While Salome has been the dominant biblical woman on the dance stage, other seductive women have appeared. In telling the story of Joseph, which involves eleven chapters of the Book of Genesis, describing the love of his father, the treachery of his brothers, the constancy of his work for the Egyptians, the care for his family, choreographers have primarily focused on one episode, that of Potiphar's wife's attraction to Joseph. This instance of a woman trying to seduce a man has been given prominence in twentieth-century dance.

In 1914, Diaghilev asked Michel Fokine to choreograph the music written by Richard Strauss, and Leonide Massine portrayed Joseph with the singer Maria Kusnetzova as Potiphar's wife. The lead character Joseph brought in as a slave was depicted as very young and innocent. Potiphar's wife went to him while he was sleeping, awakening him, and tried to seduce him with a sensual dance. When he resisted she tried to strangle him. This failed so she had chains and tortures prepared for him. An angel miraculously saved him and then she committed suicide. The story of Joseph was also done in dance by Kassian Goleizovsky, Heinrich Kroller, George Balanchine, Anthony Tudor, Aurel von Melloss, Margarethe Wallman, Pia and Pino Mlakar.

Balanchine choreographed *The Prodigal Son*, which was performed by Diaghilev in 1929 (fig. 2); another version was done in Copenhagen in 1931. This ballet has been revived frequently. The younger brother takes his inheritance and goes to a foreign land where he squanders his money on loose living and women. Within the ballet, this passing comment was given the specific form of a siren who attracts the son. She is another variation of the stereotype of woman as the source of evil. Balanchine also choreographed *Samson and Delilah*. Delilah, a Philistine woman, seduced Samson to reveal to her the source of his strength. When she discovered that it was his hair, she cut it off and he was taken captive.

Good or Ambiguous Women

With the exception of Martha Graham, women choreographers who have developed dances of strong and good biblical women have not received as much public attention as choreographers, whether male or female, who develop dances about biblical women who are interpreted to be evil or seductresses. Loie Fuller created *Miriam's Dance* in 1911 telling the story of leaving the bondage of Egypt and crossing the Red Sea. In 1918, when the husband of Ruth St. Denis, Ted Shawn, went into military service, she set out on a vaudeville tour to earn money to buy the Liberty Bonds to which she had pledged herself. At this time, she developed the dance *Jephthah's Daughter* that may have been an allusion to women who have to sacrifice for warriors. The next year, she performed *Dancer at the Court of King Ahasuerus* based on the story of Esther.

In 1919, Ruth St. Denis and her husband were the leads in *Miriam, Sister of Moses*, a play with dance performed in the Greek Theater in Berkeley (fig. 14). The plot is centered in Miriam's being struck by leprosy as a punishment for her jealousy. The biblical Miriam is described favorably for leading the people in praising God in song and dance after their departure from Egypt. Many modern Scripture scholars believe that the episode of her having leprosy is a later patriarchal interpolation to discredit a woman for having so much power. Miriam's leadership of the people in a religious ritual is considered a threat to patriarchal dominance.[12]

In 1944, Anna Sokolow created a series of dances on biblical women including Sarah and Miriam that was called *Song of a Semite*. The Inbal Dance Company in Israel under the direction of Sara Levi-Tanai, created a dance-drama on the story of Ruth in 1961. Judith, Deborah, Esther, and Ruth were often developed: Pearl Lang's *Song of Deborah* (1959); Graham's *Judith* (1950/1962/1970) (fig. 28); and Ze'eva Cohen's *Mothers of Israel* (1975). Sokolow created *Esther the Queen* in 1960, and the next year John Butler produced another version of that story.

Deborah was a judge and prophet of her people. She ruled them and led them against their enemies. Deborah has sometimes been depicted and her story was used by the Batsheva Company of Israel as the structure for a dance of lamentation for those killed in the Yom Kippur War. The Batsheva Company was originally trained by Martha Graham. Both Graham, in 1965, and the Batsheva Company, in 1970, have done versions of the *Witch of Endor*. King David, the strong male leader turned to this wise woman for advice when he was afraid.

Yvonne Georgi did solos based on the story of Ruth in Vienna in 1959 and Sophie Maslow developed Ruth in 1964. Eve and Adam appear in many diverse works such as José Limón's *Exiles* (1950) and Graham's *Embattled Garden* (1958), (figs. 21 and 25). In John Butler's *After Eden*, the expelled couple search for meaning and for comfort, and find some in being with each other. Doug Adams associates this flowering of choreography of dances of biblical women with the growing influence of women in modern society. He also notes that the violence of the 1960s and 1970s led to many dances on the crucifixion, among them Bella Lewitzky's *Pietà*.[13]

Judith Jamison, A Strong Dancer Imaging Evil Women

Joseph Neumeier recreated *Josephlegende* at the Vienna State Opera in 1977 using a "Symphonic Fragment" of the music of Richard Strauss's earlier work on Joseph. Judith Jamison danced the wife of Potiphar (fig. 29) and Kevin Haigen danced Joseph. By focusing on one American black woman dancer, Judith Jamison, I ask if sex-

29. Judith Jamison, *Josephlegende*. Photograph ©
Helmut Koller.

30. Martha Graham, *Primitive Mysteries*. Photograph © Barbara Morgan.

ism and racism are sometimes reinforced by the choice of content in the contemporary dance world.

Neumeier felt that Joseph needed more development than Fokine in 1914 had given him before the seduction incident, so the work began with Joseph dreaming about an Angel before he was sold into Egypt. In an atmosphere of opulence and decadence, the slave Joseph was brought into the palace of Potiphar. He was kind to Joseph who then danced to show his gratitude. Potiphar's wife was attracted by this handsome and sensitive youth. Joseph then slept and dreamt of the Angel. Potiphar's wife came, and kissed and caressed Joseph who was confused and then tried to flee. Potiphar heard the noise and encountered the fleeing Joseph and his wife holding his cloak. She said that he tried to lie with her. Potiphar then had Joseph beaten. The wife said nothing, but Judith Jamison with poignancy and beauty empathetically contracted as the man she desired suffered each blow. Joseph was sent to prison and the Angel came to console him, promising future peace.

Jamison's powerful performance was widely acclaimed. While the Bible gives little description of this temptress, Neumeier's version of her was "tall, dark, slender, graceful, and powerful, a woman of icy hauteur warmed and melted by concupiscence," according to Olga Maynard, Jamison's biographer.[14] Maynard notes that Jamison's portrayal was so effective that people began to speculate if the wife was really an African Princess wedded to an Egyptian or of a negroid line in Egypt. Praise such as this is confusing because it often masks racial prejudice that types black women as particularly seductive.[15]

In the introduction to *Judith Jamison, Aspects of a Dancer*, Maynard notes that despite Jamison's exceptional skill, she has been very vulnerable because she is dependent upon choreographers and companies. Maynard asks why women become dancers and toward what ends. By whose wish and whim do they dance? Whose ideas do they embody? She notes that the black dancers Alvin Ailey and Arthur Mitchell were successful enough to start companies and to free themselves from the domination of the white theater.[16] They could create their own pieces, rather than dance others' ideas.

When Alvin Ailey's company danced in 1973 John Butler's *According to Eve* (1972), Judith Jamison played the mother who showed favoritism to Abel and who neglected Cain. She instigated the tension between them and then watched as they fought. Eve in patriarchal interpretation through the centuries has been described as the originator of sin, but a careful reading of the Hebraic text reveals a story of dual responsibility in which the woman is the reflective, curious one and the man the nonthinking, sensuous, passive one. Butler's version makes Eve responsible, not only for the sin of her husband, but also for the sins of her sons.

Feminist biblical scholars ask how much of scriptural interpretation has been male projection. If Jamison had had her own company, would the lead roles for black women be those of evil women? How does a woman choreographer approach the choice and development of women biblical characters? Certainly, not all women are good, but the stage of modern dance has more frequently depicted strong biblical women negatively.

Martha Graham, A Strong Choreographer Recreating Women's Images

Martha Graham has been a leader in gifting the twentieth century with dance from a woman's point of view. She was born in 1894 into a strict Presbyterian home. Her father was a doctor working in psychiatry, which may have engendered Graham's interest in exploring the depths of the human psyche. The family lived in California during her adolescence, and there she began to deal with themes that flow throughout her work, inhibition and freedom, attraction and repulsion. Graham does not so much retell the stories of Scripture or mythology, but finds within them human emotions which stimulate her creative psychological dramas.

Martha Graham's story of Adam and Eve, *Embattled Garden*, (figs. 23 and 25) not only involves the primal couple but also the Stranger who represents the Serpent, and Lilith. According to Jewish midrash, Lilith was Adam's first wife who was not interested in being below her husband, so Eve was made to be a more submissive wife. Both of Graham's women are strong and intriguing, much more complex than the stereotypic woman, source of all evil. They have moved beyond girlish innocence and have taken the risks and faced the ambiguity that brings maturity.

Graham spoke about women's struggle for "dominance without guilt."[17] Whether she dealt with Greek mythology (Jocasta, Clytemnestra), biblical material, or Christian history (Joan of Arc), for Graham, women are protagonists, not supporting players in the stories of men. Graham had been attracted to dance by Ruth St. Denis's captivating portrayal of the heroine as goddess. These women did not wait to be protected by the male gods but recognized within themselves the divine image. Marcia B. Siegel suggests that Graham couldn't entirely shake off society's expectations for her, or the armor of guilt, conflict, repressed violence that society decrees for its female mavericks. Graham's heroines are all nonconformists — artists, doers, women with power beyond their sexuality. And they all suffer for their unorthodoxy.[18]

Graham's women have strength because of her conviction that women have as much dignity, creativity, and inner depth as men. In her two self-satires, *Acrobats of God* (1960) and *Every Soul Is a Circus* (1938), Graham seems to be frustrated when she has to depend on a man. Siegel suggests that Graham only displayed a traditional feminine stance as a weapon or as a sign of weakness. Graham does not seem to be comfortable expressing women and men as equals.[19]

Graham created two dances about Judith. The biblical story of Judith written during the first century B.C.E. in which the nation is saved "through the hands" of Judith, is similar to the story of the Exodus in which the nation is saved through the hands of Moses. The story is also similar to that of David defeating Goliath. Judith, a young, wise, and beautiful widow managed a wealthy estate. She rebuked the elders of the town of Bethulia who were ready to surrender to the enemies of God. She said that she would defend the town. She went into the enemy camp with her maid; there the soldiers were smitten by her beauty and took her to their general Holofernes. He was attracted to her and entertained her, but when he was in a drunken stupor she cut off his head and took it back to the cowardly leaders of Bethulia. After she had slain the leader, they gather courage to defend themselves.

The feminist biblical scholar, Elisabeth Schüssler Fiorenza writes,

> True, Judith is a woman who fights with a woman's weapons, yet far from being defined by her "femininity," she uses it to her own ends. Far from accepting such circumscription by feminine beauty and behavior, she uses it against those male enemies who reduce her to mere feminine beauty and in so doing seriously misjudge her real power.[20]

She is wise, faithful, courageous, and devoted to her people. In Renaissance visual art, Judith was an example of courage and justice similar to David.[21]

Martha Graham captured the womanly courage, wisdom, beauty, and power in the story of Judith, and did not get lost in a reduction of her to a seductress. Graham's *Judith*, the first version of the story done in 1950, has a simple structure of the chaste widow of Manasse enticing Holofernes with her beauty and then killing him.

The *Legend of Judith*, which Graham did in 1962, is a reflection of the aged heroine (fig. 28). She is visited by three angels and remembers herself as the young bride with Manasse, her bridegroom. Then in a rich mixture of emotions, Manasse and Holofernes become the same man. Judith and the man are entwined in a sort of totem with the angels' wings. As this dissolves, the elderly Judith entices and kills Holofernes again. Though the elderly Judith is haunted by questions about what the young Judith did, she makes the same choice again. She chooses the heroic and the good, but she must live with the ambiguity of the process.

Clytemnestra of Greek mythology and Judith can be compared: Clytemnestra killed the man who slayed her child, Judith killed the man who was about to slay her people. Both Agamemnon and Holofernes dwelt in the patriarchal world of the sparkle of military glory divorced from the flood of mothers' tears. A passage in Graham's notebook about Clytemnestra may shed some insight on Judith. Graham writes of Clytemnestra:

> The woman whose creative instinct — her child Iphigenia —
> has been killed by her husband —
> > by her need for home,
> > (her woman's nature has betrayed her)
> > In a sense she is a 'career woman' or a woman with
> > creative gifts — in that part masculine in her strength
> > of will & need to propagate her power —
> passionate
> autumnal woman —
> she kills her womanhood in killing Agamemnon, her husband.[22]

Betty Friedan's feminist classic, *The Feminist Mystique* (1963), appeared about the same time as Graham's comments. Both women with their spiritual sensitivities seem to articulate, as Virginia Woolf had before them, the tension of creative women within patriarchal structures. People have recoiled at the violence of Clytemnestra's and Judith's deeds. Christians seem to be desensitized to David's similar deed. The myths of these women raise a contemporary question. Do women have the courage to slay the relationships that destroy their creativity? The aging Martha Graham with no husband, no children, no "ladylike" securities, as the aging Judith, can struggle with the unpleasant images. Yet Judith again makes the choice to slay the force of destruction (though that force has professed love for her) that there may be life.

Graham's dance *Primitive Mysteries,* developed in 1931 and revived in 1964 and 1977, has been called a seminal achievement of
the twentieth century (fig. 30). The dance is a strong exploration of
the myth of the Virgin Mary and reveals some of the influence of
Roman Catholic imagery on Martha Graham. The dance does not
deal with the historical Mary of Scripture, but the Roman Catholic
mythical sense of her as Virgin Mother. In *Le Sacre du Printemps* in
1930, Graham was the sacrificial virgin who brings the life of spring
by dancing herself to death.[23] Mary was the willing virgin who brings
the life of Christ. Both Ruth St. Denis and Martha Graham had
male disciples who married them, but they later separated to pur-
sue their arts. Both women were virgin mothers in the archetypal
sense of independent women who are fecund. Contact with earthly
males is unimportant and at times an impediment to their spiritual
destinies.

Primitive Mysteries was developed after Graham had been studying
the Indians of the Southwest who merged Roman Catholicism with
their primitive sense of the sacred. The central female moves little,
but at times seems to be telling a story to the twelve other female
dancers around her, leading them in ritual, and at other times to be
receiving their adoration. Each of the three sections — Hymn to the
Virgin, Crucifixion, and Hosannah — is framed by a processional and
a recessional. Marcia B. Siegel has written of the women of *Primitive
Mysteries:*

> They have not taken up dancing to be looked at as beautiful, sexually
> attractive, ingratiating, or in any way idealized or "feminine" figures.
> Yet the fact that they *are* women, fully capable of conducting a religious
> observance, that they do not need male priests or teachers to channel
> their worship or intercede for them with God, is one of the boldest of
> *Primitive Mysteries'* many achievements.[24]

Looking Back to Look Forward

I have not mentioned every professional dance about biblical women
during the last hundred years, rather I have cited enough examples to
illustrate the patterns of choice. The patriarchal stereotypes of strong
women as seductive women have predominated. Women choreographers and a few men have worked with some strong and good women.
The examples of Judith Jamison's roles as biblical women raised the
unsettled, but provocative question if contemporary dance continues
to reinforce sexism and racism. Martha Graham has shown rich char-

acter development of her women, but she seems to struggle with the unresolved tension that one experiences as a woman in a patriarchal culture.

I did not cite all of the outstanding women choreographers of the second half of the twentieth century who have not chosen to work with stories of biblical women. Biblical material may have been omitted because the choreographers have moved toward abstract works, but choreographers may have felt, as did the feminist theologian Mary Daly, that the Judeo-Christian tradition is irretrievably patriarchal. For a woman to attain her full potential, she must move beyond these symbols and stories.

Yet there are feminist scholars such as Phyllis Trible, Elisabeth Schüssler Fiorenza, Letty M. Russell, Rosemary Radford Ruether, and Elizabeth Moltmann Wendel who invite fresh interpretations of Scripture through glasses not so tainted with patriarchal stain. Dancers today can claim the remnant of a lost history of women and explore where there are intersections of stories of ancient and modern women living in patriarchal culture. Dancers can use creative imagination to ritualize biblical foremothers. Hagar might dance as an abused woman today, Deborah as a leader of a nation, Jephthah's daughter as a victim of war, Miriam as a leader of liberation, Tamar as a victim of rape, or Mary Magdalene as the first witness of resurrected life in a world of too much death.

Notes

1. Methods for gender analysis of dance can be found in Judith Lynne Hanna, *Dance, Sex, and Gender: Signs of Identity, Dominance, Defiance, and Desire* (Chicago: University of Chicago Press, 1988).

2. Edwin Mullins, *The Painted Witch: How Western Artists Have Viewed the Sexuality of Women* (New York: Carroll & Graf Publishers, 1985) 16.

3. William A. Carroll, "The Bible in Dance and Drama at the Jesuit Colleges of the 16th to 18th Century" in *Papers of the International Seminar on the Bible in Dance* (Jerusalem: The Israeli Center of the International Theatre Institute, 1979) 7.

4. Phyllis Trible, *Texts of Terror, Literary-Feminist Readings of Biblical Narratives* (Philadelphia: Fortress Press, 1984) 114.

5. Letty M. Russell, ed. *Feminist Interpretation of the Bible* (Philadelphia: Westminster Press, 1985) 14.

6. Giora Manor and the editors of *Dancemagazine, The Gospel According to Dance* (New York: St. Martin's Press, 1980) 52–73.

7. Richard Bizot, "Salome in Modern Dance" in *Papers of the International Seminar on the Bible in Dance*, 14.

8. Diane Apostolos-Cappadona, " 'The Lord has struck him down by the hand of a woman!' Images of Judith," in *Art as Religious Studies*, ed. Doug Adams and Diane Apostolos-Cappadona (New York: Crossroad, 1987) 94.

9. Hanna, *Dance, Sex, and Gender*, 183.

10. Elizabeth Kendal, *Where She Danced* (New York: Alfred A. Knopf, 1979) 77.

11. Salome dances were developed by Gertrude Kraus, Michel Fokine, Boris Romanov, Nicola Guerra, Alexander Gorsky, Kassian Goleizovsky, Ruth Sorel, Serge Lifar, Ruth Page, Birgit Cullberg, Joseph Lazzini, Peter Durrel, Lindsey Kemp, André Leclair, Lester Horton, Carman de Lavallade, James Truitte, Flemming Flindt, Maurice Béjart, and Bill Cratty.

12. For further discussion of the power of women as leaders of ritual, see Martha Ann Kirk, *Celebrations of Biblical Women's Stories: Tears, Milk, and Honey* (Kansas City: Sheed and Ward, 1987).

13. Doug Adams, *Changing Biblical Imagery and Artistic Identity in Twentieth-Century Liturgical Dance* (Austin: The Sharing Co., 1984) 8–9.

14. Olga Maynard, *Judith Jamison, Aspects of a Dancer* (Garden City: Doubleday & Company, 1982) 158.

15. About ten times as many black women as white are raped in the United States. As black feminists have complained about this, they have often been told that black women asked for it because they are more sexy than white women.

16. While there are twenty-five million blacks in the United States, the number of black artists and actors in major companies and performances is minimal. Often they are not chosen for parts because of "aesthetics," which seems to be an elitist word for racism. White skin is "prettier" than black, but the exception is in having blacks play the dark evil characters.

17. Hanna, *Dance, Sex, and Gender*, 205.

18. Marcia B. Siegel, *Watching the Dance Go By* (Boston: Houghton Mifflin Co., 1977) 204.

19. Ibid., 204–5.

20. Elisabeth Schüssler Fiorenza, *In Memory of Her: A Feminist Theological Reconstruction of Christian Origins* (New York: Crossroad, 1983) 117.

21. Apostolos-Cappadona, "Images of Judith," 88–90.

22. Martha Graham, *The Notebooks of Martha Graham* (New York: Harcourt, Brace, Jovanovich, 1973) 258.

23. Graham choreographed Stravinsky's "Rite of Spring" for her ninetieth birthday.

24. Marcia B. Siegel, *Shapes of Change: Images of American Dance* (New York: Discus Books/Avon Books, 1979) 58.

PART III

Theory and Practice
of Liturgical Dance

11

...And the Word Became Dance:
A Theory and Practice of
Liturgical Dance

Carla De Sola

Liturgical dance is viewed as a living, moving, breathing epiphany of God and creation. As the paced movement of a liturgy unfolds and the dancers emerge, we find ourselves feeling and seeing an embodiment of the "word." Liturgical dance can lead both the viewer and participant to new understandings of religious and spiritual realities. The "word" becomes dance.[1]

As a communal form of worship, liturgical dance offers a renewed awareness of who these people are as a community. When bodies sway in unison, and arms lift in prayer, the congregation can become conscious, in an experiential way through the workings of the spirit, that they are a living, breathing family of God.

Practiced by liturgical artists, dance serves and functions as a conduit from the inner workings of the spirit to the outer expression of today's worship. As an art form that is fleeting, evanescent, and transient, dance makes an indelible impression upon the viewer. Communication is body-to-body with the distance between sanctuary to pew being traversed kinesthetically. The viewer is in living communication with the dancer, sharing the configurations of space, form, movement qualities, musical, and visual elements.

This reflection begins by looking, as if from the inside, at the dancer's experience. The liturgical dancer hears a call and responds with a dance from the heart. The desire to communicate what has occurred inwardly in the soul arises.

> The voice of my beloved: Behold, he comes, leaping upon the mountains, bounding over the hills.... Arise my love, my fair one.[2]

Crafting a dance with clear form and focus requires vision, faith, and inspiration, and patient work.

Dances for the liturgy change with the seasons: fall, winter, spring, and summer match Advent; Christmas, Epiphany; Lent, Easter; and Pentecost. Becoming immersed in the cyclical process, a dancer discovers that he or she has become a student of religion. Dances are designed from personal reflections on the spirituality of the liturgical season. Scripture and prayer, mingled with the urgings of the dancer's soul, and enriched by the experience of life, are shaped through the medium of dance.

One of my early explorations in liturgical dance was the choreography for the Feast of the Assumption. In this instance, I practiced the dance that would be auditioned for the priest I hoped would include it in his service. As I worked, I felt my way through instinct and prayer, and drew upon my dance training to explore the way into a mystery. This mystery proclaims that Mary, human and like us, was lifted in body and spirit into heaven.

Lying on the floor, I arched my chest upward and continued this upward lift while leading with my heart. Head and hands slowly followed the arch of the chest. I attuned my spirit to the music *In Paradisum* from Fauré's *Requiem*. The coordination of body and spirit with the music released a burst of joy that I allowed to take over and guide me through the next sequences. In a grace-filled time of practice, I learned from my body a feeling of "assumption." In dance language, this "feeling" is comprised of an "active" impulse, enriched with passion, followed by passive moments. Within a few hours, I experienced from the primary text of my body this mystery of Catholic teaching. The body/text was guided by the spirit and the tradition of my faith.

A Theory and Practice of Liturgical Dance

Although defined and comprehended by its liturgical function, the value of liturgical dance is inseparable from the quality of inspired movement. To understand the unique contributions of this art form, we must, therefore, take into account the aesthetic, spiritual, and religious values that uniquely underline its expression (fig. 31).

A *theory* of liturgical dance considers the role of the dancer in the liturgical community; the role of dance in the liturgical structure, including the varieties of religious themes which may be danced; and the communal nature or dimension of dance and worship. The *practice* of liturgical dance may be divided into the preparation of the dancer and community and the shared experience of the liturgical dancer and the community during the liturgy. In the context of dance as religious studies, special attention is given to two components of the preparation of the liturgical dancer: the practice of embodying and dancing prayers and the use of dance in the study of biblical passages. Both of these underline the presupposition that we *learn* by dancing. Further, both elements are ideally part of the preparation and training of a liturgical dancer and choreographer. Both of them, in their own right, are valuable practices for religious studies, and may be done independent of liturgical consideration.

The Role of the Dancer. The dancer's essence is founded on a unity of body, mind, and spirit. The intuitive, nonverbal faculties receive the sources of inspiration that lead the dancer to express interpretations or restatements of ancient or modern concepts, freshened as they were by the spirit. The ministry of the sacred dancer is multifaceted. At times, the dancer serves as "teacher," "prophet," "gatherer," "evangelist," "witness," and "priest." These roles are a part of the dancer's contribution to the liturgy and to the community.

Ruth St. Denis reflected that a sacred dancer's training was twofold; the dancer must train not only the body, but also be concerned with the development of the spirit. St. Denis can be considered a "foremother" of liturgical dance, having performed as early as 1910 at the Riverside Church, New York City. Ted Shawn, her longtime influential partner, remarked that the dance and the dancer are inseparable: "Dance is the only art in which we ourselves are the stuff of which it is made." The dancer/choreographer, uniquely, with body and soul, convey the message and meaning of the dance. The richer the dancer/choreographer is in spiritual and life experience, the more profound will be the message. Martha Graham has frequently been

quoted as saying "the body does not lie." Clearly, if a dancer is inspired, the body will be a reflection of an inner process, manifested
according to the type or orientation of the training the person has
undergone.

The liturgical dancer spends many years polishing the craft, much
as a priest who dedicates a life to learning to experience, reveal, and
clarify the sacred dimensions of life. Primarily drawing upon a kinesthetic dimension, a dancer will connect feelings, body shapes, forms,
and rhythms to bring forth in a heightened way the spirituality of
everyday incarnated life.

The dancer is a mirror that reflects and magnifies what is hidden
or not accessible to the eyes alone. By grounding these perceptions
in the body, a dancer then becomes as a mirror of the "within" of
things. Paying attention to both physical and human realities and
their spiritual dimensions, while simultaneously interpreting Scripture, the dancer is able to give new life and meaning to the passion
of human emotions.

While interpreting abstract forms of spirituality, the dancer draws
attention to the exquisite grace of the human body — the beauty of
the arching spine, encircling arms, with the limbs alternately supporting weight, gesturing, and reaching out into space, or retracting, with
weight, into the depths. Thus, the dancer connects the same elements
with the viewer who empathetically feels the ground, the weight, the
movements in space, the feelings of the body, and the movements of
the spirit.

The dancer/choreographer is perceived both as a teacher and a prophet — prophetic in the sense of pioneering dance in the church when
it is still unclear about the role of movement and dance in the liturgy.
Doug Adams and Judith Rock have noted that a dancer can be prophetic when choosing to dance and interpret Scripture in ways that
lead a community toward new and more vivid awareness.[3] This may
be a result of the treatment of the subject matter, or by the quality
of the demonstrated technique.

A dancer assists by serving the celebrant in a deaconlike fashion. As
dancers usher the gifts forward, for example, their bodies manifest a
reverence that can only be articulated through body and arm gestures.
This is a helping role which quietly illuminates the gospel values of
purity of heart and devotion. Mary, whose life seemed to embrace
aspects of both servant and prophet, is a model for many a female
liturgical dancer.

While leading communal circle and processional dances, the dancer
serves as a "gatherer," welding the community together with dance

32. Carla de Sola, ...*And the Word Became Dance.* Photograph by John Greim, Philadelphia.

31. Carla de Sola and the Omega Liturgical Dance Company during a worship service. Photograph courtesy of the Omega Liturgical Dance Company.

interpretations of songs or chants. The term "gatherer" expresses the role of the dancer who calls forth movements of dances from the people, and tests them out for use or further development. As with any folk dance, the movements which work will last and inappropriate or artificial movements simply disappear.

The dancer serves as a living "icon" of the "good news" and enables people, through dance, to rejoice, wonder, and open their hearts to their innermost feelings. A trained and sensitive body is like the lamp set on a stand, illuminating the way for others. Ideally, the dancer is part of the community, in touch with its life, and can reflect back to the community in heightened form a part of its spiritual journey. The dancer reminds the community that they are indeed people with feeling who can rejoice, weep, move, be freedom-loving, physical, and capable of "resurrection." As a witness, the dancer brings into heightened awareness what is already present in the community. The contributions of dance range from demonstration of the ways a congregation becomes more open and spontaneous with movement and gesture to being an integral part of an entire liturgy.

And the Word Became Dance. A review of various aspects of this work illustrates tangibly the role of dance within a liturgical structure. The function of the dance for the Entrance Procession was to set the tone for the service, and to introduce the celebrant and dancers along with the sacred objects each dancer carried (fig. 32). These included: two candles, a bell, a censer, the book, and a bowl of water. The spacing of participants is an important consideration in any liturgy. Such spatial relationship is critical in a procession of dancers, who move and weave as they pass down the aisle to the altar. Spacing is an aesthetic value in a liturgy that sets off each person in the procession while maintaining the integrity and connection of the whole line.

Suppleness and flowing movements are aesthetic values acquired by combining both training and the natural personal abilities of participants. In the Entrance Procession for *And the Word Became Dance,* each dancer was directed to move his or her torso to the right or left every few steps. The slight spiral movement showed the objects to congregants on either side of the aisle. In addition, the movement brought forth the dimension of sacred space as watching eyes followed the spiral. An awareness of the curve, height, and breadth of the church was recognized. The religious value of the procession lay in the witness of a community, represented by the dancers, moving forward toward a goal that would be fulfilled in the course of the service. Symbolically, the entire procession was a prototype of the people of God in procession, building the kingdom. The value of the procession depended upon each dancer's awareness of who they were, the role they were fulfilling, and how they were doing it. The ensuing spiritual intercommunication of the congregants and the dancers presupposed the congregation's openness of heart and willingness to freely join and participate in the experience. For the dancers, every step was important. Their commitment was shown by the way their feet touched the floor, the alignment of their bodies, and what their eyes conveyed.

In dance, each movement has the potential for spiritual value. For instance, when the dancer becomes grounded by connecting to the floor or earth with sureness so does each viewer. We are helped to feel the presence of a base of support of which we are not ordinarily aware. When the dancer's body is aligned, the harmony is facilitated and energy flows freely from one body part to another, imparting beauty in grace-filled movements. Alignment of the body is a source of awareness and grace both for the dancer and the viewer. The dancer who moves with an open and generous heart communicates a sense of warmth and inclusiveness that envelops all within it. Thus, a congregation is able to participate with the dancer on a heart-to-heart level, and a free flow of shared energy occurs.

Attention to details seems complicated, but for a trained dancer this is assimilated during the hours of preparatory practice. In "performance," intention flows in harmony with the previously learned steps and counts. Ultimately, the combination of training and the power of the spirit facilitates the expression of beauty.

The Role of Dance in the Liturgical Structure and the Variety of Religious Themes.   Thomas A. Kane has presented a helpful analysis of the role of dance within the liturgical structure.[4] In brief, he bypasses the impossible task of describing all possible places and ways of dancing in the liturgy, and directs us to consider dance according to its function in the liturgy. Liturgical dance can fall into five different categories: processional, prayer (including acclamation and invocation), proclamation, meditation, and celebration.

Religious themes are interwoven within this structure and the variety becomes endless. The dancer can express the multiple and sacred dimensions of life — joys, fears, dreams, questions, disappointments, themes of peace and justice, faith, action, and the sacredness of everyday life. Two dances from *And the Word Became Dance* are concrete examples of the diversity of subject matter and style of interpretation available to the liturgical choreographer.

One of these dances, *The Beatitude Blessing*, emphasized the blessings of the beatitudes. Envisioning the crowds who climbed the mountain to hear Jesus and who were comforted and blessed by the Sermon on the Mount, the dancers in their own way intended to impart to the congregation the blessings of the beatitudes. The dancers moved in flowing ways that began with directed and focused gestures of blessing. With the celebrant's raised hands of blessing, the dancers began with the same gesture and like a seed of movement developed and expanded upon it, adding movements for the torso, patterns for the feet, directing hands and arms in endless variations with subtleties of feeling. The dancers moved throughout the sanctuary and down the aisles reaching out in blessing toward the people.

The focal point of the service was a dance based on the conversion of Paul, *The Road to Damascus*. This segment was a combination of both proclamation and meditation dance as the dancers proclaimed words from the Book of Acts and Paul's letters while they danced the choreographer's interpretation of Paul's experience on the way toward Damascus. The blinding light was represented by a huge spinning cloth. Characters from different times of Paul's life — his mother, the students in the school of Gamaliel, and Stephen — all emerged and merged throughout the segment. Ultimately, we realize that when Jesus says, "Saul, Saul, why are you persecuting me?," this Jesus *is* indeed all people.

From these two examples, we see the variety of religious themes that can be conveyed through dance. What is needed is for congregations and leaders of churches to become more aware of the potential for dance and dancers to express this richness and complexity. The inclusion of dance in a sacred context is not peripheral, ornamental, or a diversion from the service. On the contrary, the dancer embodies unrealized hopes and dreams of the people. A trained and spirit-filled body is an image of the incarnation. The dancer teaches through dance as does an icon, a religious painting, or a fine piece of music.

The Communal Dimensions of Dance and Worship. Dance is a natural, primary expression of every human being. It is founded on the beat of our hearts, the rhythms of our breath, and the flexibility of our joints. It is manifested as an inexplicable desire to turn a walk into a pattern or a run into a leap. Dance is an integral part of who we are as whole, religious, and expressive persons.

In my description of the dance choreographed for the Feast of the Assumption, the body was spoken of as a primary text. As a solo dancer listens to his or her body and learns, so the congregation, when dancing together, feels the combined energy of all the people moving. They are led to comprehend, in a lived, felt way, what their community is about. This may give rise to a new understanding of what is implied in the phrases "the body of Christ," "the prayers of the faithful," and "the celebration of the banquet."

People learn from the dance itself. There is an ancient Greek sacred folk dance, *Cyrtos*, which was practiced by the whole village. The dance steps were designed to unite the people with heaven and earth. They were repeated over and over again. Dance became the vehicle for living and learning about a mystery moving toward deeper religious understanding. This is true for primitive or traditional folk dances. Implicitly, they are sacred dances that teach as a myth is reenacted and are derived from the people's longing for reunion with their spiritual source. The sacred, communal dance of today has the same potential for involving people in a learning and living experience of their religious beliefs.

Practice of Liturgical Dance

Practice implies both the preparation of the liturgical dancer and the actual experience of sharing and dancing in the liturgy. The preparation of the liturgical dancer can be divided into several components — spiritual, technical, analytic, as well as preparation of the community, materials, and environment — which should be approached in inclusive, wholistic ways. Each of these categories will be examined independently.

Spiritual training includes embodied ways of prayer as well as aspects of traditional religious education such as ongoing worship involvement, and studies and instruction in prayer and meditation, such as personal and centering prayers, group prayers, and the reading of Scripture.

Technical training involves the dancer's preparatory warm-up prior to the liturgy, such as loosening-up exercises to activate the body through stretching and other techniques. These are abbreviated extensions of the dancer's eternal training, encompassing various dance technique styles, dance composition, music and voice training, acting, and experience with improvisational approaches to learning.

Analytical training, or development of subject matter, consists of studies in Scripture, liturgy, and ritual, together with study of psychological and spiritual components of the personality. Additionally, attention to the themes and subject matter of dances and development of a point of view about the material are based on personal experience that has political, sociological, and economic dimensions.

The preparation of the worship community includes assisting in the religious education of the people by workshops or preliminary instructions with the congregation. The dual objective is to prepare the community to participate in the dances and to create collaborative work with the celebrant and/or liturgical team.

The physical dimensions of the ceremony are a significant consideration for the preparation of materials and environment. On the practical side, in preparing a rich and successful dance liturgy, attention must be given to space, lighting and color, sacred objects, costumes, and music. Space involves attention to sight-lines; physical details of the church, such as arrangement of seats, aisles, overall architecture; and an awareness of the function of, and feelings conveyed in the different physical areas. Lighting and color include exploration of the flexibility of lighting control where possible, and awareness of the color scheme throughout the church. Sacred objects require attention to the handling of the candles, incense, book, processional cross, and gifts in a reverent manner. Costumes need attention to design, colors, and fabric in coordination with the colors of the church, season of the liturgical year, and needs of the dance. Music requires coordination with music director and liturgy team, and the setting of cues and sound levels for recorded music.

An Embodied Way of Prayer. This session includes both personal and group prayer. Students are instructed to sit comfortably. There may also be a flower arrangement, icon, or other religious points of focus. This arrangement must be simple and beautiful. The beauty of the physical objects affects the sense of beauty felt toward one's own body.

After a few minutes of quiet, focused attention, which may include an awareness of one's breath, the leader invites all to participate in a simple danced gesture of prayer set to a line of Scripture. For example, "Be still and know that I am God," is a good beginning passage for this exercise.[5] The gesture(s) will reflect the intention of the phrase. It is not mimetic; that is, it does not describe the phrase in a literal way, but leads the student to a deeper connection with the prayer. The student learns about stillness by the timing of the gestures, the coordination of arms and torso, the shapes of the sequence, and the transference of feeling from instructor to student, or from student to student.

The full meaning of a phrase such as "Be still and know that I am

God" cannot be understood only by the mind. It needs to be felt and perceived by the whole body. There is no one way of gesturing a phrase, for there is an unfathomable richness to each line of Scripture. They are doorways to contemplation. The dancer, teacher, or student is led to know what to do from within. The movement is right when it makes sense both bodily and spiritually; this might occur when hand, heart, and mind pause at the exact same moment.

In a more extended movement prayer, the instructor shapes the study according to the objective sought. For example, it may be important for students to be led to discover their own relationship to God. The instructor sets aside movements to traditional modes of prayer, such as prayers of petition or praise or thanksgiving, and encourages the students to improvise to questions such as "Who are you?," "Who am I?," "Where are you, God?," "Are you there?" The results can be far-reaching. Students, through dancing with these questions, discover something on a nonverbal level about their relationship to the world, the self, and God. In this process, experience comes first. Later it can be translated into a verbal, cognitive form for which the body has been consulted. This leads to a new level of spiritual enrichment.

An important aspect of dance/prayer sessions is in group sharing of movement prayers. Each person is enriched by learning to emulate, copy, and feel from within the source of another's movements. In a typical session one person's prayer/movement sequence might reflect the phrase, "Taste and see the goodness of the Lord." Another's movement might be a rose opening, and a third's a full chalice held in reverence. Another's movement might convey personal anguish, and take a form of sorrow and the shape of the cross. Sharing dance prayers feels as if one is experiencing "the one vine, with many branches," to which Jesus referred in John's gospel. In such a moment, the sap of the spirit courses through many limbs; and participants are enriched by a commonly shared spiritual experience.

A Bodily Approach to Biblical Study.   Danced biblical study is exemplified by a session based on the story of the Demoniac.[6] Entitled *Alien Energies*, this session is based on a reflection of the Gerasene demoniac wandering "among the shards of the dead...Abused and abusive, occupied by alien energies." Later we read, "Sometimes we are healed in the presence of one who hears our cries, asks our names and holds us, trembling."[7]

Designed as a workshop, this is a ninety-minute dance meditation that utilizes movement studies, creative improvisation, role-playing, sound and music, and guided interaction. The objectives are multiple, as participants of a healing workshop first encounter the story of the demoniac. They become empowered toward a deeper healing while personalizing their movements through the story and relating it to their own life issues. Our purpose is to show how a body, interacting with Scripture, leads to a dynamic and personal involvement with the story, enabling a participant, who may be both dancer and student of religion, to realize dimensions of the narrative otherwise unsuspected.

This session is introduced by a comforting and protective movement prayer of blessing, which gives assurance and serves as a base from which participants can move with greater daring and freedom of expression. The participants are then led in strong, open, centered, and expansive movements. They are encouraged to move around freely, developing patterns of confidence, and of being "in their right minds."

The facilitator then reads the gospel narrative while participants note phrases of significance to them. All rise and improvise in movement as key phrases from the story are called out loud. These are spoken in random order, one tumbling out after another. For example, one person might call out the word "possessed," and initiate movement in response to the word. All then repeat out loud the word *possessed* and move in a similar way to the person who began. After a few seconds another word is called out and everyone repeats the new word or phrase and follows the new movement. This continues for a while as people find phrases that stimulate them to get in touch with their own similar feelings. The process may release surprising reactions that provide new openings for personal explorations.

The group then sits down and people share their experiences. They reflect with the leader on the "chaotic health" of the "madman," "breaking fetters," released by "snapping chains." They then speculate on the "demons" beyond the man's reach and reflect upon the demons within themselves, deposited either by their own acts or the acts of another, and beyond their reach.

The facilitator then guides them through the dance study, based on an abstract from the story of the demoniac. Grouped in pairs, each person experiences in turn the roles of being healer and being the recipient of healing. They are led to reenact through movement the casting out of Legion. The study concludes with the facilitator moving among the people, blessing them, saying, "It is good and right that you are beautiful, and healed. Go and spread the good news of your healing."

For the dancer, and the student of religion, the story becomes personalized, and a connection develops from which new points of view emerge. When a biblical story is danced it becomes "part of one's bones." As an integrated, living memory, it has the potential to affect one's life in far-reaching ways. Through our bodies, we have entered into an integral relationship with the gospel. Reading the Scriptures and prayers with and through the body is a new kind of hermeneutics.

The Shared Experience of Dancing the Liturgy. We have learned from the spirit, from our bodies, and from Scripture. Our minds and hearts have united and standing before the presence of God, we move! "In God we live and move and have our being."[8] When a dancer is fully engaged in performance, and the spirit moves, a unifying experience of dance and prayer occurs. This is exalting! However, this is not always the case and yet a dancer continues, sensing a goal worth the effort.

During preparation time, and even after sharing the dance, tests of faith often occur. A dancer/choreographer wonders whether the dance vision will communicate clearly and be well received, whether it will serve people spiritually, and whether the congregation and ministers will be united with and through the dance. A spiritual goal of dance is to open new channels for prayer and worship. Ultimately, the liturgical dance serves to transform and become a common praise and "work of the people."

When dance is first introduced to a congregation, there may be initial ambivalence on the part of some people toward accepting it as a true ministry. Some members may be concerned that dance will trivialize worship. Others may draw back, perhaps anticipating criticism from their peers for considering an unconventional approach to worship. Some may fear participating in that which is unfamiliar. However, once resistance to expression through dance is overcome and the "first steps" are taken, an inherent joy can be awakened. The theory and practice of liturgical dance are fulfilled when people explore this added dimension to worship...when the word becomes dance.

Notes

1. An evening-length dance/prayer service, *And the Word Became Dance*, was performed by the Omega Liturgical Dance Company, which is in residence at the Cathedral Church of St. John the Divine, New York City. This dance/prayer service was directed by Carla De Sola, Thomas A. Kane, C.S.P., and Allan Tung. *And the Word Became Dance* was commissioned in part by the Paulist Fathers in conjunction with their evangelization program in Canada and the United States for the fall of 1988.

2. Song of Solomon, 2:8, 10.

3. See Doug Adams and Judith Rock, "Biblical Criteria in Dance: Modern Dance as Prophetic Form," in this collection.

4. Thomas A. Kane, "Shaping Liturgical Dance," in *Introducing Dance in Christian Worship*, ed. Ronald Gagne, Thomas A. Kane, and Robert Van-Eecke (Washington, D.C.: The Pastoral Press, 1984) 93–118.

5. Psalm 46.

6. Mark 5:1–20.

7. Robert Raines, "Alien Energies," *The Ridgeleaf* 168 (July 1988).

8. Acts 17:28.

12

Dance as Performance Fine Art in Liturgy

Susan Bauer

Most resources on the history and theory of dance in liturgy refer to dance performed by the entire church: in some cases by the lay community, in other cases the clerical community, or at times the two together. From the early church through the Middle Ages, dance was not a rehearsed event but a spontaneous set of steps and patterns that consisted of simple walking, hopping, or jumping done in lines and circles. The performance quality was pedestrian in nature. The dance steps and patterns came to symbolize more than physical movement for the community or were used to induce an altered state of mind in the performer; dancing was the community's physical expression of its faith and concerns. The development of dance as a performance fine art in the Western Christian liturgical context is a twentieth-century phenomenon.

Dance as performance fine art is defined as being choreographed around particular themes to be performed with or in place of the liturgy. Neither spontaneous nor pedestrian in nature, this dance is well crafted with a clear intention and carefully selected movement material. The dance is technically articulated in performance. Dancers are designated by a church community to minister in dance. These dancers are committed to the development of their technique and creative potential to serve in this artistic ministry. Referred to by Forrest Coggin as the "priesthood" of dancers, they function much like a choir.[1] The dancers move beyond the pedestrian, ritual, and folk movement to an abstract, symbolic expression of themes. The community experiences the physical expression of the dance vicariously.

When working with dance as performance fine art in liturgy, there are several issues that need to be considered. Some relate directly to the choreographer, others to the dancers and the choreographer. The worshipping community that incorporates dance into liturgy needs to be cognizant of all these issues. The choreographer must consider that the dances move beyond a literal, subjective level; have other criteria than just being beautiful or warmly inspirational; be perceived as more than a way to attract the youth; not exclude the congregation or remain a private experience for the dancers; be choreographed for all parts of the liturgy, not just the prayers; and be seen as integral to liturgy rather than as experimental worship. Dancers and choreographers need to affirm their instrument, the body, through movement and costume selection; not to separate or assign different value to "sacred" and "secular" experiences; to continue to study technique, movement theories, and choreography; and, to continue the process of critical reflection personally and professionally.

For the worshipping community to have a meaningful experience, the choreographer, dancers, and congregation need to spend time reflecting on these issues, which can be studied and discussed from several different perspectives. The history of dance and movement in Western Christianity is one perspective. While this history seldom refers to dance as performance fine art in liturgy, it informs us of the occasions, reasons, steps, and patterns for incorporation into contemporary choreography. The artistic perspective informs us of the craft of choreography and the means by which choreographers and dancers can technically and creatively develop their full potential. This perspective enables the congregation to work with the perception process, whereas the practical perspective highlights the choice of costumes and music, use of the space, time frame, congregational expectations, and ways of approaching a congregation. The most often neglected and perhaps most important perspective is that of biblical and systematic theology, which clarifies the ways the dancers and choreographers embody their theology through their understanding of God, the incarnation, worship, and community. This theological perspective also shapes the dancers' view of performance of artistic creativity.

I explore the ways these issues can be clarified by the historical, artistic, practical, and theological perspectives. From this framework that raises theoretical and practical considerations can be established a process for the development and evaluation of dance as performance fine art in liturgy. This framework is not necessarily the same for all choreographers, dancers, and congregations.

Historical Perspective

Much has been written about the ways in which dance was incorporated into the life of the Christian community. Researchers continue to find ways that dance and ritualized movements were an important part of a community's actual physical expression of their faith. This history heightens our awareness that there is a heritage which can be drawn upon for understanding and creatively broadening contemporary liturgical dance.

Early liturgical dance occurred at particular times during the year; the dances celebrated and reflected the church calendar. Liturgical seasons, themes, and celebrations provide choreographers with thematic and movement ideas and music, e.g., the Easter *pelota* dance of the clergy as they sang the hymn, "Praise to the Paschal Victim." This hymn is still sung by some denominations. Early liturgical dance is a source for steps and patterns. The *tripudium*, or three-step dance, consisting of three steps forward and one step back, can be incorporated with any number of variations; for example, the processional to Ecternach in honor of St. Willibord, when a hop was added to the three to five steps forward and the one to three steps back as the change in direction occurred.[2] The movement around a labyrinth as in the *pelota* dance suggests some floor patterns.

An important aspect for the historic consideration of liturgical dance is the study of the symbolism of the early steps and patterns. The forward steps of the tripudium symbolize the positive occurrences in life and the backward steps the setbacks in life. Movement into the center of the labyrinth represented the death of Jesus, and the movement out of the circle the life and resurrection of Jesus. Historical symbolism should be reflected by choreographers, dancers, and the congregation. First, a choreographer should work on a variation of a historic idea and inform the congregation of the history of the symbolic patterns being incorporated into new choreography. Second, the actual pattern and symbolism could be set to other pieces of music. For example, the hopping dance or processional to Ecternach works very well with the hymn, "Joyful, Joyful, We Adore Thee." Third, a study of the historical symbolism can clarify the use of contemporary movement rituals and symbols in our lives as individuals and as community. Overused movements such as the upraised arms and circle floor pattern can symbolize a variety of meanings, so the choreographer's intent must be clear. Such movements may be only a choreographic device without any intended symbolism. This may not, however, be true for the congregation. The history of liturgical dances and symbolism focuses on acquired meanings of movement.

Historical data is one aspect of our heritage for performance dance in liturgy. History is the primary source for incorporating performance dance in liturgy today. Beyond the examples of dancing during worship, many dances occurred outside the church at various festival celebrations or as processionals from shrine to shrine. Hebrew Scripture references indicate little evidence that dancing occurred in the synagogues or temple as part of the liturgy; instead it was a part of celebrations — weddings, bar mitzvahs, and processionals to the holy site.[3] While future research may uncover examples of choreographers preparing specific dance pieces for incorporation into liturgy, it is important to recognize that dancing in liturgy was a spontaneous response by the community that physically expressed their faith. From these historical experiences, we gain ideas and movement material for dance in liturgy with designated dancers.

Artistic Perspective

If dance as performance fine art is to be incorporated into liturgy, the considerations given to concert dance by choreographers, dancers, and audiences must hold true for dance in the sanctuary. From the artistic perspective, these considerations include the craft of choreography; the discipline of the dancer's instrument, the body; the perception process; and the development of creative potentials.

Necessary skills to be developed to work with the choreographic process are the ability to identify themes and move from subject matter to content; a working understanding of the movement vocabulary; an increase in observation and movement analysis skills; movement from literal gestures to their abstraction and intensification; selection and arrangement of movement materials in a coherent, unified manner; and an ability to critically reflect personally and with others. Generally, the theme or subject matter can be easily identified for dance in liturgy. What is not so easy to identify is the content or intent to be expressed: what one wants to say. The purpose of performance dance is not the literal restatement of a particular theme but the discovery of what the theme has to say personally to the choreographer or to the community. Many times we have participated in "dancing," a spontaneous expression of skipping and turning of joy or a handwringing huddled shape of sorrow. The "dance" through the choreographic process objectifies, intensifies, and abstracts those feelings and associated movements. The performance dance universalizes and focuses the individual or community's felt, spontaneous, or conditioned movement responses.

The movement from subject matter to content raises the following questions: What are the facets of this theme? What do others say and how does that affect me? How else has this been communicated through sermons, visual art, music, drama, and literature? If the general theme or subject matter is anger, for example, several different types of anger can be expressed. Anger can be unexpressed and contained within the individual. Anger can be expressed in a very indirect manner; or the anger could be fully expressed toward a particular person or object. Even though a clear focus may not be apparent at the beginning of the choreographic process, these questions and reflection on them should be. The selection of one focus or contrasting idea is an important decision for the observation, analysis, articulation, and selection of the appropriate movement materials.

During the development of an intent or focus, reflection on past experiences, observation of current life situations, and analysis of movement occur simultaneously. Choreography arises from life experiences that are informed in, by, and through the community. Choreographers need to be involved and aware of events from a personal, local, national, and global perspective. Openness to a variety of experiences and careful observation (either as spectator or participant) provide a data bank of observed movement, feelings, and kinesthetic responses.

Development of a clear understanding of movement vocabulary and its use for analysis of movement extends beyond a purely subjective response. Objectivity facilitates critical reflection and the ability to select movement material. Carefully selected and articulated movement facilitates an affective response in the congregation. The choreographer rejects the use of literal gestures and extends dance beyond the realm of pantomime and theater.

Literal or pedestrian gestures can be movement vocabulary for choreography such as in *Anger*, where a kick or pushing-away gesture is evident (fig. 33). However, to engage a particular mood or to generate response from the congregation, these gestures need to be abstracted and intensified. While the choreographer works with a specific intent, what the congregation sees establishes the range of their possible responses. This is similar to the experience of looking at a watercolor print or a photograph taken with a soft-focused or starburst lens — there is an image that is open to a variety of responses and interpretations. Dances are not choreographed in black-and-white, but in shades of grey. Lengthening the amount of time a gesture takes, exaggerating the range of motion, changing normal use of energy, using different body parts, and repeating or rearranging parts are simple ways of exploring the abstraction and intensification of literal gesture.

These aspects of the choreographic process — analysis, intensification, and objectification — enable the dance to move beyond a subjective, personal experience to one that vicariously involves the worshipping community. Feelings are closely examined and their associated movements clearly articulated for varied and active communication with the congregation. The entire body, not just the face, takes on expressive responsibility. These aspects of choreographic process also expand movement possibilities. It is important to recognize the limitations of the raised arms and the circle and to see other movement possibilities. Further questions or challenges arise to the previously accepted definitions of beauty, as only those movements that leave a congregation warmly inspired are expanded to the new movements observed and articulated. Beauty and inspiration in dance also mean enabling a congregation to reflect on aspects of life that disturb or frustrate. The choreographer needs to consider and to express all facets of the community's life.

During this entire process, a choreographer has the responsibility to critically reflect on the choices made. Is the piece going in the direction intended? Is there more clarity in a new direction which should be considered instead? Is the movement chosen communicating clearly? Are the movement choices based on favorites or ones the dancers do well, rather than what communicates the intent? Feedback can come from the dancers. One of the best sources for critical reflection are friends who are both familiar with the arts and will be gracefully honest. In the end, it is the choreographer who makes the final decisions. Nevertheless, continual feedback keeps the intent and selected movement focused.

One thing that the choreographer needs to be sensitive to is the amount and kind of training the dancers have had. It is possible to choreograph for the nondancer as well as the highly trained dancer.

33. Susan Bauer, *Anger.*
Photograph by Kim J. Klose.

34. Susan Bauer, *Homecoming.* Photograph by Kim J. Klose.

The selection and arrangement of movement materials are done carefully so that both the performer and the audience will be comfortable. This may mean exploring new movement material rather than what has been considered traditional, beautiful, graceful, and inspiring. In such a case, it is useful to begin from pedestrian movement and then to move toward a comfortable range of abstraction. For example, in *Homecoming* (fig. 34), the congregational participants are asked to work with the pedestrian movements of leaning forward with arms extended in anticipation, rising and waving in excitement, falling back in disappointment, sinking in sadness, and narrowing in boredom — all possible responses to coming home. These are repeated in unison and with different timings as gestures are eliminated so that the group simply moves through the motion of advancing, rising, retreating, sinking, and narrowing. Eventually, the motion rebuilds to include gestures found in a religious context. Congregational members participating include children as young as six or seven, young people, and adults, some as young as eighty-two.

If the "priesthood" of dancers includes nondancers, then they along with the choreographer need to work on training their instrument, the body. They should be taking technique classes on a regular basis. While historical or traditional forms of technique — classical ballet, Martha Graham, José Limón, and Merce Cunningham — are important and valuable, whenever possible, this training should also include various movement theories, i.e., Rudolf Laban and Irmagard Bartenieff, or Bonnie Bainbridge Cohen. The former tend to be "form-oriented," working with an outside image. The latter tend to be "motion-oriented," working from the inside out. The movement vocabulary and all its implications need to be worked with consistently for continual growth in kinesthetic awareness and articulation. While regular exercise is a side effect of dance classes, the primary motivation is a greater understanding of the body from a kinesiological/functional perspective for safe and efficient movement, and from a creatively expressive perspective to fulfill the potential to communicate. The body is a very subtle, complex, wonderful instrument. As the primary means to communication in dance, dancers have a responsibility to learn as much as possible about their own bodies.

A willingness to explore one's own creative potential is essential. Incorporating improvisation into sessions is one avenue. Improvising with a particular focus is a good way to create new material, to find new ideas, and to build kinesthetic awareness between dancers. Trying different movement theories or genres of dance also triggers new awareness of creative potentials. This work helps break down ideas as to what "dance should look like" and builds up a basic vocabulary from inner to outer impulses. As dancers become comfortable with their own bodies, they rethink the qualitative energies that emerge from an inner core.

As dancers and choreographers work with performance dance in liturgy, they find that technical and creative work is not an occasional activity but an ongoing commitment. There is a responsibility to both the art form and the congregation/audience to present and maintain the best dance possible. This does not happen in a vacuum, but rather in continual interaction with others in one's own art form, artists in other forms, and nonartists.

The congregation also has a role in the artistic perspective. As they vicariously experience the physical expression of the dance piece, the congregation should actively experience and participate in the perception process. They should be made aware of the movement vocabulary and learn how to actively observe the dance. Congregations need to be encouraged not to look for literal meaning in every movement but to sense the overall mood or feeling that is being conveyed. The observation becomes one of overall patterns and the flow of movement rather than specific gestures. The perception of dance can be expanded if the congregation discusses their expectations or "baggage." What has been their past experience with dance? What do they prefer and why? What do they know of or about the theme? How do they personally relate to it?

The next step in the perception process is the description and/or interpretation of the dance. These steps happen simultaneously and support each other. The interpretation is the sensed mood or feeling along with ideas regarding the choreographer's intent. Description of the movement supports the interpretation. Even the most basic understanding of the movement vocabulary is useful. Interpretation/description enables a congregation to analyze the piece from the whole to the parts, and to the whole again.

Describing the parts does not destroy the piece but facilitates a fuller and richer "new" whole in the end. When the piece *Anger* is used to illustrate this part of the perception process, the congregation is asked before the dance to decide if it is about contained or released anger. Following the dance a show of hands indicates a group consensus of contained anger with attempts at releasing. The congregation is then encouraged to describe the movements that led to that interpretation. At this stage, words are often introduced, e.g., "pushing away." They are asked to describe this — hand/foot remain flexed while arm/leg is flexed and extended in a bound manner. The description may challenge the initial interpretation, point out other ones, or as indicated deepen the interpretation and experience with the dance.

Although evaluation often occurs when the audience enters the perception process, e.g., "I liked or did not like the piece," evaluation should happen with the full support of description and interpretation. Questions that aid in evaluation are: Should the piece be performed again? Was the piece coherent and did it have a logical sequence? Was the theme universal or timeless in nature or narcissistic in nature? Did the piece enhance the liturgy? Evaluation helps the choreographer, dancers, and congregation grow in understanding the art form, the role of dance in liturgy, and the values or concerns that have been expressed. Evaluation with support of description and interpretation encourages fuller participation in the artistic process and performance.

Those individuals who create and perform dances for incorporation into liturgy have a responsibility to stay attuned to the artistic aspects of dance. Learning about the art form and how the body communicates in an articulate manner is a never-ending process. It is a disservice to everyone involved not to take the artistic aspect seriously. If a church community is committed to performance dance in liturgy, the perception process — perceiving, describing, interpreting, and evaluating — needs to be presented, discussed, and used throughout. Gaining recognition for a general understanding of the artistic elements and the specific perception process are part of the practical perspective.

Practical Perspective

The interrelationship of the historical, artistic, practical, and theological perspectives toward dance in the liturgy becomes apparent. Artistically, a choreographer draws from historical steps and patterns. The practical considerations are: How to educate a congregation about dance as an art form? Where in the liturgy and in what space will dance take place? Will the music be composed or is it something already written? When does one need to start choreographing, teaching, and then rehearsing? What will the costume be like? All of these considerations affect and/or are affected by artistic decisions.

There are a variety of ways that a congregation can be exposed to dance as an art form and simultaneously provided with information toward understanding the process and responsibilities. Meeting in small groups is one of the best ways, e.g., youth groups, women's circles, committee meetings, or other small groups that the church normally divides itself into. By working with these smaller groups information can be geared toward their interests. Additionally, small groups of people are often more willing to discuss their "baggage" and expectations. Information presented to these groups should include historical aspects of dance in the Christian tradition, movement vocabulary, the creative process, and the perception process. In one meeting with a women's circle sewing quilts, the question arose as to the selection and arrangement of movement. The quilt became a metaphor for the dance as someone chose the particular pattern and colors of squares, and sewed them in a particular order or arrangement. People often see the creative process as beyond their understanding, even while obvious examples exist in their everyday lives. Although time consuming, meeting with these groups is productive and rewarding.

The personal contact that emerges from such small groups is preferable, as it is the basis for a trust relationship. The choreographer/dancer/congregation relationship is enriched by the personal sharing of stories and experiences. The choreographic process draws upon life experiences and the community plays a very important role in shaping those experiences. Reflection on those experiences is valuable for both the congregation and the choreographer/dancers.

Another way to disseminate information is through newsletters and bulletins. Articles that are informative, well researched and written, and yet personal, reach members of the congregation who need facts to understand that dance in liturgy is not just "emotional gushing." Additionally, abbreviated versions of such texts can be presented three to five minutes prior to the beginning of a service, or adapted for insertion and presentation in the liturgy prior to the dance. A congregation needs information; they are a captive audience, one usually unfamiliar with performance fine art dance. For the well-being of the congregation, the choreographer/dancers, and the dance, every opportunity for the dissemination of adequate information must be used. These presentations will also weaken the idea that dance in liturgy is condemned to being experimental or a way to attract youth. Far too often it is the minister, the youth director, and an arts committee, who think it would be a good idea to incorporate dance in liturgy. They do so without seeing the need or taking the time to build a broad congregational base of understanding and enthusiasm.

The physical place for the dance performance in the liturgy must be arranged with the key people involved, i.e., minister, music director, and lay liturgist; attention must be paid to the flow of the movement.

Processional, Scriptures, sermon, hymns, and prayers are all possibilities. Transitions into and out of danced sections of liturgy are crucial so that a flow is maintained. The dance becomes a part of liturgy rather than a special interruption within it.

The physical space needs to be carefully selected. A choice of space just because it is new and unusual is not sufficient. The purpose of liturgy, the overall theme of the service, and the choreographer's intent are the primary considerations for physical space. Part of the artistic challenge is to work with existing spaces, including the aisles. Compromises are made for traveling patterns and level changes. For example, the space may not be large enough to choreograph patterns that travel a great deal; the space may not be elevated enough for the congregation to see movements at low level. Navigating steps becomes a real challenge. The acquired inherent meaning of places and objects within the space must be articulated and discussed before the choreographer's work begins. For example, some ministers will not consent to having the altar or communion table placed in a different position to provide more physical space for the dance. Choreographers and dancers must be willing and ready to adapt to a variety of spatial configurations.

Music may or may not be used for accompaniment. Silence or the spoken word can be effective and appropriate for some pieces. If music is selected, it may already be part of the liturgy such as the chanted liturgy or the hymns. Another option is to have the music commissioned by the choreographer/congregation. This is the ideal as the choreographer is free to work with movement ideas and arrangements without the constraints of previously composed music. A dialogue develops between choreographer and composer that integrates the art forms, causing each to reflect on the ideas and intent of the dance and how it is best expressed. Each artist learns of the other's materials, form, and process, and how to best articulate that in order to have a creative, constructive, and collaborative experience.

Whether the music is precomposed or commissioned, a live performance is a special experience. Working with musicians, instrumentalists, or vocalists, solo, duo, quartet, small ensemble, or choir, expands the base of active participation in and understanding of dance in liturgy. A wonderful give-and-take during the performance enhances both art forms and the experience. Depending on the ability of the musicians, different arrangements may have to be considered. The requirement of rehearsal time is a consideration in the selection of the number of people and the musical arrangement with an awareness of what will be manageable and work best. For example, choreography to Psalm 23 can be adapted to a variety of musical arrangements, and the Brother James Air is most suitable for many church choirs or small vocal ensembles.

Precomposed, taped music requires several precautions. The quality of the recorded music and the available sound system should be checked. Bad recordings or poor amplification can break the flow of both the liturgy and the dance. The music written for solo, duo, or small ensemble is more appropriate for certain spaces, the number of dancers, and the scope of the dance. In working with inexperienced dancers, the choreographer should be as sensitive about the music chosen as the movement vocabulary; both need to be manageable.

Another crucial area is costuming. The body is the dancer's instrument; costuming should allow the body its fullest visibility and articulation. A sensitive choreographer should be aware of the congregation's position on what they feel, rightly or wrongly, is appropriate or inappropriate. Any decision should be based on the artistic direction of the dance; then if need be, make a compromise. If the costumes are to be used over a long period of time, the design needs to be simple and appropriate so that accessories can be added. For women a simple cowl neck, long-gathered sleevetop, and full skirt works well, as a stole or tunic can be added. For men, a similar top with loose-fitting slacks works well by itself or with a stole or tunic. A costume that "suggests" both dance and pedestrian wear works best.

One of the more frustrating things for a choreographer is to be asked to choreograph for a service that is only two weeks away. For some choreographers/dancers, this may be a possibility. What the request generally indicates is a lack of awareness on the part of the congregation of how much time is needed to create, teach, and rehearse a piece. Many dances tend to be first drafts that would have benefited from more time. The choreographer needs to be consulted early enough so that a reasonable time frame and rehearsal schedule can be established. Pieces generally do not come easily; material set for certain dancers may not work and then has to be reworked, while the reflective process requires time. There needs to be sufficient time for the give-and-take between choreograph and dancers. The dancers may also be asked by the choreographer to be a part of the recreative process. While collaborative endeavors may generate ideas, it works best for one person to make the final decisions.

Everyone involved in the piece must be aware of and committed to the time frame and schedule. It is difficult to create and teach a piece when dancers are missing; this is unfair to all involved. Rehearsals are the time when "the whole" becomes a reality and the dancers become comfortable with the movement and space. Discomfort and lack of confidence communicate quickly and easily to a congregation.

Theological Perspective

The last perspective to be considered is the theological one. How does dance in liturgy communicate a community's faith and concerns? How does the dance embody a theology? A particular understanding of God and the incarnation will be reflected in the dance piece; this holds true for the way in which worship, community, and performance are understood. As these particular concepts are reflected in the dance, the choreographers, dancers, and congregation are physically expressing, reaffirming, and at times, challenging their individual and collective faith. My analysis will center on an understanding of the dancer's instrument — the body — and worship.

If dance in liturgy is to have a significant and meaningful role, the affective-physical dimension as a means of expression and affirmation of faith must be fully understood. We both know and communicate through the physical dimension of the body. In Western Christianity, the rational mind has been emphasized at the expense of how we know through the body. There is a body knowledge or kinesthetic intelligence that facilitates an understanding of our world and relationships with people. The vitality and more fully informed perceptions that result from a unity of body and mind need to be recognized. Dance, through a heightened sensitivity to functional and expressive movement, can enable congregations to attune themselves to the body by accepting and affirming the physical.

An understanding of God and incarnation is reflected in the expressiveness of the physical dimension. God is often seen as directing life from above, and the focus becomes one of "upness" or "out-there-ness." This perception results in the overuse of the upraised arms, choir robe costuming, and a light use of energy, thereby denying the body as a primary means of expression. When God is perceived as a creative source of being who acts in and expresses intentions through human bodily form, arms reach out to and/or touch others, costuming facilitates bodily expression, and use of energy is also strong and quick. As James B. Nelson suggested,

> [T]he body can be word itself.... the Word made flesh...Christian faith is an incarnational faith, a faith in the repeatable and continuing incarnation of God. God is uniquely known to us through human presence, and human presence is always embodied presence.[4]

We know and experience God, the creative source of being, through the unity of the body and mind.

Nonverbal communication occurs through body language. We know and communicate through the body. A great deal of time is spent studying and articulating the verbal and written forms of language, while the observation, analysis, and articulation of movement vocabulary — body movements as words and language — is almost unknown except to dancers. Choreographers create from experiences felt and known through the body and mind with body language. Choreographers enhance incarnational activity by careful selection and phrasing of movements that communicate individual and collective experiences of God and the Word as embodied in human relationships.

Dance in liturgy provides a visible and moving affirmation of a congregation's faith in the incarnation, the Word made flesh through Jesus as Christ and the ongoing incarnation in our lives. Faith in the incarnation enables congregations to fully celebrate and affirm the physical, the body as instrument. Choreographers and dancers see and understand their work in liturgy as God's intent, a way in which the unity of body-mind knowing and communicating is presented and openly affirmed by the collective.

Louis Gunnemann has called worship the "public face" of the Christian community.[5] Worship is the occasion in which the community publicly makes itself visible. A time when praise and thanksgiving are expressed, worship is also a "building-up" of community by sharing experiences and strengthening the sense of mission.[6] The idea of community praising and building, as a primary focus of worship, is reflected in dance. The overuse of circles closes off community building and creates private experiences for the dancers. Upraised arms express praise that needs to be balanced with outstretched, community-inclusive arm gestures and eye focus. Faith issues expressed in dance must share the challenges as well as the joys to strengthen a congregation's mission. Dance in liturgy becomes a meaningful body-mind experience for the entire community, not just the youth or those involved in "experimental" worship. As a congregation becomes more attuned to their own physical being and more knowledgeable about dance, the heightened kinesthetic, vicarious experience of dance in liturgy builds the community through a physical affirmation of mission.

One line of the *Kyrie* in the Lutheran Liturgy is "Help, save, comfort and defend us gracious Lord." Choreographed for groups of three dancers, the *Kyrie* is performed in the aisles, facilitating a sense of community as the dancers and congregation physically affirm the comfort of God. The dancers embody the comfort of God not through raised arms but by movements toward one another. The dancer in the center, as she slowly bends to the side, is comforted by one dancer embracing her shoulders from behind, while the third dancer faces her and cradles the side of her head. With the contact maintained, the center dancer is gently brought back to an upright position. This idea of embodied comfort has been expanded so that the dancers embrace friends in the pews; hence the congregation actively participates in the physical affirmation. God's comfort is embodied by our relationship to one another; this physical action is intentional and intensified through the choreography and performance of the dancers. In the *Kyrie*, the congregation participates through the sung or spoken response, "Lord have mercy," which heightens the shared experience. A congregation could include an action with the sung response or continue to experience the physical affirmation vicariously through the dancers.

A choreographer is called to respond to all areas of community life without judging aspects of them as either secular or sacred. Dance that reflects the faith and concerns of the community will not assign different values to secular and sacred, but sees God's creative energies and intentions revealed in all of life. Dance can challenge and enable a community to reflect on all of God's creation.

Worship is important, as this is congregational praise, building-up, and reflection in a public, visible manner. Worship as the community's "public face" allows for understanding the incorporation of dance in liturgy and as a "performance." Choreographers and dancers who see dance as a gift from God fulfill that gift in the public place of worship. Their public statement is that God's intent is fulfilled with integrity. In their public performances in liturgy, dancers and choreographers make visible their call to be cocreators in the life and mission of the church.

The four perspectives, historical, artistic, practical, and theological, are so intertwined and interdependent that any framework to develop and evaluate performance fine art dance in liturgy must consider all of them. The establishment of a framework is always in process as choreographers, dancers, and congregations share and grow with reflection on the significance of the unity of body and mind as an expression of faith. This is expressed through dance, as what is embodied is raised to a conscious level for discussion, reflection, and affirmation. To know and communicate through the physical dimension enriches the perceptions of and responses to God's work in the world.

Notes

1. Conversation with Forrest Coggin, 1974.

2. E. Louis Backman, *Religious Dances in the Christian Church and in Popular Medicine* (London: Allen and Unwin, 1952).

3. Dance as a performance fine art in liturgy is not found in Jewish history.

4. James B. Nelson, *Embodiment: An Approach to Sexuality and Christian Theology* (Minneapolis: Augsburg Publishing House, 1978) 35–36.

5. Louis H. Gunnemann, "On Being Honest About Worship," *Theological Markings* (Autumn 1971) 1–2.

6. For example, see Oscar Cullmann, *Early Christian Worship* (London: SCM Press, 1956).

13

Dance, Texts, and Shrines

Judith Rock

Arepresentative for a "Christian arts organization" recently remarked that before considering the use of an art work in one of her organization's projects, she must find out about the artist's intention in making the work. She seemed to imply that what matters about art in relation to Christianity is not the work itself, but the artist's religious sincerity and moral perspective. This approach to art and religion is not uncommon. Unfortunately it reflects and perpetrates misunderstandings of both art and biblical Christianity.

The biblical narrative, the primary source of our Christian self-understanding, points in another direction. As so many wrestlers with the Christian tradition have said, the trouble with the Bible is that it can be read in support of almost any vested interest. This annoying refusal to pick one point of view, preferably our own, and stick to it, must be read as an affirmation of the diversity and richness of creation and human history, a richness in which God seems to have a vested interest. The Bible, then, in its structure and form, asks us to be attentive to events in themselves and to respond to and learn from them. Our attention is not necessarily directed toward holy or uplifting events, but toward anything that suddenly flames into a light for someone's path to God. A biblically grounded case can be made against the supremacy of intention over event as a guideline for the relationship of art (including dance) and the church.

Several biblical texts and reflections direct us to the complexity and event-fullness of creation, suggesting that questions of orthodoxy and morality are answered by living in and waiting on events themselves rather than by examining intentions. In making, choosing, and facilitating dance in the church, we will do well to orient ourselves by God's gaze, at least as that passionate attention is depicted in the biblical stories. These tell us that God is interested in people who vote with their feet, who catch the tail of the divine kite and hang on for a wild ride, who make new and startling realities out of the endless diversity of the world. As someone has said, whatever has given us the idea that God is primarily interested in recognizably religious people?

The business of the artist, including the choreographer, is to help us to see the world around us. The choreographer helps us suspend our interpretations of events so that, at least momentarily, we come closer to seeing and experiencing the events themselves. Of course, any human framing of events is itself interpretation; but the choreographer's interpretations are made to invite and startle us into fresh seeing.

Our chance for fresh seeing is reduced when we are more concerned with a choreographer's intentions or theological allegiances than with the actual dance the choreographer makes. If we examine our tendency to focus on the human maker's intention in the light of the biblical narrative, we begin to see that a dance in a religious setting is often regarded as a "text" or as a commentary on a text. Our concern for intention can be an attempt to make sure that a religious work "follows the text," whether a biblical or theological text or simply some local canon of good taste. In commissioning dance for the church, we tend to expect the "revised standard version" of some part of our tradition. One important function of dance and all the arts in the church, is to remind us of a basic fact about our primary religious texts: they routinely include more than one version of a story. Further, this often puzzling diversity of account and interpretation was recognized by those who fixed the scriptural canon as being centrally important for the health of the faith.

The Bible begins with two creation stories and continues as a rich and tangled tale in which at least three distinct narrative traditions are intertwined in a complex "dance" of event and interpretation. "Oh," Christians are tempted to say, "but that's the Old Testament." When we come to the New Testament the chorus of diverse and excited voices only gets louder. Our tradition is founded on four gospels, four different versions of one story. All four of them are "The Good

News." At every point, those who defined the Bible and canon recognized that the mystery of God and of God's self-revelation is so
complex, so endlessly full of nuance and facet, that the story can only
be told from many points of view by many voices, all talking at once!

Like all storytellers, these storytellers were interested in what happened, what is happening, and what is going to happen. Unlike some
storytellers, they were more interested in what people actually did,
than in what they meant to do or in how they felt. Significantly,
they were more often concerned with present response to God's mystery or call to justice than with virtue or morality. Moses and Judith
were murderers, Esther contracted a sexual relationship for political
purposes, Jacob was a devious character out for his own self-interest,
Paul was a ruthless fanatic who retained much of his intolerant tunnel
vision after his conversion, and even the disciples wavered between
dreams of glory and laughable foolishness. Nevertheless, all of them,
murderers and fools alike, saw God in the events around them and
risked everything for a vision of divine-human partnership. They
staked their lives on the revelatory significance of events in the created world, and on their ability to shape and call attention to those
events, however strange or disconcerting.

At the heart of this passionate commitment, however, is stamped
a surprising hallmark of biblical faithfulness: a willingness to admit
to a limited vision about God. Even Paul, who, perhaps more than
any of them, needed to be right, underwent a complete and humil-
iating change of perspective. What saves the faithful people in the
Bible from the blindness of their limited individual vision and what
can save us, is close attention to what is really happening around us.
Even Jesus' disciples seem rarely to have been right in their conclu-
sions about their leader or their own courses of action. Yet they were
almost always willing to hear and see, and to do something different
as a result of their hearing and seeing. They became models of faithfulness for us not because they were always right, but because they
never stopped altering their course whenever they got a new glimpse
of God. At the Transfiguration, when Peter, James, and John see Jesus
shining with light and talking with Elijah and Moses, the only thing
the disciples can think to do in response to this bewildering event is
to build three "tents" or shrines to mark the holy spot. When they
suggest the shrines to Jesus, however, their suggestion is ignored. Instead, a voice tells them to "Listen," and Jesus tells them not to talk
about what they have seen.[1] They do as they are told, though no doubt
with private regrets for the shrines. The gospel emphasis is on paying
attention to the event and incorporating it, in all its strangeness, into

the ongoing business of discipleship. At the Ascension, the disciples stand staring up at the sky, where they last saw Jesus.[2] It is easy to imagine that if they stood there long enough, one of them would get the idea of marking this especially holy place with a shrine. Two angels come along and ask bluntly, "Why are you standing there looking up at the sky?"[3] The disciples shake themselves out of their reverie and go back to Jerusalem.

If the twofold hallmark of discipleship is willingness to admit that our concept of response to God is always too small, and to alter our course when we see something new about God's mystery, then the artist, whose task and gift are to help us to see with new eyes, is potentially a contemporary prophet. Just as the biblical prophets startled Israel by calling her to see God's presence in something as secular as the invading Assyrian army, so the contemporary choreographer enlarges and sharpens our vision of creation — and therefore of God — by offering us work that has no religious intention or content. The Assyrian army was not concerned with the God of Israel.

Contemporary choreography can invite us simply to see and respond to the movement and relationship of bodies in space, to feel our own physical response to the movement, to enjoy the beauty and excitement the bodies and their movement create, without overlaying what we are seeing with "religious meaning" or any verbal meaning at all. A dance, regardless of its conceptual content, can call us to be momentarily quiet and receptive to reality in much the same way that contemplative prayer does. It can call us to wait, to look, to listen, so that we can receive something new, see something new, and travel to a new place.

Jesus seems to have reserved his wrath for those who were sure they had all the answers about God and religion, those who were sure they knew exclusively where to look for divine revelation and insight. As soon as a religious expert, rich man, thief, or any sinner opened up even a little to new perceptions and new behavior, he or she began to find a place in the kingdom.

Our task in recognizing, choosing, and commissioning dance in religious settings is not to decide whether the choreographer's intentions, behavior, or institutional loyalties warrant a place in the kingdom or in our particular version of it. The point is whether the *work itself* opens us to new perceptions, possibly even new behavior. If it does, our vision of the world and of other people (that vision from which we weave spirituality and theology) will then include more charity, courage, delight, humility, and humor. The point is what happens to and for us when we experience a choreographer's work. Emily Dickinson wrote that real poetry made her feel as if the top of her head were taken off. When we look at a dance, does the cold water shock of fresh vision break over us and leave us breathless? Does the beauty of line and movement and musicality pierce us to the bone? Do we laugh until we cry? Or cry until we laugh?

When John the Baptist sent messengers to ask Jesus whether he was the Messiah, Jesus did not say, "I am the Messiah because I feel very strongly about God," or "because I want everyone to believe in God," or "because I think of my work as prayer." He said:

> Go back and tell John what you have seen and heard: the blind can see, the lame can walk, the lepers are made clean, the deaf can hear, the dead are raised to life, and the Good News is preached to the poor.[4]

In other words, he directed the messengers' attention to what was happening to people as a result of his work. He did not base his identity or authority on religiously orthodox intentions, loyalties, or feelings. His authority was grounded in event: what happened to and for those who experienced what he did.

A Christian perspective on dance as a source of religious insight and understanding extends beyond the assumption that dance which is useful or appropriate in this connection will show us traditionally religious images, characters, and stories. It moves beyond the assumption that what we see is or ought to be a representation or an "acting out" of some religious event we already know about: the story of Moses, the passion of Jesus, the conversion of a sinner, and so on. Dance presents all of these things, poorly or well, but there are other complex and important patterns of relationship for dance with religious concerns.

One of these can be called catalyst imagery. A dance that works in this way can be about anything, made with any and every imaginable intention on the choreographer's part. It can be a Merce Cunningham-type abstraction, playing with allusion and non sequitur, and using a nondramatic technique and style; a passionate Martha Graham-type narrative, drawing the viewer into the cave of the human heart, to paraphrase one of Graham's own titles; or a wild and funny slice-of-kinetic-life by window-designer-turned-choreographer David Gordon. Whatever the dance's style or the choreographer's intention in this pattern of relationship between dance and religion, the relationship is discerned by the viewer. The viewer does not attribute to the choreographer intent or content that are not really present in the piece. The viewer is startled and delighted by a unique kinetic and visual image that suddenly throws a new light — its own unforeseen light — on tradition, theology, or spirituality. The choreographer has not made a "religious dance." He or she has given the viewer a new and potent kinetic image, which, set side-by-side with religious tradition, theology, or spirituality, brings something there into new and sharp focus.

An example of such a dance is Paul Taylor's *Esplanade*, which is in no sense a "religious dance." Yet its opening and closing sections, for some Christian members of the dance audience, cast a new and joyous light on the traditional verbal images of "kingdom of God," "body of Christ," and "communion of saints." The radiant physicality of the piece and the choreographic use of a group of dancers working together so deftly and with such apparent delight make the viewer long to be part of *Esplanade*'s exuberant community.

The Christian viewer may say something like, "Ah, what the theologians try to point to with their language about 'kingdom' and 'body' and 'communion' must be something like this kind of delight in and deftness of connection." This response to the dance arises in the viewer, out of his or her own interests and musings. The viewer is not "deciphering" the dance and discovering that Taylor intended a commentary on the communion of saints. He or she is making one of many possible responses to a potent, kinetic image. For the viewer who responds in this particular way, the image has nudged his or her theological thinking. A dance like *Esplanade* is a physical creation that appears in our world and reorders reality for us. Profane in the best sense of the word, it draws us "outside the temple" of our canon of religious images and renews our vision so that we can see more clearly what is in the temple as well as what is outside it.

Another pattern of relationship for dance with religious concerns is kinetic exegesis. In this case, the choreographer chooses explicitly religious material, a familiar text from the faith tradition, as a conceptual starting point for the piece. He or she then extends the material from its usual frame of reference so that the audience experiences it in a new way. The choreographer uses the nature of dance itself to reorient the text.

The best way to communicate what this approach does for our relationship with the already known text is with a dream image. I once dreamed of a familiar church building that suddenly got up on enormous feet in black slippers, and red and white striped stockings, turned itself around a few paces so that its orientation was slightly but strikingly different, and then "sat down" again. Dance as kinetic

35. Body and Soul Dance Company. *3-in-1 and 1-in-3*. Photograph by
Kingmond Young.

exegesis does just this with text: reorients it so we experience it from a completely new perspective.

3-in-1 and 1-in-3, a trio choreographed by the members of Body and Soul Dance Company, is an example of kinetic exegesis of a traditional text (fig. 35). The choreographers juxtaposed the text of the Nicene Creed, other words (both sense and nonsense), movement, and rhythmic, vocal sound so that the familiar religious text became part of a completely new communicative image. Because the audience experiences it as part of a new and startling image, the Creed takes on fresh point and meaning. The Creed becomes approachable, a text to work with and move through, because it is seen as what it is, a humanly created set of verbal images created by people trying to wrap words around a theological idea. Dance reminds the viewer that our theological formulations have to keep moving to keep up with the relational reality of the Holy. *3-in-1 and 1-in-3* ends as the three dancers land simultaneously from a jump, turn to each other and say, "I believe in one God-Maker!"

As Dorothy L. Sayers pointed out, the first image the Bible offers us for God is that of Creator.[5] The first thing it tells us about ourselves is that we are made in the image of the Creator. Therefore we too are, first and foremost, makers. None of us can ever make the ultimate image of anything. Even in our records of divine revelation, we need more than one version of the story to make sure that as much of the event as possible is communicated to future generations.

If we invite choreographers to offer as many diverse kinetic images as possible in religious settings, if we go to the theater to encounter varied kinetic perspectives, then dance will do what it does best in relation to religious concerns: it will help us to see as much reality as possible. The more we see of the reality God has made, the better theology and liturgy we will make, and the clearer our vision of God will be. Of course, being human, we will perhaps never see very clearly. However, we will do well to curb our tendency toward shrines, deciding instead to press on with the business of discipleship, always with one ear cocked for the rustle of wings, and one eye scanning the horizon for the next vision-bringing event.

Notes

1. *Good News Bible*, Matthew 17:1–13; Mark 9:2–13.
2. Ibid., Acts 1:6–11.
3. Ibid., Acts 1:10.
4. Ibid., Luke 7:22.
5. Dorothy L. Sayers, *The Mind of the Maker* (San Francisco: Harper and Row, 1968 [1941]) 22.

14

Movement as Mediator of Meaning: An Investigation of the Psychosocial and Spiritual Function of Dance in Religious Ritual

Valerie DeMarinis

This exploration of the psychological and spiritual function of dance and movement in religious rituals, liturgies, and ceremonies focuses on the participants of Macumba-Christianity in Salvador, Brazil.[1] In this grass-roots movement, dance serves as the central mediator of religious meaning for both the individual and the community.

My initial introduction to Macumba-Christianity and to the power of dance in it came through my work as a pastoral psychotherapist. In an atmosphere empathetic to cross-cultural and intercultural concerns, a woman whom we shall call Anna came to me for an initial clinical interview. In the course of our first meeting, Anna presented a series of interconnected facts about herself: her African-Brazilian heritage, her Macumba-Christian faith, her attachment to "her" people and "her" land, her interest as a college student in cross-cultural anthropology, her difficulty in the decision-making process of North American students, her sense of isolation, and her fundamental, perhaps, unshareable, secret.

A bright, likable, intense young woman, Anna was determined to be "at home" enough in the United States to do her work and survive the complexities of life and relationships. I was intrigued by her recognition of the need to share something "secret" and perhaps, not "safe." As time passed, she became confident of my trustworthiness. One day, she began the necessary process of sharing her secret with me. From her sack emerged shells, oils, candles, a crucifix, and two little statues, one male, one female. As she lit the candles, Anna arranged the items in a circle. She stepped into the circle, and began to move and to chant. With very deliberate movements, the volume of the chanting and speed of her motions increased. After five minutes, Anna stopped, knelt down in silence, took a deep breath, and moved back into a chair. Then, she freely told me about all that I had just seen and heard. This was Anna's special "secret," her inherited spiritual and cultural dance of Macumba-Christianity, which was practiced by her people whose roots were African, Brazilian, Native South American Indian, and Christian.

Anna's caution about her "secret" was rooted in earlier attempts of sharing that had resulted in ridicule and disrespect. In our relationship, however, she had come to sense a bond of trust and therefore wisely determined the propriety of sharing her secret. From that time, Macumba-Christianity and its integral use of dance and movement, became a foundational dimension for Anna's therapy. From a clinical perspective, Anna's progress and eventual creative strategies were dependent upon the entry into the therapeutic process of the dance of Macumba-Christianity. For Anna, the power of this dance consisted of communication and mediation, to translate struggle and hope into movement which then moved into meaning. My encounter with Anna resulted in a clinical and personal hunger to learn more about Macumba-Christianity and the power of dance.

Five years after my first meeting with Anna, I was able to do primary field research on Macumba-Christianity with the people of Salvador, Brazil. The assumptions and approach with which I began my exploration are important in identifying my investigative method and its parameters. As a researcher and clinician in the field of theology and psychology, examination of the nature and function of a religious belief system in the thought and daily life processes of its followers is essential. My assumption and approach in this investigation are grounded in the interest of exploring both the function of religion for psychological and spiritual health, and the function of psychological and spiritual health for religion. The various theological observances made here serve to identify the internal points of belief for Macumba-Christianity.[2]

This exploration began with an investigation of the dimensions of influence on and integration of movement and dance in intrapersonal and interpersonal communication. This topic emerged through my clinical work with persons such as Anna, whose religious and cultural expression was dependent upon the inclusion of movement and dance in the therapeutic process. Similar work within social and religious frameworks from a variety of cultural and intercultural situations had allowed for a rethinking and a reshaping of my pastoral psychotherapeutic orientation, which is built upon depth psychology, feminist theory, and pastoral theology.

Depth psychology utilizes the memories of someone's past experiences to offer clues and interpretations for approaching the complex workings of current experiences and perceptions. Feminist theory understands the therapeutic relationship to be an important relationship for building trust and for modeling adult-to-adult responsibility, while working toward an integration of mind and body. Feminist theory emerges from a base that simultaneously examines the social and personal foundations and implications of issues. Pastoral theology begins with an understanding that spiritual concerns are important for effective therapy in exposing areas of psychological pathology and as a vital resource for constructing and reconstructing ways of understanding and approaching reality. My therapeutic orientation saw that Macumba-Christianity provided a rich religious faith system and culture for the study of the meaning and function of religious dance.

The history of Macumba-Christianity began in the 1500s when people from the West African Portuguese colonies were brought to Brazil to work as plantation slaves for the Portuguese colonists. As a result of this enforced immigration, families were divided as tribal members and scattered with the intention of making communication and traditional bonding patterns impossible. Names were changed, surface identities stripped, and individuals forced to convert to Christianity, most especially to the Portuguese form of Roman Catholicism.[3]

These African men, women, and children, coming from the Yoruba tradition, culture, and spirituality, understood exactly what horrors were being done to them. The Portuguese colonists did not realize the resources, creativity, and perseverance the Yoruba people brought with them. Their culture and ritual, steeped in music, rhythm, and dance, provided a way for these slaves to keep alive their tradition, to communicate with one another, and to maintain hope in the midst of terror.

Much of the communication took place through forms of movement and dance. These combined with religious ceremonies in which the dance evolved and through which a system of communications developed. Each small group or community worked to develop its own system of communication and particular dance patterns or rituals. The tradition was preserved and passed on through oral communication. Therefore, each group or individual community developed dance and ritual patterns particular to itself, but emerging from the Yoruban tradition.

For some Africans, the Yoruban traditions were preserved with the Christian influence as only a surface symbol system. As one Macumba priestess stated, "the Christian symbols were forced upon us, and so we used them as the top layer, but underneath we were worshipping the gods of Yoruba. It was only a kind of surface Christianity."[4] Other groups sought intentionally to allow Yoruban Macumba and Roman Catholicism to encounter each other. A Macumba-Christian priestess noted that

> Our Yoruban tradition of Macumba is deep and wise. We believe it is better to do what you have to do to stay alive than become a martyr for the next world. This world and life is our focus. So, some Macumba believers felt that the gods of Yoruba, the *orixás*, were telling them to let Christianity and Macumba meet, not get mixed together, but meet.[5]

Macumba-Christianity arose as the culture and religion of the Macumba practices and beliefs began to dialogue with Christianity's beliefs and practices. As a Macumba-Christian priest indicated:

> This is not a simple syncretistic tradition as it has been described. My fathers and mothers let the traditions speak to each other and both Macumba and Christianity became stronger. The Catholic or Protestant structure may or may not recognize this, but the people of Salvador know the wisdom here.[6]

Thus, several dimensions of this culture and religion need to be kept in focus for this exploration of the central role and function of dance in contemporary Macumba-Christianity. First, culture and religion are so intertwined for Afro-Brazilian people that any approach which is premised on their separation inevitably leads to a misunderstanding. Second, the tradition of small group and community gatherings remains the structural model for Macumba-Christians. Oral tradition is the normative form leading to great varieties of expression in the cultural and religious ceremonies, and in dance forms. Third, many Salvadorans who identify themselves as Macumba-Christians also attend Roman Catholic mass or other Christian worship services as a separate activity.[7]

Fourth, the theological focus of Macumba-Christianity is on this world and not on the hereafter. Energy and resources are directed toward the improvement of life in this world. There is no dichotomy between body and soul or spirit and flesh.[8] Fifth, the community is essential to the individual and the individual to the community. Sacred ritual times are communal events during which the community works through problems and invites the wisdom of the gods, spirits, and saints — Macumban and Christian — on behalf of individual persons and the community.[9] Sixth, the relationship between the people and the gods is distinct but interdependent. The gods, the *orixás*, are invited into the gatherings and their wisdom is sought to benefit the people. Specially initiated members of the community function as mediums, who act within the community to translate the message of the particular god or spirit to those seeking assistance. On the other hand, the gods and spirits rejoice in the role of helper and in the community's effort to work through its problems.

In Macumba-Christianity, there are two kinds of sacred rituals, religious rituals and spiritual rituals. The former occur in the *terreiro*, a special place of meeting, while the latter are not site specific. The religious rituals tend to follow a more specific, repetitive pattern. The spiritual rituals tend to be more spontaneous. Central to this community-based culture and religion, both styles of sacred rituals employ movement and dance as the critical means for centering energies for either the individual or the gathered group. However, the spiritual rituals use movements and dances different from the religious ones.

The spiritual rituals use movements that do *not* have as their intention the calling of the gods, but rather, the spiritual energy of the gathered community. Religious rituals, however, use movements that call upon the gods to enter the community for specific purposes. For example, a ritual gathering to celebrate the birth of a child or to mark a celebration in the community would not include movements or dances to summon the presence of the gods. Nevertheless, the gods are believed to be present more as spectators than as invited participants, whose spirits stand on the outer edge of the gathered circle. A ritual gathering to address a community problem or problem for individual persons within the community (e.g., spouse abuse, loss of job, death), would employ movements and dances that invite the gods' attendance through the initiated mediums, so that divine wisdom comes to the people who are requesting it.

Religious rituals are for preventive care or for problem-solving; spiritual rituals are for celebrations and for social occasions. However, both are sacred for Macumba-Christians, since they serve to center spiritual energy and to organize meaning. Not necessarily religious in this context, the sacred is equated with that process and experience whereby energy is brought to focus on meaning and action.

From the outset of the religious ritual gatherings, there is physical (bodily) movement. The gathering community moves into a seated circle around the border of the *terreiro*. All rise as one, bringing the circle closer together. If the gathering place is small, several circles form and people are free to move in and out of them. The drum is beaten constantly, as the individuals close their eyes and seek to move to the drum-rhythm or in time with clapping. Opening their eyes, individuals settle into a regular but distinct pattern of movement. Despite these varied patterns, the assembly appears to blend into a common motion. As the movement continues, the circle moves around the room in occasional unison.

In spiritual rituals, members of the community will move either into the center or to the periphery of the circle to initiate a dance of a particular god. This is not a call to that god, but a community acknowledgement of the god's assistance. Each of the gods, the *orixás*, has different dances for spiritual rituals and religious rituals. Whenever an individual person within the circle either feels intense energy or the need, he or she stops the movement or dance and stands apart from the circle. Then the individual's eyes are closed in an attempt to recenter their energy, or, if necessary, other community members may assist that individual.

In religious rituals, a similar pattern of movement is followed. Special dances are performed by the initiated mediums to call to and invite the gods to come upon them. When these dances are held, the community waits with an electric measure of energy; the god's arrival may come upon the initiated medium in any number of ways. For example, the medium may begin to dance at a frantic pace or to shake violently. At other times, she or he may fall to the ground and appear to be in a mild or intermediate state of convulsion. A third possibility is the medium's alternating between swift movements and absolute stillness.

Once the particular god has come upon the medium, he or she then moves around the circle to communicate the divine messages face to face to the individual members of the community by offering a special touch, specific words or greetings, silent greetings, invitation to join in a special dance, or any combination of these. Even though the medium called forth a particular god or goddess to benefit an individual's problem or a specific need, the medium communicates with each and every member of the assembled community. After these individual visits, the medium takes leave of the god or goddess through the group activity of dancing back into the community. The assembled members act as the physical perimeters of containment for the medium and for the power of the divine energy. The community needs the medium and the medium needs the community.

After the medium returns to the present reality state, the community remains in its circle to talk, sing, dance, and work through the meaning, nature, and implications of the god's messages of wisdom. The formation of the circle is significant as a literal and symbolic form of containment. Though there is continual activity and movement, there is also a tangible sense of positive control and centering. Individual members of the gathered circle are encouraged to put their internal questions and concerns "into" the center of the circle — to let them "dance" there for the community to move around. At the end of the ritual, each person comes to rest in a particular place. With eyes closed, each individual takes back their energy and the now newly energized questions and/or concerns that were put into the center of the circle.

When the ritual is finished, the community remains gathered for a ceremonial meal or drink together. The mediums move around the room and persons talk with them about the meanings of the god's words or message. The medium also learns what the people have observed, so that a reconstruction and remembrance of the time in the trance state can occur.

One final use of movement and dance needs to be noted. This function is performed by the priestess or priest of the local *terreiro* with the initiated mediums to ascertain whether or not that medium is "free enough of problems so that the energy can be used to bring the god and not lose the person."[10] Unlike other forms of religious trance, these Macumba-Christian mediums do not totally lose or empty themselves of their individual identities. The desired state is that of allowing enough room for the god with the ego-self so that the medium may communicate to others on behalf of the god. The dance between the priestess or priest and the medium helps to determine the medium's appropriateness to call upon the god at the time.

Psychological and Spiritual Function of Movement and Dance as Mediator of Meaning

A psychological and spiritual analysis of the functions of movement and dance in the sacred rituals of Macumba-Christianity begins with the oft-repeated description of participants that "Dance for us is not a performance but a presence."[11] In these sacred rituals, movement and dance do not signify a spectator event but a participatory individual and communal event.

Seven dimensions of dance as a mediator of and for meaning emerge from the sacred rituals of Macumba-Christianity. Functioning in unison, the interrelationship of these dimensions is such that when and where there is an alteration in one, the others need to be reexamined for responsorial changes. These dimensions are: intrapersonal, psychological centering and spiritual balancing; interpersonal, social centering and spiritual balancing; releasing and containing of physical and spiritual energy; focusing of community social energy; mediating of powers inside and outside of self; bridging energies of gender, age, and class; and, caring at both the preventative and primary levels.

From my first experience with Anna and throughout my experiences in Salvador, it was obvious that movement and dance were used by the individual person for intrapersonal, psychological centering and spiritual balancing. As Anna indicated, movement serves "as a bridge, bringing together body and soul, inside and outside thoughts, and all of the energies."[12] Whether it is impromptu, freeform, or stylized movement from a learned dance of one of the gods, the power of dance to concentrate the individual's focus and strength is obvious. As the Macumba-Christian priest Ezeckiel noted, "Our dancing can both relax and make tense, that is its power. The person needs both calmness and excitement, and the dance is a way for this state to come."[13]

Dance movement is designed to focus the individual's energy to arrive at this balance. During both religious and spiritual rituals, once individuals felt overcome by the excitement of the dance itself, or by an excitement created internally, that person would stop dancing and remain still. Only when in spiritual balance would that individual resume the dance.

Dancing in the circles of the spiritual and religious rituals brings the individual members of the community into an interpersonal centering and spiritual balancing. There is a dual centering of the individual intrapersonally and interpersonally within the circle of dance. Particular dimensions of the dance, such as each person's movements of extending and throwing "problems and concerns" into the circle's center, and reaching for "helping energy" reveal the critical link between an individual's centering process and that of the assembled community. The gathered circle serves as both a literal and symbolic means of containment, a perimeter within which it is safe to move and to risk the sharing process responsibly.

These centering processes through movement and dance are built upon an understanding and appreciation of human psychological, spiritual, and physical energy. A Macumba-Christian priestess defined the approach to energy as it has been handed down to her through her family and community.

> Energy is not what you can see but what you can feel and what works in and around people. It is not magic nor can it be made to change by some outside god or spirit. It is the power and motion that is inside a person and that also combines with the power inside other people too. There is no magic at work here, only a true understanding of how people are.[14]

This is a physical and metaphysical philosophy for understanding human nature and interaction. Energy is simultaneously intrapersonal and interpersonal. As with other aspects of Macumba-Christianity, there needs to be a balance between things. In this instance, there needs to be a balance between the process of releasing and of containing energy. Since nothing is judged in and of itself but always in relationship, energy is neither "good" nor "bad." Rather, a problem exists when an interruption of movement or one's inability to release or contain energy occurs.[15]

In the ritual circle, the movement of dance is an enactment of the intrapsychic process and the communal activity of releasing and containing energy. Such a process permits each individual member of the community to move within and outside of the circle, to find the best way to balance the complex life process.

The physical and metaphysical understanding of energy as a balancing of the life force is clearly symbolized in the community by the circle dance. This movement progresses through six steps in the energy focusing process. First, the dance brings each individual into focus with her or himself. This focus is necessary for the individual to be present as part of the community. Second, this newly focused energy of the individual members is concentrated within the circle of the community.

Third, the community is informed of the special needs, concerns, problems, or issues of those present or their representatives as brought to the attention of the gathered group. Using special movements to focus their energy, the community concentrates its movements and stillness to create an atmosphere appropriate to summon the gods, and/or to harness the spirit of those gathered to bring wisdom to address the concerns.

Fourth, once the gods are called, the initiated mediums perform a special dance to summon the energy of the particular god or gods. Meanwhile, the rest of the community focuses its energy on movement designed to facilitate the arrival of the god's energy. Safe arrival will not overpower the medium, but will be powerful enough to bring insight and wisdom. The community then works with the medium to translate energy and wisdom into action.

Fifth, the arrival of the god's energy results in the formation of a communal circle including within it those who acted as mediums. In this final movement, the community begins the process of moving from ideas to address the announced problems, concerns, issues, and needs. Sixth, before leaving the circle, each person moves to refocus their individual energy. In this process, there is an assurance that the community's energy will remain within each individual to help with any new issues that may arise prior to the next gathering.[16]

The multidimensional quality of movement and dance used during both the religious and spiritual ritual gatherings reflects the Macumba-Christian understanding of the nature and function of energy and power. Simultaneously, the physical and metaphysical definition of human nature informs its philosophy and theology. Power is critical to understanding the nature of the gods and human beings. The gods, including Jesus as the Christ, are understood to be sources of energy and power. Neither expecting nor accepting sacrifices, these gods desire to assist human beings who learn to use energy in focusing power to solve problems in a nonviolent manner. The body, earth, and nature work in unison with the world — the realms of the spirits and the soul. The gods join with human beings in focusing energy on the common interest of understanding the importance of life on earth. Life is a gift from the gods to be appreciated and respected.

The understanding of power and energy in Macumba-Christian philosophy and theology is distinct from the power structure prevalent in Brazilian society. The nature and position of women and children in Macumba-Christianity are also separate from that of the society at large. In Macumba-Christianity, as well as other Afro-Brazilian-derived cultures and religions, women play a central role of leadership at every level and stage of organization.[17] Women compose the majority of initiated mediums and leaders of local *terreiros*. This exists in marked contrast to the invisibility of women in societal and economic decision-making positions in the general culture, where, at its worst, women are treated as little more than the property of their fathers or husbands.

Children, who have little or no voice in the larger society, have a special role in Macumba-Christianity. All are welcomed to attend the rituals and be a part of the community; there are no age restrictions. During ritual gatherings, young children wander freely in and out of the circle, as they learn the process of energy-focusing. In the midst of considerable movement and activity, the children feel at home. One can observe their natural orientation to experiment with dance and to become a part of the gathered.

Observance of women and children in ritual gatherings resulted in a recognition that their cries and problems regularly voiced situations of physical and/or emotional abuse in their families or communities. The ritual circle allowed them a special freedom which their home life did not. One middle-aged woman expressed this frustrating and terrifying reality, "I pray for the strength to face the struggle to keep hoping when I leave this safe *terreiro*."[18]

The movement and dance during the ritual gatherings reflect both the emotional and physical power of the hope and the anguish of the Salvadoran people. Despite a popular movement of Macumba among members of Brazilian society not of Afro-Brazilian heritage, the center of Macumba and of Macumba-Christianity remains the Bahia state, home to the original African slaves and their descendants. One of the poorest areas of Brazil, this state struggles to address the problems of poverty, illiteracy, and impotence in the country's economic and governmental structures.

In recent years, the Macumba-Christian community within Salvador has attempted to use its gathered energies for nonviolent change. Efforts have been made to address the poverty of the children of Salvador, including the poor or nonexistent educational systems, and to address the secondary status and role of women. Special ritual gatherings have been organized among varied Afro-Brazilian groups to mobilize energy and power. The ritual movements and dances have played a critical role to call upon the wisdom of the gods and to work toward strategies of action. Violence is supported only as a last resort or for self-defense. Macumba-Christianity is responsible for many projects and networks that will insure the physical, psychological, and spiritual survival of the children — the survival of the Afro-Brazilian people and cultures.

Movement and dance are an integral part of Afro-Brazilian life as it bridges energies of gender, age, and class. Walking through the streets of Salvador, one hears music and drumming everywhere in the large city. Throughout the spiritual and religious rituals, dancing is an essential element, for "dancing is presence."[19] This is the medium through which and by which energy is focused and power is gathered. Dancing serves to make the senses, the intellect, the body, and the soul present at that moment and focused on the issues at hand. Dance as presence goes beyond the ritual gatherings as it has emerged from the daily traditions the original Africans brought to Brazil. Dance is popular, secular, and religious; the same forms are used and adapted to meet the needs of the particular nature of the gathering. Movements and dances to summon the gods differ from one religious gathering to another, reflecting the distinguishing characteristics of each community as passed on through tradition.

Spiritual and religious rituals bring together persons of all ages, genders, and classes. Children may be invited into the rituals, although those under the age of seven are restricted from certain ceremonies. As communities are usually formed within neighborhoods, it is common to see children, parents, and grandparents gathered together. As in North American cultures so too in Brazil, grandparents maintain a close and observable link with their grandchildren. For example, in two ritual gatherings, I observed that when a child wanted to leave the ritual circle, she went to a grandparent to escort her from the circle.

Throughout the life cycle, the centrality of dance is understood and incorporated into daily existence. Although not specifically taught, there are dance forms learned by boys and by girls as part of the tradition. The necessity for understanding the nature and function of dance as a key to human survival for focusing energy and power is instinctive to and intuited by children. This fascination with movement and dance is encouraged and incorporated throughout the stages of the life cycle.

The meaning and purpose of movement and dance in Macumba-Christianity continue to be directed to human survival — preventative and primary care. Preventative care anticipates needs; primary care addresses existing problems or concerns. The medical interpretation of these different functions of care is helpful as illustration. Preventative care would involve giving children a vaccine so that their systems would be able to produce antibodies to resist a given disease. Primary care would involve attending to the nonvaccinated children who have been stricken with the disease.

A considerable parallel between the medical functions of preventative and primary care and the psychosocial and spiritual functions of dance in Macumba-Christianity can be drawn. Dance as presence focuses on preventative and primary care. From its Yoruban roots and from the cultural and religious traditions begun by the African people in Brazil, dance has been essential for survival. The idea of survival is a sophisticated one, incorporating preventative and primary care. Survival means having the wisdom to understand the difference between primary and preventative care, and developing a strategy to assess the needs of a particular situation. As the Macumban-Christian priestess explained:

> Surviving is a knowing and a thinking ahead.... There are the things like food and home and protection, but it is deeper than that. Surviving means feeling inside the way of energy and using that way to understand things, to work ahead.... In our ritual circle we bring energy to look ahead and to look at the present. In our dance and energy we always ask the question, "What do we need to take place for there to be a future here?" This is the question for surviving looking at today and yesterday but for the sake of there being a day to come.[20]

Preventative and primary functions are at work in ritual dance. These are the movements that bring the individual members of the community into spiritual focus, ready to address what is coming and anticipating the required energy necessary. These movements are simultaneously preventative and primary in function — they both anticipate and address the needs at hand. The dance that summons the gods combines these elements as particular needs are recognized (a primary care function), while the will and desire to call upon the gods for the energy to address these needs is a preventative orientation.

The philosophical and theological underpinnings of Macumba-Christianity provide the foundation for this orientation toward preventative and primary care; for example, the value and nature of human life, the desire for body and soul to work in cooperation, and the positive evaluation of nature and the physical life that allow a holistic structure for and approach to life experiences. The points of conjunction between the physical and the metaphysical; the nature and function of community; and the approach to energy and power are particular dimensions of approach that allow the inseparability of religion and culture. Sustained by the medium of dance, the literal and symbolic representations of preventative and primary caring for life itself are integral aspects of Macumba-Christianity.

Therapeutic Principles for Understanding the Place of Movement in Pastoral and General Psychotherapy

My encounter with Anna and my experiences in Salvador revealed new areas for research and clinical thinking about the nature of movement in therapy and in a philosophy of the therapeutic. Six themes have emerged from my research: clinical sensitivity and responsibility to understand cultures and religions in which movement and dance are central; attention to designing a safe therapeutic environment; appreciation of the power of movement and dance for focusing internal energy; incorporation of ritual movements as a way to access belief systems; attention to bringing body and soul into a working dialogue; and, understanding of the importance of community in individual and familial therapy.

In a cross-cultural context, a clinician or researcher needs to develop special clinical and diagnostic sensitivity and responsibility to understand cultures and religions in which movement and dance are central. In such situations, the therapeutic context must find a way to welcome and invite movement and dance as irreplaceable resources. The therapist needs to find a comfortable way to access and assess the movement dimension as part of the client's history and the person's present and future development.[21]

Concerns of safety and containment in the therapeutic process have emerged as critically important from my own experiences. When movement or dance is brought into the therapeutic setting, a greater vulnerability results, and new areas of memory and energy that need careful containment are opened. Attention to designing a safe and therapeutic environment (for both therapist and client) is crucial. A safe context is required that can serve as a containment for the experience and energy that such movement is meant to generate. Religious and/or spiritual movement and dance will tap a complicated and complex energy core, thus testing the safety of the therapeutic environment. A critical dimension of safety is the flexibility necessary to name, examine, and approach the roots of the complexity and its ensuing multivalent issues.

My experiences with Macumba-Christianity have been intentionally cross-cultural, an opportunity to share across cultures and for learning to be exchanged. As a result, I have come to appreciate in a new way the power of movement and dance for focusing and directing energy. The need for this kind of focusing to become part of the therapeutic setting is essential. The nature of movement accomplishes this by bringing, literally and symbolically, mental and physical energies together. As I have worked with other clients to create strategies to focus energy, some kind of movement usually has resulted. In several cases, this has been a first-time experience or experiment with movement, an intentional effort to bring body and mind into a cooperative mission. It is one thing to talk about the need for the integration of mind, body, and soul. It is quite another to witness the integrating process as the energies of each come together in movement.

The power of movement to invite, nurture, and necessitate the inclusion of religious practice and influence into the therapeutic process has been impressive. Using either ritual movements from a person's past or working to create a movement pattern that expresses different stages of belief can provide access into belief structures and patterns, and a means for researching the formation of new beliefs. Movement can provide clues for approach and access to vital information that may otherwise be inaccessible or only partly accessible.

The performance itself and the shared memory of this movement provide a therapeutic resource that cannot be duplicated. They provide concrete access to a person's way of approaching reality and assigning meaning. Movement can signal the presence of different belief systems coexisting within an individual, and highlight the tensions of this present reality.[22]

Accessing and assessing the presence of different, perhaps, conflicting belief systems for an individual is of concern to clinicians and researchers in pastoral counseling, care, and psychotherapy. Therapists need to investigate the ways in which movement might serve to access an individual's or group's religious and/or spiritual approach, and to facilitate bringing body and soul into a working dialogue. This is important in the reconstructive aspects of the therapeutic relationship for those therapists and clients who come from belief systems where body and soul have been separated and dichotomized. Movement can enact the underlying religious dimensions of the separation, and the possibility for integration — the need for a reframing of religious dimensions.

The patterns of movement emerging from Macumba-Christianity emphasize the importance of community as the way one conceptualizes the nature and understands the behavior of human beings. The emphasis on the community's defining role and function for its individual members is important for effective therapy. Movement can be used to bring forth interpretations of past communities, including

their understandings of negative and positive conceptions of relationships. Movement can also assist in designing the characteristics
of relating and relationship necessary for the interdependence and
growth of individuals. This offers a unique resource for enactment of
the past and projection of future actions. The therapeutic context is
a "world" that must be able to connect with the communities from
which an individual has come and into which the individual is going.
It provides a relational situation in which one can "move through"
different understandings of community and relationship.

Is there a relationship between the nature and function of movement and dance from the pastoral and general psychotherapeutic
standpoint and the nature and function of American liturgical dance?
The relationship seems an important one worthy of future investigation. At the present, however, three dimensions of American liturgical
dance present an already established basis for hypothesizing about
this relationship. First, liturgical dance attempts to bring a wholistic
approach to liturgy — the uniting of body and soul in the expression of faith. Second, liturgical dance involves, at least at some level,
both individual and community; therefore, it recognizes and needs
the social and corporate dimension of participation for its context
of meaning-making activity. Third, liturgical dance, engaged in during communal worship, serves as a preventative care activity for both
body and soul, individual and community, for spiritual, personal, and
social healing and strengthening through faith. If these dimensions
of American liturgical dance are understood and nurtured, the relationship between liturgical dance and the use of religious dance and
movement in pastoral care and counseling would be a working pastoral partnership for preventative and primary caring throughout the
life cycle of faith.

Notes

Special thanks and appreciation to the people of Salvador, Brazil; the Rev-
erend Gerusa Sanil dos Santos, interpreter; Dr. Lyn Cowan, cotraveller,
photographer, and Jungian analyst; and the American Academy of Religion
for a research grant that made this project possible.

1. In Salvador, Brazil, there are different names used with variations of
meaning to refer to the African-rooted belief systems. The most common are
Macumba and Candomble. Macumba is usually associated with the area of
Rio de Janeiro and Candomble with Bahia. The group I was researching,
however, though based in Bahia, incorporated more of the Macumba rituals
and thus maintained the term Macumba to be coupled with Christian.

2. I am not functioning here as a Christian critical theologian. Therefore, there are no theological judgments about the inclusion and function of Christian theology in the Macumba-Christian religion. Rather, exclusion of such judgment was appropriate for the nature of this investigation. Likewise, I am not functioning here as a history of religion investigator. Therefore, the observations made emerge from the present-day understandings of religion and culture from the Macumba-Christian community members. These "living human documents" share perspectives not necessarily found in the texts of Western researchers.

3. There are several resources that provide useful background information on the religious and cultural dimensions of Brazil. See especially, Roger Bastidde, *The African Religions of Brazil: Toward a Sociology of the Interpenetration of Civilizations* (Baltimore: Johns Hopkins University Press, 1978); Fred G. Strum, "Afro-Brazilian Cults," in *African Religions: A Symposium,* ed. Newell Booth (New York: N.O.K. Publishers International, 1977); Lawrence E. Sullivan, *Icanchu's Drum: An Orientation to Meaning in South American Religions* (New York: Macmillan Publishing Company, 1988); and, Pierre F. Verger, *Orixás: Deuses Iorubas na Africa e No Novo Mundo* (São Paulo, Brazil: Editora Corrupio Comercio Litda, 1981).

4. From field interview with a thirty-three-year-old woman, a Macumba priestess.

5. From a field interview with a thirty-five-year-old woman, a priestess of Macumba-Christianity.

6. There is considerable tension among Christian churches in Brazil, Roman Catholic, Protestant, and the Macumba-Christian groups.

7. In a field interview, one man explained,

> We do not see it as going against Salvadoran belief. The Church may have a problem with this, but we Afro-Brazilians do not. Going to church gatherings or mass is not the Christian part of being Macumba-Christian, it is a different past.

8. In a field interview with a thirty-five-year-old Macumba-Christian priestess, she remarked, "The body and spirit must work together to give us wisdom and for us to work together to settle things."

9. In a field interview of an eighty-eight-year-old participant in a Macumba-Christian community, he said, "When I come here I can get more calm and think better than when I am off alone. The people are all separate and the movement brings us together."

10. From a field interview with a female medium, age fifty-seven, member of a Macumba-Christian community.

11. Ibid.

12. Used by permission from a therapeutic session with client Anna.

13. From a field interview with seventy-eight-year-old Ezeckiel, priest in a Macumba-Christian community. He asked to be identified by name in any publication on this field research.

14. From a field interview with a thirty-five-year-old priestess of Macumba-Christianity.

15. In a field interview, the priestess offered an explanation of this containing and releasing process:

> Moving is the key to understanding how life is. Things, especially things like
> thoughts, concerns, dreams, problems, need to be moving in and out of us. We
> need to know how or learn how to balance between a holding on and a letting
> go. There is stillness also in movement and there is movement also in stillness.

16. Normally, these gatherings are held on a weekly basis.

17. For an understanding of the position of women in Afro-Brazilian re-
ligion and culture, see especially Carole A. Myscofski, "Women's Religious
Role in Brazil: A History of Limitations," *Journal of Feminist Studies in
Religion* 1.2 (1985) 43–57; and, idem., "Women's Initiation Rites in Afro-
Brazilian Religions: A Structural Source Analysis," *Journal of Ritual Studies*
2.1 (1988) 101–18.

18. From a field interview with a Macumba-Christian participant, age fifty-
nine.

19. Words echoed by many in Salvador to describe the function of both
dance and drum.

20. From a field interview with a thirty-five-year-old woman, a priestess of
Macumba-Christianity.

21. Important resources for exploring the use of movement and dance in
therapy are Elaine and Bernard Feder, *The Expressive Arts Therapy* (Engle-
wood Cliffs: Prentice-Hall, Inc., 1981); Hans Kreitler and Shulamith Kreitler,
Psychology of the Arts (Durham: Duke University Press, 1972); Arthur Rob-
bins, *Expressive Therapy: A Creative Arts Approach to Depth-Oriented Treatment* (New York: Human Sciences Press, 1980); and, Audrey G. Wethered,
*Drama and Movement in Therapy: The Therapeutic Use of Movement, Drama
and Music* (London: MacDonald and Evans Ltd., 1973).

22. Important resources for investigating the nature and function of ritual,
and the role of ritual in religion include Anthony J. Blasi, "Ritual as a Form
of the Religious Mentality," *Sociological Analysis* 46 (1985) 59–71; Ronald
L. Grimes, "Sources for the Study of Ritual," *Religious Studies Review* 10.2
(1984) 134–45; Arthur Kleinman, *Patients and Healers in the Context of
Culture* (Berkeley: University of California Press, 1980); August G. Lager-
man, "Myths, Metaphors, and Mentors," *Journal of Religion and Health* 25.1
(1986) 58–63; Ninian Smart, *Worldviews* (New York: Charles Scribner's Sons,
1983); and, Charles E. Winquist, "Theology, Deconstruction, and Ritual Process," *Zygon: Journal of Religion and Science* 18.3 (1983) 295–309.

PART IV
Bibliography

15

Sources for the Study of Dance and Judaism and Christianity

Doug Adams

$\mathbf{T}$o relate dance and religion, religious studies first focused on passages in biblical and historical sources that explicitly included words for dance. Recent critical scholarly methods allow distinction between actual dance and metaphorical uses of the word *dance* in those passages and perception of a wider range of dance forms even in other passages where the words for dance are not mentioned. Similarly, dance studies first focused on choreographies that were based on biblical or religious subject matter. Contemporary attention to dance form aids us in discerning the religious dimension in a wider range of choreographies that contain no biblical or religious subject matter. This discernment also allows us to question whether a choreography is religious even when it is based on a biblical or religious subject.

Attention to the wider context of the biblical or historical text or dance is important in assessing its religious and choreographic dimensions. Often taken out of context, many texts and dances are cited as arguments for or against dance in contemporary religious practice. A similar redaction of the material is evident in the primary biblical and historical sources and results in a wide range of interpretations. Often the original context of the material has been partially or wholly lost so that no definitive interpretation is likely. Assessment becomes more complex as historical church restrictions or negative comments on liturgical dance are interpreted as witnessing to the presence of liturgical dance or its demise. A series of restrictions may witness to a persistence of the dance despite the negative comments. The lack of any comment on dance may be attributed to either the absence of the dance or its prevalence. A customary feature of worship does not occasion comment. While several of the following studies disagree on method and interpretation, each remains a source for glimpsing the different dimensions of dance as religious studies.

Earlier twentieth century religious studies traced the derivations of the varied biblical terms for dance and attempted to see in each term (or cluster of terms) a different dance form and purpose. The best of these attempts in the order of their publication were Julian Morgenstern, "The Etymological History of the Three Hebrew Synonyms for 'To Dance' " (*American Oriental Society Journal* 36 [1916] 328–46); W. O. E. Oesterley, *The Sacred Dance* (Cambridge University Press, 1923); and Dvora Lapson, "Dance" *The Universal Jewish Encyclopedia* (Jewish Encyclopedia Co., 1941) III, 455–63. Subsequent studies have given attention to the larger contexts of those terms to reveal additional nuances. Investigations into the Sumero-Accadian milieu alter Oesterley's evaluations of the continuity and distinctiveness of Hebraic dances: Alfred Haldar, *Association of Cult Prophets Among the Ancient Semites* (Almquist and Wiksells, 1945). In two studies, Mayer I. Gruber differentiates between actual dance and metaphorical use of "dance" by noting other physical acts in conjunction with the former and abstract expressions with the latter: *Aspects of Nonverbal Communication in the Ancient Near East* (Biblical Institute Press, 1980) and "Ten Dance-Derived Expressions in the Hebrew Bible" (*Biblica* 62 [1981], 328–46), reprinted in *Dance as Religious Studies* (Crossroad Publishing Co., 1990), edited by Doug Adams and Diane Apostolos-Cappadona. Bathja Bayer doubts whether the biblical terms are really as specific as Gruber and earlier authors delineate: "Dance in the Bible: the Possibilities and Limitations of the Evidence," *Papers of the International Seminar on the Bible in Dance* (The Israeli Center of the International Theatre Institute, 1979). The communal character and effect of each biblical dance rather than its individual movements are the foci of Doug Adams's *Congregational Dancing in Christian Worship* (The Sharing Co., 1984 [1971]), portions of which appear as "Communal Dance Forms and Consequences in Biblical Worship" in *Dance as Religious Studies*. That work traces the positive correlation of the rise and fall between liturgical dance and a community's sense of freedom and responsibility.

The pervasiveness of dance in worship of the first and second temple periods resulted in the word *dance* not being mentioned. Commonly accepted practices occasion little or no comment, as summarized in Norman Gottwald's *Hebrew Bible, a Socio-Literary Introduction* (Fortress Press, 1985, 138–40). Such pervasive dancing probably carried over into early Christian worship where rejoicing was synonymous with dancing, as Matthew Black suggests in noting that an Aramaic term for *rejoice* also means *dance* and allows us to see dancing where there is rejoicing in the spirit in Christian Scriptures: *The Aramaic Approach to the Gospels and Acts* (Clarendon, 1967). While a first-century Jewish reader would understand the presence of dancing when "rejoicing" was mentioned, such as in Matthew 5:12 (where Jesus says, "Rejoice and be exceedingly glad,"), dance must be specified when writing for a Greek audience, as in Luke 6:23 (where Jesus says, "Rejoice ye in that day, and leap for joy.") For modern audiences who might miss the meaning even of that rendering, the latter phrase is translated as "dance for joy" in the *The New English Bible* (Oxford University Press and Cambridge University Press, 1961). Similarly, those studying Hebrew music and poetry see dancing when "festival" is mentioned in Hebrew Scriptures and detect patterns of movement in the rhythm of biblical lyrics: Alfred Sendrey, *Music in Ancient Israel* (Philosophical Library, 1969) and Olaf Hoeckmann, *Dance in Hebrew Poetry* (The Sharing Co., 1987). The question remains when such terms ceased to suggest dance to readers.

Sharing insights from form criticism, Hal Taussig suggests the original liturgical events and accompanying movements for hundreds of Hebrew Scriptures and Christian Scriptures. Identifying which biblical verses were most likely hymns and which were communion rites or baptismal rites, he not only reveals possible historic dance movements where the word *dance* is not mentioned in the texts, but also provides guidance for contemporary choreographers. Knowing that a text had a likely relation to baptismal or initiation rites, the dance may be meaningfully shaped around the font; knowing that a text may be related to communion rites, the dance may form around the table. Taussig's works include *Dancing the New Testament: A Guide to Texts for Movement* (The Sharing Co., 1977); *New Categories for Dancing the Old Testament* (The Sharing Co., 1981); and *The Lady of the Dance: A Movement Approach to the Biblical Figure of Wisdom in Worship and Education* (The Sharing Co., 1981). A substantial portion of his first two works appear as "Dancing the Scriptures" in *Dance as Religious Studies.*

At the 1979 Jerusalem international seminar on the Bible in dance, several dance scholars focused on the many choreographies based on biblical subject matter. Giora Manor digests such choreographies with accompanying photographs in *The Gospel According to Dance: Choreography and the Bible from Ballet to Modern* (St. Martin's Press, 1980). Similar approaches are evident in Martha Hill's "José Limón and His Biblical Works," Gunhild Schueller's "Legend of Joseph — from Fokine to Neumeier," and Richard Bizot's "Salome in Modern Dance" in *Papers of the International Seminar on the Bible in Dance* (The Israeli Center of the International Theatre Institute, 1979). Also at that conference, Selma Jean Cohen presented a portion of her study on how leading choreographers have treated or would treat the Prodigal Son story. Her earlier book provides more extensive information on that subject, including observations by José Limón, Erick Hawkins, Pauline Koner, Paul Taylor and others: *The Modern Dance: Seven Statements of Belief* (Wesleyan University Press, 1965). Doug Adams and Judith Rock's paper presented a different approach at the Jerusalem conference; it applied Paul Tillich's categories to reveal biblical dimensions in choreographies without explicit biblical subject matter. Their study explored an affinity between the styles of biblical prophets and pioneering modern dance choreographers. That work was published in both English and Hebrew: "Biblical Criteria in Modern Dance: Modern Dance as Prophetic Form" (*Israel Dance* [1980]). A revised form of this essay is included in *Dance as Religious Studies.*

Hundreds of dance references by historic church leaders were translated in Eugene Louis Backman's *Religious Dances in the Christian Church and in Popular Medicine* (Allen and Unwin, 1952). His work is accurate when dealing with quotations from the Middle Ages; but his translations are less reliable for earlier centuries. Backman tended to cite only those texts that include words for dance and often failed to provide the surrounding contexts that would aid in discerning whether the sources refer to actual dance or metaphorical use of the term. Of many authors who have relied heavily on Backman's work, Margaret Taylor is the best of those whose work is most readily available: *A Time to Dance: Symbolic Movement in Worship* (The Sharing Co., 1967 [1981]. A revision of the historical portion of her work appears as "A History of Symbolic Movement in Worship" in *Dance as Religious Studies.* Attempting to correct errors in translation or interpretation by Backman and others, John Gordon Davies tends to judge all references to dance as metaphoric unless there are surrounding indications of actual dance: *Liturgical Dance: An Historical, Theological and Practical Handbook* (SCM Press, 1984). His approach is an overly conservative one, which probably classes as metaphor a number of historic references to actual dance. Nevertheless, his method may be a corrective to the tendency by others to interpret every dance reference literally.

The later history of liturgical dance is best documented by definitive books on particular periods or peoples. Edward D. Andrews provides a comprehensive study of nineteenth-century American Shaker dances with each folk dance fully described: *The Gift to Be Simple: Songs, Dances, and Rituals of American Shakers* (Dover Publications, 1962 [1940]). With some attention to sacred dances in Africa and America, Lynne Fauley Emery provides the best overall source on American black dance: *Black Dance in the United States from 1619 to 1970* (National Press Books, 1972). Charles Johnson carefully and exhaustively documents formal marches and informal dance manifestations in camp-meeting worship that renewed so many Protestant denominations across the midwest and upper south in nineteenth-century America: *The Frontier Camp Meeting* (SMU Press, 1955). Martha Ann Kirk details the inculturation of many Indian and Mexican dances in Catholic worship of the southwest: *Dancing with Creation: Mexican and Native American Dance in Christian Worship and Education* (Resource Publications, 1983); evidence of such inculturation with dance appears widespread throughout Mexico, documented by Michael Calderwood and Michael Kelly: *Máscaras Rituales de México* (Centro Cultural de la Villa de Madrid, 1978). Studies of the recent history of liturgical dance include Carlynn Reed's *And We Have Danced: A History of the Sacred Dance Guild: 1958–1978* (The Sharing Co., 1978) and Mary Jones, *The History of Sacred and Biblically Inspired Dance in Australia* (Christian Dance Fellowship of Australia, 1979).

Also reflecting the most recent history of liturgical dance are dozens of books recounting choreographies currently occuring in worship services. The most influential of these is Carla De Sola's *The Spirit Moves: A Handbook of Dance and Prayer* (The Sharing Co., 1986 [1977]). Juilliard-trained and capable of the finest modern dance technique with her Omega Liturgical Dance Company, she develops not only choreographies for the soloist and ensemble but also simple movements for the whole congregation to dance. Other approaches include use of folk dance as the idiom for liturgical dance choirs, such as Constance Fisher's *Dancing The Old Testament: Christian Celebrations of Israelite Heritage for Worship and Education* (The Sharing Co., 1980); use of folk dance for the whole congregation to move in worship, such as Margaret Taylor's *Hymns in Action for Everyone: People 9 to 90 Dancing Together* (The Sharing Co., 1985); and use of gesture by worship leaders and congregations, such as Carolyn Deitering's *Actions, Gestures, and Bodily Attitudes* (Resource Publications, 1980). Revealing the widest survey of different approaches in contemporary liturgical dance is Doug Adams's *Dancing Christmas Carols* (Resource Publications, 1983 [1978]), in which ten liturgical dance leaders share their best choreographies for congregations and performing dance groups utilizing folk dance, jazz dance, modern, and ballet. Among the most theologically perceptive writers on dance in worship are Cynthia Winton-Henry in *Leaps of Faith: Improvisational Dance in Worship and Education* (The Sharing Co., 1985); Ronald Gagne, Thomas A. Kane, and Robert Ver Eecke in *Introducing Dance In Christian Worship* (The Pastoral Press, 1984); and Judith Rock and Norman Mealy in *Performer as Priest and Prophet: Restoring the Intuitive in Worship through Music and Dance* (Harper and Row, 1988).

Dance and Biblical Studies

Adams, Doug, and Apostolos-Cappadona, Diane. *Dance as Religious Studies.* New York: Crossroad Publishing Co., 1990.

Adams, Doug. *Congregational Dancing in Christian Worship.* Austin: The Sharing Co., 1984 (1971).

Adams, Doug, and Rock, Judith. *Biblical Criteria in Modern Dance: Modern Dance as Prophetic Form.* Austin: The Sharing Co., 1979.

Bayer, Bathja. "Dance in the Bible: the Possibilities and Limitations of the Evidence." *Papers of the International Seminar on the Bible in Dance.* Jerusalem: The Israeli Center of the International Theatre Institute, 1979.

Black, Matthew. *The Aramaic Approach to the Gospels and Acts.* London: Clarendon Press, 1967.

Cohen, Selma Jean. *The Modern Dance: Seven Statements of Belief.* Middletown: Wesleyan University Press, 1966.

Gruber, Mayer I. *Aspects of Nonverbal Communication in the Ancient Near East.* Rome: Biblical Institute Press, 1980.

———. "Ten Dance-Derived Expressions in the Hebrew Bible." *Biblica* 62 (1981) 328–46.

Hoeckmann, Olaf. *Dance in Hebrew Poetry.* Austin: The Sharing Co., 1987.

Lapson, Dvora. "Dance" *The Universal Jewish Encyclopedia.* New York: Universal Jewish Encyclopedia Co., 1941. III, pp. 455–63.

Manor, Giora. *The Gospel According to Dance: Choreography and the Bible from Ballet to Modern*. New York: St. Martin's Press, 1980.

Morgenstern, Julian. "The Etymological History of the Three Hebrew Synonyms for 'To Dance.'" *American Oriental Society Journal* 36 (1916) 321–32.

Oesterley, W. O. E. *The Sacred Dance*. New York: Cambridge University Press, 1923.

Sendrey, Alfred. *Music in Ancient Israel*. New York: Philosophical Society, 1969.

Taussig, Hal. *Dancing the New Testament: A Guide to Texts*. Austin: The Sharing Co., 1977.

———. *The Lady of the Dance: a Movement Approach to Biblical Figures of Wisdom in Worship*. Austin: The Sharing Co., 1981.

———. *New Categories for Dancing the Old Testament*. Austin: The Sharing Co., 1981.

Dance and Historical Studies

Andrews, Edward D. *The Gift to Be Simple: Songs, Dances, and Rituals of American Shakers*. New York: Dover, 1962 (1940).

Backman, Eugene Louis. *Religious Dances in the Christian Church and in Popular Medicine*. London: Allen and Unwin, 1952.

Beck, Fred., ed. *The Jewish Dance*. New York: Exposition Press, 1960.

Calderwood, Michael, and Kelly, Michael. *Máscaras Rituales de México*. Madrid: Centro Cultural de la Villa de Madrid, 1978.

Carroll, William. "The Bible in Drama and Dance at the Jesuit Colleges of the 16th to 18th Centuries." *Papers of the International Seminar on the Bible in Dance*. Jerusalem: The Israeli Center of the International Theatre Institute, 1979.

Davies, John Gordon. *Liturgical Dance: An Historical, Theological and Practical Handbook*. London: SCM Press, 1984.

Emery, Lynne Fauley. *Black Dance in the United States from 1619 to 1970*. Palo Alto: National Press Books, 1972.

Fallon, Dennis J., and Wolbers, Mary Jane, eds. *Focus on Dance X: Religion and Dance*. Reston: American Alliance for Health, Physical Education, Recreation, and Dance, 1982.

Foatelli, Renée. *Les Danses Religieuses dans le Christianisme*. Paris: Editions Spes, 1947.

Johnson, Charles. *The Frontier Camp Meeting*. Dallas: SMU Press, 1955.

Jones, Mary. *The History of Sacred and Biblically Inspired Dance in Australia*. Sydney: Christian Dance Fellowship of Australia, 1979.

Kirk, Martha Ann. *Dancing with Creation: Mexican and Native American Dance in Christian Worship and Education*. San Jose: Resource Publications, 1983.

Knox, Ronald, *The Mass in Slow Motion*. New York: Sheed and Ward, 1948.

Marks, J. E. *The Mathers on Dancing*. New York: Dance Horizons, 1975.

Mead, G. R. S. *The Sacred Dance in Christendom*. London: John M. Watkins, 1926.

Reed, Carlynn. *And We Have Danced: A History of the Sacred Dance Guild: 1958–1978*. Austin: The Sharing Co., 1978.

Rock, Judith. *Terpsichore at Louis Le Grand: Baroque Dance on a Jesuit Stage in Paris*. Berkeley: Ph.D. diss., Graduate Theological Union, 1988.

Sorell, Walter. *The Dance Through the Ages*. New York: Grosset and Dunlap, 1967.

Taylor, Margaret. *A Time to Dance: Symbolic Movement in Worship*. Austin: The Sharing Co., 1981 (1967).

Trolin, Clifford, *Movement in Prayer in a Hasidic Mode*. Austin: The Sharing Co., 1979.

van der Leeuw, Gerardus. *Sacred and Profane Beauty: The Holy in Art*. New York: Holt, Rinehart, and Winston, 1963.

Liturgical Dance Theory and Practice

Adams, Doug, ed. *Dancing Christmas Carols*. San Jose: Resource Publications, 1983 (1978).

———. *Sacred Dance with Senior Citizens*. Austin: The Sharing Co., 1982.

Champion, Marge, and Zdenek, Marilee, *Catch the New Wind: The Church Is Alive and Dancing*. Waco: Word Book Inc., 1972.

Davies, John Gordon. *Worship and Dance*. Birmingham, England: University of Birmingham Institute for the Study of Worship and Religious Architecture, 1975.

Deiss, Lucien, and Weyman, Gloria. *Dance for the Lord*. Schiller Park: World Library Publications, 1975.

———. *Liturgical Dance*. Phoenix: North American Liturgy Resources, 1984.

Deitering, Carolyn. *Actions, Gestures, and Bodily Attitudes*. San Jose: Resource Publications, 1980.

———. *The Liturgy as Dance and the Liturgical Dancer*. New York: Crossroad Publishing Co., 1984.

De Sola, Carla. *Learning Through Dance*. New York: Paulist Press, 1974.

———. *The Spirit Moves: A Handbook of Dance and Prayer*. Austin: The Sharing Co., 1986 (1977).

Fisher, Constance. *Dancing Festivals of the Church Year*. Austin: The Sharing Co., 1986.

———. *Dancing the Old Testament: Christian Celebrations of Israelite Heritage for Worship and Education*. Austin: The Sharing Co., 1980.

———. *Dancing with Early Christians*. Austin: The Sharing Co., 1983.

Gagne, Ronald; Kane, Thomas A.; and Ver Eecke, Robert. *Introducing Dance in Christian Worship*. Washington D.C.: The Pastoral Press, 1984.

Jones, Mary. *God's People on the Move: a Manual for Leading Congregations in Movement*. Sydney: Christian Dance Fellowship of Australia, 1988.

Kirk, Martha Ann. *Celebrations of Biblical Women's Stories: Tears. Milk, and Honey*. Kansas City: Sheed and Ward, 1987.

Lee, Cathy, and Uhlmann, Chris. *Collections*. Sydney: Corinthians VI, 1984.

Long, Anne. *Praise Him in the Dance*. London: Hodder and Stoughton, 1976.

Lyon, Barbara. *Dance Toward Wholeness: Moving Methods to Heal Individuals and Groups*. Austin: The Sharing Co., 1981.

Ortegal, Adelaide. *A Dancing People*. West Lafayette: Center for Contemporary Celebration, 1976.

Packard, Dane. *The Church Becoming Christ's Body: The Small Church's Manual of Dances*. Austin: The Sharing Co., 1985.

Rock, Judith, and Mealy, Norman. *Performer as Priest and Prophet: Restoring the Intuitive in Worship through Music and Dance*. New York: Harper and Row, 1988.

————. *Theology in the Shape of Dance: Using Dance in Worship and Theological Process*. Austin: The Sharing Co., 1977.

Sautter, Cynthia D. *Irish Dance and Spirituality: Relating Folkdance and Faith*. Austin: The Sharing Co., 1986.

Taylor, Margaret. *Dramatic Dance with Children in Education and Worship*. Austin: The Sharing Co., 1977.

————. *Hymns in Action for Everyone: People 9 to 90 Dancing Together*. Austin: The Sharing Co., 1985.

————. *Look Up and Live*. Austin: The Sharing Co., 1980 (1953).

Troxell, Kay, ed. *Resources in Sacred Dance: Annotated Bibliography*. Peterborough, N.H.: The Sacred Dance Guild, 1987.

Winton-Henry, Cynthia. *Leaps of Faith: Improvisational Dance in Worship and Education*. Austin: The Sharing Co., 1985.

Wise, Joseph. *The Body at Liturgy*. Phoenix: North American Liturgy Resources, 1972.

Notes on Contributors

DOUG ADAMS is Professor of Christianity and the Arts at the Pacific School of Religion and a member of the doctoral faculty in arts at the Graduate Theological Union, Berkeley. A past national president of the Sacred Dance Guild, he is author of *Congregational Dancing in Christian Worship* (Austin: The Sharing Co., 1984 [1971]) and editor of many books on dance including *Dancing Christmas Carols* (Saratoga: Resource Publications, 1978). He and Diane Apostolos-Cappadona coedited previously *Art As Religious Studies* (New York: Crossroad, 1987).

DIANE APOSTOLOS-CAPPADONA is Professorial Lecturer in Religion and Art, Georgetown University. She is editor of Isamu Noguchi's published papers; Jane Dillenberger's *Image and Spirit in Sacred and Secular Art* (New York: Crossroad, 1990); and Mircea Eliade's *Symbolism, The Sacred and the Arts* (New York: Crossroad, 1987). A contributor to the forthcoming *Dictionary of Art* (London: Macmillan), she is the Core Consultant for the WNET/THIRTEEN "Dance Project," an eight-week educational series, scheduled for the 1991–1992 television season.

SUSAN BAUER is Associate Professor of Dance in the Dance Department at St. Olaf's College in Northfield, Minnesota, where she has developed the college's B.A. major in "dance and religion" and also directs dance companies.

VALERIE DeMARINIS is Associate Professor of Religion and the Personality Sciences at Pacific School of Religion and on the doctoral faculty at the Graduate Theological Union, Berkeley. Her current research focuses on the use of ritual in counseling contexts and the therapeutic role of dance in rituals such as the worship of Macumba-Christianity, which she has studied in Brazil.

CARLA DE SOLA is a graduate of the Juilliard School and director of the Omega Liturgical Dance Company in residence at the Cathedral of St. John the Divine, New York. She teaches liturgical dance each summer at Pacific School of Religion in Berkeley, California; and she is author of *The Spirit Moves: a Handbook of Dance and Prayer* (Austin: The Sharing Co., 1986 [1977]).

MAYER I. GRUBER is Senior Lecturer in the Department of Bible and Ancient Near East, Ben-Gurion University of the Negev, Beersheva, Israel. He is the author of *Aspects of Nonverbal Communication in the Ancient Near East* (Rome: Biblical Institute Press, 1980); *Rashi's Commentary on the Book of Psalms in English with Introduction and Notes* (Philadelphia: Jewish Publication Society, forthcoming); and a contributor to *Encyclopedia Judaica, The Illustrated Dictionary and Concordance to the Bible* (New York: Macmillan, 1986), and numerous scholarly periodicals.

MARTHA ANN KIRK, C.C.V.I., is Associate Professor of Religious Studies and Art at Incarnate Word College, and Director of the Peace and Justice Studies Graduate Program. She earned the Ph.D. in arts from the Graduate Theological Union, Berkeley, with a dissertation that has been published under the title *Celebrations of Biblical Women's Stories: Tears, Milk, and Honey* (Kansas City: Sheed and Ward, 1987). She is also the author of *Dancing with Creation* (Saratoga: Resource Publications, 1983), a study of the inculturation of Mexican and Native American dances in Roman Catholic Church worship.

NEIL DOUGLAS-KLOTZ is the editor of the first edition of *The Divine Dance*, a collection of unpublished writings (1933–1960) on spiritual dance creation from the Ruth St. Denis manuscripts, papers, and poetry. He teaches religious dance and body prayer in the graduate program at the Institute for Culture and Creation Spirituality, Holy Names College, Oakland, California. He is also codirector of the Center for the Dances of Universal Peace, a member of the Somatics Society, and the Sacred Dance Guild.

JUDITH ROCK is a professional dancer, choreographer, and writer who received her M.A. in dance at Mills College, Oakland, and her Ph.D. in theology and dance from the Graduate Theological Union, Berkeley, with a dissertation entitled *Terpsichore at Louis Le Grand: Baroque Dance on a Jesuit Stage in Paris* (1988). She is the author of *Theology in the Shape of Dance: Using Dance in Worship and Theological Process* (Austin: The Sharing Co., 1977). Her most recent book was coauthored with Norman Mealy and is entitled *Performer as Priest and Prophet: Restoring the Intuitive in Worship through Music and Dance* (New York: Harper and Row, 1988).

HAL TAUSSIG is a United Methodist clergyperson with a Ph.D. in New Testament Studies. His most recent publications include *Wisdom's Feast: Sophia in Study and Celebration* (San Francisco: Harper and Row, 1989);

"The Lord's Prayer" in *Foundations and Facets Forum 4.4*; and *Sophia: The Future of Feminist Spirituality* (San Francisco: Harper and Row, 1986).

MARGARET TAYLOR has introduced liturgical dance in hundreds of churches around the world. She teaches dance for worship and education each summer at Pacific School of Religion and is the author of many books on this subject, including *A Time To Dance: Symbolic Movement in Worship* (Austin: The Sharing Co., 1981 [1967]); *Dramatic Dance with Children in Education and Worship* (Austin: The Sharing Co., 1977); and most recently *Hymns in Action for Everyone: People 9 to 90 Dancing Together* (Austin: The Sharing Co., 1985).

Scripture Index

General Index

Abraham, 7, 8
According to Eve (Ailey), 7, 143
Adams, Doug, 156
Ailey, Alvin, 7, 143
Allan, Maude, 104, 105, 107, 138, 139
American Genesis (Taylor), 7
Apostolos-Cappadona, Diane, 138

Balanchine, George, 5, 7, 8, 140

Cain and Abel, 7
choral dancing, 16, 17, 21, 37
choreography, 155–165, 170–180
Christian Scriptures, 7, 75–78, 95, 97
circle dance, 16, 36, 49, 50
communal dance, 35–47, 160
congregational dancing, 7
Cunningham, Merce, 5, 81, 86, 174

Dance of Death, 22, 23, 24, 27
Dante Alighieri, 24, 41
David, 5, 7, 8, 17, 18, 24, 36, 37, 40, 50, 54, 55, 57, 58, 59, 70, 137, 145, 146
David the King (Shawn), 4
David Triumphant (Lifar) 5
Diaghilev, Sergei, 5, 8, 104, 140
Duncan, Isadora, 110

Early Christianity, 16–19,
Early Middle Ages, 19–25
Eliade, Mircea, 96

Embattled Garden (Graham), 7, 119, 122, 123, 124, 126, 130, 141, 144
Eve, 7, 95, 96, 98, 119, 122–124, 126, 128, 135, 143, 144

Fokine, Michel, 4
Fuller, Loie, 4, 104, 137, 138, 140

Genesis, 122, 139
Graham, Martha, 4, 5, 7, 9, 84, 85, 86, 104, 105, 107, 109, 118–133, 134, 140, 141, 144–147, 155, 174

Hawkins, Erick, 5, 86
Hebrew dancing, 16
Hebrew Scriptures, 7, 16, 35, 36, 48–66, 67–79, 95, 97, 170
Heriodiade (Graham), 5, 105
Herodias, 95, 100, 105, 107, 137, 139
Humphrey, Doris, 5, 85, 86, 109

Isaac, 7, 8

Jacob's Dream, 8
Jamison, Judith, 134, 141, 143, 147
Job, 4, 7, 8, 37, 80
Joseph, 8, 139
Joseph the Beautiful (Goleizovsky), 8
Joseph's Dream, 7
Josephlegende (Neumeier), 141
Judith, 7, 16, 98, 103, 119, 128–131, 135, 136, 138, 141, 145, 146